TOO BEAUTIFUL FOR
THIEVES AND PICKPOCKETS

A HISTORY OF THE
VICTORIAN CONVICT PRISON
ON SPIKE ISLAND

Cal McCarthy is the author of *Cumann na mBan and the Irish Revolution* (2007), *Green, Blue and Grey: The Irish in the American Civil War* (2009) and is co-author of *The Wreck of the Neva: The Horrifying Fate of a Convict Ship and the Irish Women Aboard* (2013). In 2005 he received his MPhil for a thesis entitled, 'The 1918 General Election – The swing to Sinn Féin'. Cal has participated in numerous radio and television productions dealing with various aspects of 19th- and 20th-century Irish history. He has worked for the Department of Transport, the Department of Arts, Heritage and the Gaeltacht and is a former Secretary of the Council of National Cultural Institutions. He currently works for Cork County Council.

Barra O'Donnabhain is a graduate of UCC and the University of Chicago. His publications include the edited volumes *The Dead Tell Tales* (2013) and *Archaeological Approaches to Human Remains: Global Perspectives* (2014). Barra has directed and collaborated on archaeological projects in a number of world areas. He began excavations at the 19th-century prison on Spike Island in 2012. He teaches in the Department of Archaeology at University College Cork and is on the Board of Directors of the Los Angeles-based Institute for Field Research.

TOO BEAUTIFUL
FOR THIEVES AND PICKPOCKETS

A HISTORY OF THE
VICTORIAN CONVICT PRISON
ON SPIKE ISLAND

Cal McCarthy & Barra O'Donnabhain

First published 2016 by Cork County Library
Carrigrohane Road, Cork, Ireland.
Tel: +353 (0)21 4546499; Website: www.corkcoco.ie

ISBN Paperback: 978-0-9929970-1-4
ISBN Hardback: 978-0-9929970-3-8

First edition: 2016

Cover photograph: Con Brogan, National Monuments Service
Edited by Rachel Pierce at Verba Editing House
Designed and Printed in Ireland by Lettertec

lettertec

An Roinn
Ealaíon, Oidhreachta agus Gaeltachta
Department of
Arts, Heritage and the Gaeltacht

IFR Institute for Field Research
ACADEMIC EXCELLENCE IN FIELD TRAINING

UCC
University College Cork, Ireland
Coláiste na hOllscoile Corcaigh

Dedication

We dedicate this book to the volunteers and staff of today's Spike Island in acknowledgement of their devotion to the island's past, present and future.

Table of Contents

A Note on the Book's Title

The title of this book is taken from the words of Rev. Gibson:

'The inhabitants of the beautiful villas around the harbour, and on the River Lee, are as free from the intrusion of the convicts of Spike as they are from those of Norfolk Island. Indeed, I know but one objection to Spike Island as a convict depot - and it is a sentimental one. The site and situation appear too beautiful for such a set of thieves and pickpockets as we have congregated there.'

Reverend Charles Bernard Gibson,
Presbyterian Chaplain on Spike Island, 1856–1863.

A Note on Primary Sources

Our source material is referred to in the footnotes at the end of each page. We are aware that some readers find that footnotes tend to interrupt, clutter and fragment the narrative. We are equally aware, however, that some will find the process of turning pages to check each source intensely irritating. We hope that those readers of the former category will forgive our accommodation of the latter, try to ignore the footnotes and continue with the main narrative as they desire.

The following is a note of all the major primary source material consulted during research of this text. Such material is listed in order of the archive or repository in which it may be accessed and all relevant acronyms are explained.

NAI – National Archives of Ireland

CSORP – Chief Secretary's Registered Papers: these are the original letters of the various arms of government (civil service) that formed the Chief Secretary's Office. Each piece of correspondence was given a unique number and entered in the correspondence index of the year in which it was received. Consequently, each reference beginning with CSORP will next refer to the year from which it dates (mostly 1847–1883 in this text) and, finally, will quote the unique identifier number. Some of the earlier numbers will be preceded by a letter. These letters refer to the category of the correspondence.

As an example, NAI, CSORP/1847/G9844 refers to the 9,844th piece of correspondence registered during 1847 in Category G of the Chief Secretary's Registered Papers. Where no letter identifies a category, the correspondence comes from a year when no categories were created.

The number referred to here may not be the call number that will produce the document in the NAI. This is because most pieces of correspondence were subsequently attached to others and, over time, formed a file. Consequently, G9844 may have been attached to G10451, which may have been attached to H7542, which may not have been attached to any other papers. In that case the call number CSORP/1847/H7542 will produce the document. One can trace the subsequent correspondence to which any of these pieces of correspondence were attached by referring to the CSORP indexes in the NAI.

OP – Official Papers: the Official Papers are the papers of the Chief Secretary that were not recorded among the registered papers. They were filed in a similar manner to the registered papers, by year and individual correspondence number. However, as the collection is smaller, the individual correspondence number will usually be identical to the call number used by the NAI.

GPO – General Prisons Office: records which once belonged to the General Prisons Office. This text refers to two categories of such records:

LB – Letter Books, into which outgoing correspondence was copied;

XB – Minute Books, recording the details of internal meetings.

Call numbers should include the number of the book, which is the first number quoted after the LB or XB prefix. The final number within these references refers to the piece of correspondence within the individual book.

GPB – General Prisons Board: records which once belonged to the General Prisons Board, the successor to the General Prisons Office. This text refers to two categories of such records:

LB – Letter Books, into which outgoing correspondence was copied;

MB – Minute Books, recording details of internal meetings.

Call numbers should include the number of the book, which is the first number quoted after the LB or MB prefix. The final number within these references refers to the piece of correspondence within the individual book.

OPW – Office of Public Works: records which once belonged to the OPW.

CON/LB – Chief Secretary's Correspondence Letter Books, into which outgoing correspondence was copied.

TR – Transportation Register: records details of many of the convicts transported to the colonies we now know as Australia.

CRF – Convict Reference Files: these files were generated by correspondence regarding some specific convicts – usually appeals of their sentences.

NLI – National Library of Ireland

Most of the newspapers referred to within this text are available for consultation at NLI, online via various subscription sites or online at www.irishnewspaperarchives. ie, which can be accessed at most county libraries.

Published Primary Documents

Gibson, Rev. Charles Bernard. 1864. *An Irish Convict in the Federal Army.* In: *Once a Week,* 27 August 1864.

Gibson, Rev. C.B. 1863. *Irish Convict Reform: The intermediate prisons, a mistake.* Dublin: McGlashin and Gill.

Gibson, Rev. C.B. 1863. *Life Among Convicts, Vols I and II.* London: Hurst and Blackett.

Mitchel, J. 1982. *Jail Journal.* Dublin: University Press of Ireland.

Von Holtzendorff, Baron Franz. 1860. *The Irish Convict System: More Especially Intermediate Prisons.* Dublin: W.B. Kelly.

Von Holtzendorff, Baron Franz. 1863. *Reflections and observations on the present condition of the Irish convict system.* Dublin: J.M. O'Toole and Son.

Manuscripts

MS 3016, Convict register of an Irish prison (Spike Island Government Prison?) giving detailed particulars of prisoners, including many transported to Bermuda, Van Diemen's Land and Gibraltar, 1849–1850.

PRO – Public Record Office

The Public Record Office is one of four bodies amalgamated to form the National Archives (United Kingdom). The following PRO material was consulted during work on this text:

CO – Colonial Office

AO – Audit Office

HO – Home Office

T – Treasury

TS – Treasury Solicitor

WO – War Office

MPF – Maps and Plans originating in the State Paper Office

MPH & MPHH – Maps and Plans originating in the War Office

MFQ – Maps and Plans originating in other Departments

All numbers quoted after the above prefixes should locate the individual document, or the book, folio or box in which it is contained.

HMSO – Her Majesty's Stationery Office

Her Majesty's Stationery Office is one of four bodies amalgamated to form the National Archives (United Kingdom). The HMSO documents referred to in this text are published documents and are available in various libraries, and sometimes online. The major HMSO collections consulted were:
Annual Reports of the Inspectors General on the General State of Prisons of Ireland 1846–1852.
Annual Reports of the Directors of Convict Prisons in Ireland 1854–1877.
Annual Reports of the General Prisons Board, Ireland 1879–1883.

British Library

Published Primary Documents

Balme. 1863. *A Reply to Mr. Burt's 'Wakefield Figures in relation to Convict Discipline'*. London: Simpkin, Marshall and Co.

Burt, John Thomas. 1862. *Observations on the Treatment of Convicts in Ireland With Some Remarks on the Same in England*. London: Simpkin, Marshall and Co.

Burt, John Thomas. 1863. *Irish Facts and Wakefield Figures in relation to Convict Discipline in Ireland*. London: Longman and Co.

Burt, John Thomas. 1865. *Convict Discipline in Ireland: being an examination of Sir Walter Crofton's answer to "Irish Facts and Wakefield Figures"*. London: Longman and Co.

Carpenter, Mary. 1857. *Reformatory Discipline as Developed by the Rt Honourable Sir Walter Crofton*. British Library, X208/1839.

Crofton, Walter. 1857. *A Few Remarks on the Convict Question*. Dublin: British Library, Mic.A.10472(1).

Crofton, Walter. 1863. *A few Observations on a Pamphlet Recently published by J Burt on the Irish Convict System*.

Krause, T. 2003. *The influence of Sir Walter Crofton's 'Irish system' on prison reform in Germany*. Dublin: British Legal History Conference: Adventures of the Law.

Shipley, Orby. 1857. *The Purgatory of Prisoners: or an intermediate stage between the prison and the public; being some account of the practical working of the new system of penal reformation, introduced by the Board of Directors of Convict Prisons in Ireland*. British Library, 6055.df.29.

Gibson, Rev. C.B. 1878. *Cellular and Solitary Discipline*. In: *Social Notes Concerning Social Reforms, Social Requirements, Social Progress*. London: SC Hall (ed.).

Manuscripts

British Library. Loan RLF 1/1727. Reverend Charles Bernard Gibson and Mrs Margaret Gibson, his widow.

British Library. Add MS 60844–60848. Carnarvon Papers. Vols. LXXXVIII–XCII. Correspondence and papers of Lord Carnarvon relating to national and local prison and reformatory administration and policy, including correspondence with Sir Walter Frederick Crofton, formerly Commissioner of Prisons in England and Ireland; 1857 – aft. 5 April 1885.

AOT – Archives of Tasmania

CON – Convict Papers

A NOTE ON THE NAME OF THE PRISON

The Victorian Prison on Spike Island was always a place of detention for the most serious category of Irish prisoner. But during its three-and-a-half decades of operation it was known by various titles. In official and unofficial documentation all of these titles were used all throughout the period. The most common titles used during specific periods were broadly aligned as follows:

1847-1849: Convict Depot; 1850-1863: Convict Depot/Government Prison;

1863-1878: Prison/Government Prison/Convict Prison; 1879-1883: Convict Prison

A NOTE ON IMAGES

The authors would like to acknowledge the following individuals and institutions for permission to reproduce images:

S.H. Bean; Con Brogan of National Monuments Service (Department of Arts, Heritage and the Gaeltacht); F. Cole; Cork County Council; William Cumming of National Inventory of Architectural Heritage; Simon Hill/Scirebroc; HM Stationery Office; Nick Hogan, Department of Archaeology, University College Cork; Dennis Horgan; Michael Lenihan; Library of Congress; the Murphy family of Bracklyn House; National Library of Ireland; National Archives of Ireland, with particular thanks to Zoe Reid and Aideen Ireland; National Library of Scotland; Offaly Historical and Archaeological Society; Ordnance Survey of Ireland; Public Record Office, London; Tasmania Museum and Art Gallery; O.J. Walsh.

Figure 0.1 View of Spike Island from Fort Camden and the entrance to Cork harbour. (Image © courtesy of O.J. Walsh)

Introduction:
Spike Island, History and Legend

On the night of 8 October 1847, a small paddle steamer called *Minerva* emerged from the seas beyond Cork harbour. Turning to starboard and rounding the lighthouse atop Roche's Point, she sailed beneath the guns of Fort Carlisle on her starboard side and Fort Camden to port. These two forts were part of a ring of steel that had guarded the entrance to Cork harbour since the late 18th century (though Fort Camden's origins go back at least to the 16th century). The sailors on *Minerva*'s deck could probably see the third part of that ring, as an imposing island loomed above the bow. On the island's highest point was sited another commanding military fort. This was Fort Westmoreland and it was about to relieve *Minerva* of her unfortunate cargo. For beneath the steamer's decks, 109 men were locked away and tightly confined. They were convicted criminals who had been sentenced to be transported overseas. As such, they took on a moniker that was not generally applied to other criminals. These men were known as 'convicts'. After a decade of absence, when such men were held in Dublin detention centres, convicts had returned to Cork harbour.

This may not have been the first time that the island had served as a detention centre. The use of the island as a prison was mentioned by the 17th-century bardic poet Diarmaid Mac Sheáin Bhuidhe Mac Cárrthaigh, whose 1687 poem about the accession of the Catholic King James II listed the injustices suffered by Irish Catholics under his predecessors.[1] This poem mentioned how Spike

---

1 '*A n-airm le chéile d'éis gur leagadar, 'S i nOileán Spíc na mílte i gcarcar ann, Uireasba bidh is dighe agus leabtha ortha, Ag faitheamh le tríall go h-iath nach feadadar.*' (After they had laid low their armies, In Spike Island they imprisoned thousands, Without food or drink

4

Island was used as a holding place for Irish prisoners prior to their transportation to Jamaica and other far distant locations. Those 17th-century detainees may have been considered prisoners-of-war rather than common criminals. The same could not be said of *Minerva*'s convicts. Spike Island was about to encounter the first of thousands of ordinary criminals to be contained by its high walls.

Minerva passed by the island and continued upstream to the bustling harbour town of Passage. She docked there and the prisoners spent their first night in Cork beneath the decks of the ship. Soon after dawn broke through the harbour sky the men were loaded onto a smaller craft and ferried to their new home on Spike Island.[2] It was Saturday morning, 9 October 1847. Spike Island had just begun a 36-year journey into infamy.

Figure 0.2 Location of Spike Island in Cork harbour. (Image © Ordnance Survey Ireland. All rights reserved. Licence number 2016/06/CCMA/ CorkCountyCouncil)

or beds, Waiting for a journey to an unknown country.) Ó Donnchadha, T. (ed). 1916. 'Amhráin Dhiarmada Mac Seáin Bhuidhe MacCárrthaigh.' Dublin: McGill. See also: Broderick, M. 1989. *A History of Cobh (Queenstown)*. Cobh, pp.79–80. In: Martin, M. 2008. *Spike Island - Saints, felons, and famine.* Dublin: The History Press, p.37.
2 NAI, CSORP/1847/G10795. Governor Grace specifically mentioned the prisoners' arrival on Spike Island on Saturday morning (9 October). However, Turnkey Walsh's statement (see Chapter 2) mentioned that the *Minerva* arrived at Passage at 11.00pm on 8 October. It is assumed that the craft docked at Passage because the island's pier was unable to accommodate a vessel of her size. Whilst it is likely that her additional cargo was unloaded at Passage, it is highly unlikely that the ship would bypass the island if she could have unloaded the convicts first. Thus, it seems logical that the convicts were ferried to Spike Island aboard smaller craft, as John Mitchel was just eight months later. (Mitchel, J. 1982. *Jail Journal.* University Press of Ireland, p.9.)

1. Crimes and Convictions

By the standards of the 21st century, the criminal justice system that operated in Ireland and Britain in the mid-19th century was harsh in the extreme. Hundreds of crimes, most of which would now be considered relatively trivial offences, were punishable by execution, at least in theory. The implementation of a death sentence usually meant the convicted person being hanged, a punishment that was carried out in public until the 1860s. In Ireland, contemporary newspapers documented hundreds of hangings taking place in Dublin and Cork in the 18th and 19th centuries.[1] For what were considered more heinous crimes, such as treason, the penalties were even more severe, such as the vivisection involved in a sentence of being hanged, drawn and quartered, which remained on the statute books until the 1870s.[2]

Part of the reason for this brutality was that some aspects of the criminal justice system had not changed substantially since the 13th century. This was the case in relation to the crime of larceny, or the theft of personal property. In AD 1275 a distinction was made in law between grand larceny and petty larceny based on the value of goods stolen, with one shilling being set as the threshold.[3] Grand larceny was a felony or a capital offence and therefore subject to a death sentence. Petty larceny was classed as a misdemeanour, and in the Middle Ages was punished by flogging or by a period of public

---

1 Henry, B. 1994. *Dublin Hanged: crime, law enforcement and punishment in late eighteenth-century Dublin*. Dublin: Irish Academic Press; O'Mahony, C. 1997. *In The Shadows: life in Cork 1750-1930*. Cork: Tower Books.
2 O'Donnabhain, B. 2011. *The social lives of severed heads: skull collection and display in medieval and early modern Ireland*. In: Bonogofsky, M. (ed.). *The Bioarchaeology of the Human Head: decapitation, decoration, and deformation*. Gainesville: University Press of Florida, pp.122–38.
3 3 Edw I c.15.

humiliation in the stocks. Prisons were used only for the short-term incarceration of those awaiting trial or sentence. Despite inflation, the value of the threshold between grand and petty larceny was not changed; by the 19th century an offence such as stealing a handkerchief could be regarded as grand larceny and was, in theory at least, punishable by death.

In an attempt to stifle perceived increases in criminality, successive governments in Ireland and Britain had responded to the momentous social and political changes of the Early Modern Period, such as the Reformation, the Industrial Revolution and the growth of cities, by increasing the number of offences punishable by death. In England, 187 new capital offences were created between 1660 and 1819.[4] Until 1717 the courts had no discretion in sentencing for capital offences, with one exception: since the time of the establishment of the American colonies in the reign of Elizabeth I (1558–1603), a death sentence could be reprieved if the offender agreed to be transported to the colonies, where they would become a source of unfree labour.[5] Vagrants were also subject to transportation or forced military service from this time.[6] With the Transportation Act of 1717, transportation became a sentence for many offences and no longer relied on the consent of the convicted person.[7]

The loss of the American colonies in the late 18th century put the transportation system under some stress and was a catalyst for change. While jurists and others had often commented on the

---

4 Shaw, A.G.L. 1966. *Convicts and the Colonies: a study of penal transportation from Great Britain and Ireland to Australia and other parts of the British Empire*. London: Faber and Faber, p.25.

5 Renton, A.W. and Robertson, M.A. (eds). 1907. *Encyclopaedia of the Laws of England, Vol II*. Edinburgh: William Green and Sons.

6 Shaw, p.23.

7 4 Geo I c.11.

disproportionality and harshness of the criminal justice system, it was the temporary suspension of transportation after 1776 that ushered in the first substantial reforms. Campaigners such as John Howard and Jeremy Bentham had pointed out the poor conditions of existing Irish and British prisons, which were never intended to hold prisoners for long periods of time.[8] The British government formulated three key responses. First, it allowed the use of convict labour at home in Britain and in Ireland.[9] Secondly, it passed the Penitentiary Act of 1779 allowing for the construction of a network of state-operated prisons.[10] Thirdly, it provided a new venue for transported convicts with the establishment of the penal colony at Botany Bay, in New South Wales, in 1788.[11]

The earliest of the state-operated prisons were the county and city gaols that were run by the local Grand Juries. For a time, these institutions housed all prisoners sentenced to transportation (then referred to as convicts) until a ship was procured to carry them to their destination. Convicts from all 32 counties of Ireland were often congregated in the county gaols of Cork and Dublin. However, these prisons were often seriously overcrowded and their governors complained frequently at the government's failure to remove the convict class. The answer to this problem came in the form of a convict depot. This was a single location where convicts from all over Ireland would assemble prior to their transportation. In 1817, Elizabeth Fort in Cork City became Ireland's first convict depot. Dublin's County Gaol at Kilmainham continued to provide accommodation for large numbers

---

8 John Howard was particularly horrified by the Irish prisons: see Starr, J. 1995. Prison reform in Ireland in the Age of Enlightenment. *History Ireland,* **3**:21–25.

9 16 Geo III c.43.

10 Devereaux, S. 1999. The Making of the Penitentiary Act, 1775-1779. *Historical Journal* **42**:405–433.

11 Shaw, Chapter 2.

of convicts from the northern half of the island. From there, convicts were shipped to the Cork depot, or boarded the transports at Kingstown (now Dún Laoghaire) before they called at Cork.

As the sentence of transportation became increasingly common, the Irish convict operation continued to grow. Soon further accommodation for those awaiting transportation was required. It was provided in the form of decommissioned warships known as hulks. HMS *Surprize* was anchored off Ringaskiddy in Cork's lower harbour and HMS *Essex* near the landward end of Kingstown's East Pier. These hulks served as male convict depots until 1837. Elizabeth Fort continued to detain female convicts. Then, with the hulks having fallen into disrepair and the costs of running the convict operation from the most southerly county under question, it was decided to centralise the transportation mechanisms in Dublin. In the resulting reorganisation, the hulks were decommissioned and male convicts were thenceforth held in the Dublin County Gaol at Kilmainham. Elizabeth Fort was closed and female convicts were moved into a special wing of the new all-female gaol in Dublin's Grangegorman Lane, which had opened in 1836. Kilmainham Gaol suffered serious overcrowding due to the influx of convicts. This situation was allowed to prevail for seven years, until a male convict depot was opened at Dublin's Smithfield in 1844.[12]

The onset of the Great Famine (1845–1852) and the associated perceived rise in criminality (mostly involving larceny) quickly rendered Smithfield (with accommodation for just over 300 prisoners) incapable of accommodating the male convict population. The situation was also exacerbated by a growing reluctance on the part of

12 To trace the development and locations of the various Irish convict depots (and hulks), see HMSO, *Reports of the Inspectors General on the General State of the Prisons of Ireland, 1817-1848*; see also: NAI, CSORP/1847/G9844.

Australian colonists to welcome the inmates from Irish and British prisons who frequently turned up on their doorstep. With nowhere to transport to, and with Smithfield filled to capacity, the authorities resorted to overcrowding Kilmainham once again. An unused building associated with the Richmond Bridewell was also converted to accommodate 250 convicts.[13] After the Summer Assizes of 1846, with Kilmainham, Smithfield and Richmond completely overcrowded, there was little option but to leave the convicts in the county and city gaols where they had been initially detained. This made the convict population a problem for every gaol and every prison governor in Ireland. As county and city gaols filled to levels often in excess of four times their official capacity, and their governors complained loudly and sought increased funding from central government, it became very apparent that a new convict depot had to be found.

The shape of that new depot was not immediately apparent. Although an entirely new structure had been proposed for Dublin some years earlier, it was quite evident that this could not be built in time to relieve the overcrowded gaols. In the meantime, the authorities had to look elsewhere. For a time they considered placing new hulks in the harbours at Cork and Dublin,[14] but permanent buildings were always preferable. In the end the government began to turn its eyes southwards, to a harbour that hadn't seen convicts in a decade – Cork.

In the lower reaches of Cork's vast harbour, the 104-acre Spike Island caught the government's attention. The island had formed part

---

13 HMSO, *Report of the Inspectors General on the General State of the Prisons of Ireland 1847* (hereafter *Prisons of Ireland Report 1847*; reports from other years will have the same title excepting the relevant year).
14 The siting of hulks in Cork and Kingstown was considered again as Spike Island's depot expanded rapidly in 1847 and into 1848. See NAI, GPO/Minute Book (XB)/3/268. The idea was mooted again in the early 1850s (see NAI, GPO/Letter Book (LB)/4/92).

of Cork harbour's military defences for almost eight decades. In order to protect transports of both matériel and personnel across the Atlantic during the American Revolutionary Wars, a gun battery was erected in 1779 on the eastern side of Spike Island (Fig. 1.1).[15] After the Treaty of Paris in 1783, when Britain recognised the independence of the USA, the Lord Lieutenant ordered that the battery on Spike Island should be dismantled.[16] However, the topography of the island was to be transformed soon after this as part of the intensification of the militarisation of the harbour when France became the main threat to British interests. With the outbreak of the French Revolution (1789–1799), the military function of the island was once again considered important.

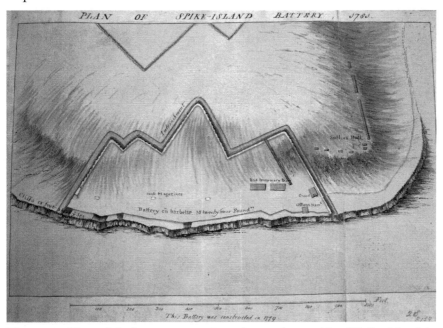

Figure 1.1 Plan of the battery erected on the southeast side of Spike Island in 1779 and dismantled after 1783. (Image © PRO: MPH1/188)

---

15 PRO, MPF 1/159.
16 PRO WO 1/611; McEnery, J.H. 2006. *Fortress Ireland: the story of the Irish coastal forts and the River Shannon defence line*. Bray: Wordwell, p.42.

The site of the early battery was incorporated into a larger pentagonal fort that was built under the direction of General Charles Vallancey at the east side of the island (Fig. 1.2). This fort was still under construction when the site was visited in October 1790 by John Fane, 10th Earl of Westmorland, who served as Lord Lieutenant from 1789 to 1794 and after whom the new fort was named.[17] (Contemporary maps use the spelling Westmoreland rather than the version preferred more recently, Westmorland.) However, the French invasions of Ireland in 1796 and 1798 convinced Vallancey and others that fortifications in Cork harbour were still inadequate. After the Act of Union (1801), the Irish Board of Ordnance was suppressed and its functions were taken over by the much better-resourced Board of Ordnance, based in London. A report on the defences of Ireland was commissioned and was delivered in November 1801.[18] The report's author, Colonel Hope, suggested replacing the first Fort Westmoreland with a much larger fortress capable of holding 2,000–3,000 men. The foundation stone for the expanded fort was laid with some pomp on 6 June 1804.[19] The new, larger fortress (which also came to be referred to as Fort Westmoreland) consisted of six bastions connected by ramparts and surrounded by a dry moat.

The basic walls of the hexagon were almost complete by 1815 and two barracks buildings (one for officers, one for 'the men') had been completed in the southwest corner of the fort by 1820 (Fig. 1.3). However, construction was halted that year and three decades later the remnants of Spike Island's original hilltop still sat in the middle of the fort, whilst its buildings, casemates and glacis also remained

---

17 Tuckey, F.H. 1837. *The County and City of Cork Remembrancer; or Annals of the County and City of Cork.* Cork: Osborne Savage and Son, p.204.
18 McEnery, p.42.
19 Tuckey, p.223.

unfinished.[20] Now, with a potential source of free labour overcrowding gaols all over the country, the location of convicts on Spike Island seemed to offer a credible solution to two separate problems.

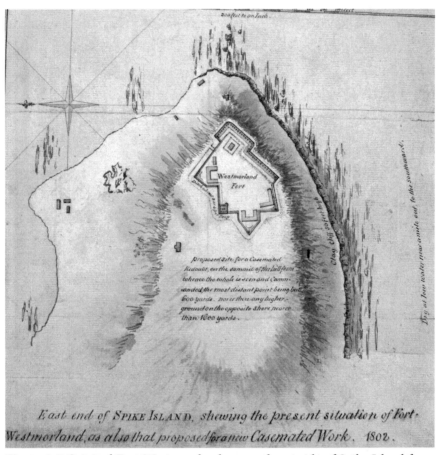

Figure 1.2 Original Fort Westmoreland on southeast side of Spike Island from 1802 planning for extant fort. (Image © PRO: MPH1/158)

The idea of converting Spike Island's fort into a convict depot was first suggested in February 1847, in a letter from the Surveyor General of Convict Prisons in Britain, Joshua Jebb, to Sir William Somerville, then Under-Secretary in the Home Department.

---

20 PRO, MPH 1/191, MPH 1/188 & MFQ 1/1335. See also: NAI, CSORP/1847/G8814.

Curiously, Jebb's suggestion seemed to fall on deaf ears, although inquiries about the availability of the island's buildings were made. In June, the Inspector General of Prisons, Clement Johnson, repeated Jebb's suggestion and emphasised the urgency of the matter. By 2 July 1847 all parties were in agreement and the 82nd Regiment, then deployed on the island, was ordered back to England (although the military would retain some accommodation within the fort). Surveyors were then dispatched to the island under the watchful eye of one of the two Inspectors General of Irish Prisons, Major Edward Cottingham.[21]

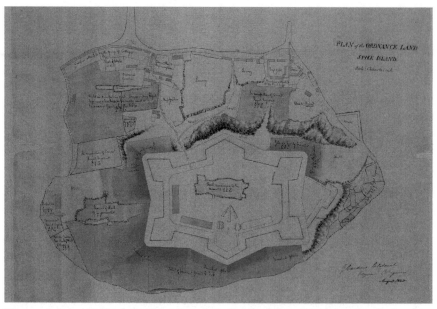

Figure 1.3 An 1820 plan of the as yet unfinished Fort Westmoreland, showing the completed Georgian barracks blocks in the southwest corner of the Parade Ground and, near the entrance to the fort, the remains of the original hilltop yet to be excavated. The remains of the most easterly bastion of the original Fort Westmoreland were still standing to the east of the fort. (Image © PRO: MPH1/188)

21 PRO, HO 45/1395. Major Cottingham was responsible for the northern half of the country while his colleague, Captain Clement Johnson, oversaw the southern district.

Within a few years, this small island in Cork harbour was to become the largest convict prison in either Ireland or Britain, housing over 2,300 prisoners by the early 1850s. The location was secure and convenient as a point of embarkation for the transportation of convicts to the Australian penal colonies in Van Diemen's Land and Swan River, as well as to the fortification-construction sites at Gibraltar and Bermuda.[22] However, in 1847 the scale, extent and devastation of the Great Famine were not fully understood. Thus, the prison was originally intended as a temporary detention centre for no more than a few hundred convicts. The first of these men arrived by sea in October 1847.[23]

---

22 Convict transportation to New South Wales had been suspended in 1840 while the first penal colony was established in Tasmania (then known as Van Diemen's Land) in 1803.
23 Marine transport was more secure than an overland route. The rail network from Dublin to Cork was under construction in 1847 and did not reach the outskirts of Cork City until 1849.

2. The First Convicts

One of the criminals disembarked on the island's pier on that October day in 1847 was Thomas O'Neill, a 15-year-old from Dublin. O'Neill was committed to Kilmainham Gaol on 17 April 1846, on suspicion of stealing three bridles and some other items. His co-accused was John Esdill, also 15 years old, but who, unlike O'Neill, had not served a prison sentence prior to 1846. When O'Neill and Esdill were brought before a judge on 18 June 1846, Esdill was acquitted; O'Neill was sentenced to seven years' transportation. He returned to Kilmainham Gaol and spent another month there before being transferred to the convict depot at Smithfield. He spent a further 14 months there and was described by the governor as 'well conducted' before he finally boarded *Minerva*, bound for Spike Island.[1]

Figure 2.1 Spike Island's first convicts would have disembarked at the same location as the modern pier. (Image © courtesy of National Monuments Service)

---

1 NAI, Smithfield Prison Register, 1844-49, 1/14/1 and Kilmainham Prison Register 1845-48, 1/10/7.

As O'Neill alighted from the boat and on to Spike Island's pier (Fig. 2.1), he carried a little secret with him. When *Minerva*'s owners rather stupidly left nothing but a canvas between the convicts and the ship's cargo, young Thomas O'Neill was one of those who couldn't help himself. He stole several silk neckerchiefs and carried them with him from the ship. Two days later, he swapped two of them with Warder Lawrence Walsh for a quantity of snuff.

When *Minerva*'s owners complained of their loss, Walsh alerted the governor. He claimed that he had received only one garment and that O'Neill had informed him that he had been given the neckerchief by his mother before he left Smithfield. Consequently, Walsh claimed, he was unaware of its provenance. His receipt of stolen goods was first acknowledged as a genuine mistake, but he was subsequently dismissed when it was discovered that he had in fact received two neckerchiefs. Lawrence Walsh holds the dubious distinction of being the first of many warders to be dismissed from service on Spike Island. He had been on the island for just eight days. Thomas O'Neill was the only other guilty party named in the correspondence relating to the theft, but multiple garments were found among the belongings of various prisoners in the days that followed. Thus, it is quite likely that several others joined O'Neill in some form of unpleasant punishment.[2] Their punishments would have ranged from '25 lashes on the bare back' to solitary confinement in a small cell without any bedding or pillows. Such punishments were common throughout the period of the island's use as a convict prison.[3] One of the changes made to the buildings on the island prior to the arrival of the first prisoners was the preparation of 11 cells for solitary confinement. These were created

---

2 NAI, CSORP/1847/G10795 and GPO/XB/3/213.
3 NAI, GPB/MB/2/2 June 1881 & 27 September 1882.

in No.3 Bastion of the fort when the latrines previously used by the soldiers were refitted as solitary cells.[4]

Thomas O'Neill had shared *Minerva*'s voyage with a number of young petty offenders. Seventeen-year-old William Frar from Co. Down had been convicted of larceny, while Joseph Cooper from Co. Laois was the same age and had a similar conviction. Bartholomew Mears from Limerick was only 15 years old but had already been convicted of theft on two previous occasions. The governor of Limerick Gaol had recorded his 'bad' conduct in that facility.[5] These young offenders seem likely participants in the theft aboard the *Minerva*. Yet thieves were not the only criminals who stepped onto Spike Island's pier on that first morning. One of the more interesting offenders was a young man from Carlow known as James Cleary, or Clarke, and his crime was one of the less common variety.

The 28-year-old Cleary had been married to Jane Maher in Tullow, Co. Carlow, in 1844. That fact did not prevent him from changing his last name to Clarke and taking the hand of Margaret Kelly in Dublin on 9 May 1846. Kelly was described as 'a pretty and well-dressed young woman' and it is certainly possible that Cleary fell for her. It is equally possible that her dowry, £60 worth of furniture, was the real object of his desire. Although Cleary claimed that he had been entrapped into his second marriage while in a state of intoxication, his plea did not impress the jury. They found him guilty of bigamy and the judge promptly sentenced him to seven years' transportation.[6]

Contrary to popular belief, Petty Crimes courts did not sentence offenders to transportation. Those who received that sentence

---

4 NAI, CSORP/1847/G8814.
5 NAI, Smithfield Prison Register, 1844-49, 1/14/1.
6 *Freeman's Journal,* 26 October 1846.

were convicted by higher courts and tended to be repeat, or serious, offenders. While it was theoretically possible to sentence petty offenders to transportation, such sentences were seldom passed down, unless the petty offences were of a repetitive nature.[7] Spike Island's inmates were always considered to be at the more serious end of the spectrum. Yet in the early days it was thought that the island should only house those sentenced to shorter periods of transportation. As Spike Island was only intended to be a temporary depot, the authorities saw no reason to change their transportation practices and as a result, Kingstown harbour was still envisaged as the departure point of all convict ships. However, fewer and fewer men were actually being transported as resistance to the system grew at the destinations. It was suggested, therefore, that only the most serious offenders be shipped out; those were the men sentenced to 10 years' transportation or more. It was considered appropriate that those definitely destined for transportation should remain in Dublin, while those sentenced to seven years or less should be sent to Spike Island. The Inspector General of Prisons, Clement Johnson, explained his policy in a letter to the Chief Secretary:

> It is necessary for me to premise that formerly all embarkations for the Colonies were carried into effect at Cork, but so many were found to be the inconveniences of this plan ...

7 McCarthy, C. & Todd, K. 2013. *Neva: The Horrifying Fate of a Convict Ship and the Irish Women Aboard.* Cork: Mercier Press, pp.261–76. Of 53 clearly defined offences on *Neva*'s convict indent, 45 might be considered serious, mostly the theft of property that was valuable at that time (i.e. animals, luxury wearing apparel, large quantities of cloth, jewellery, assorted luxury goods). Of the remaining eight, four were vagrants (usually prostitutes) and four were guilty of theft on a smaller scale, though they may have been repeat offenders. Insofar as we can ascertain, none of *Neva*'s convicts was guilty of the theft of food, though such theft was probably much more common during the famine. (The voyage of the *Neva* occurred more than a decade prior to the Great Famine.)

that the Irish Government found themselves compelled ... to discontinue this plan and since that period all embarkations have taken place in Kingstown Harbour.

Considering therefore that such will continue to be the practice, I venture to make the following observations –

It appears to me obvious that the persons hereafter to be embarked for transportation to Bermuda, Gibraltar and finally to our Australian Colonies should be those sentenced to Transportation for life and for periods of 10 & fourteen years and upwards and in special cases men only sentenced to seven years. These persons I consider it would be advisable as a general rule to confine during the period of their detention in this country in the Depots of the city of Dublin whereby they would be available for embarkation at any period that an opportunity of sending them to the Colonies might present itself.

Another good effect of this would be that persons sentenced for the more serious offences would be more immediately under the superintendence of the Inspectors General and the care of officers of more experience than those at Spike Island. By this means the prisoners confined at Spike Island would principally consist of men sentenced to periods of Seven years...

I would therefore suggest that the first body of convicts sent to Spike Island should be 300 men sentenced to seven years transportation taken from those now in the Dublin Depots and that their places be immediately filled by persons sentenced to long periods of transportation – principally from the northern and western gaols...

Another great advantage to be derived from this course of proceeding will be that we shall be able to commence our experiment – for such it must be in a degree – at Spike Island under most favourable circumstances – as the first considerable body of prisoners sent there will be in a great degree broke in and rendered amenable to discipline by their previous sojourn in the Dublin depots.[8]

So the men who stood on Spike Island's pier that Saturday morning were part of a temporary experiment. They were not the most serious offenders in the penal system, nor were they considered petty criminals. Some had proven themselves dangerous individuals, and none more so than Patrick Colliton.

Colliton was 21 years of age when he reached Spike Island. His comparative youth had not prevented him from taking part in one of the murkier facets of Irish life. By the middle of the 19th century, British law and order was contested in many areas and large tracts of rural Ireland were partially controlled by secret societies. Known as Ribbonmen, these societies were quite numerous and did not have a unified command structure. However, the groups were broadly categorised by the authorities as 'Whiteboys' (the name of an organisation from the previous century) and they attempted to rule the countryside in pursuit of a quasi-political agenda. In theory they opposed tithes, excessive rents, evictions and all the oppressive acts of a regime that governed the poor in the interests of the rich. In reality, many Ribbon groups served the interests of their members ahead of any communal cause and many (though by no means all) were transformed into groups of ruffians that terrorised communities as much as the red-coated troops of the British crown. The Ribbonmen contributed greatly to the breaking down of law and order. They also helped

---

8 NAI, CSORP/1847/G9844.

to propagate a negative image of Ireland in the minds of those who governed that island from Britain. Colliton was a 'Whiteboy' and his case illustrates the climate of fear and intimidation in which these organisations operated. On 3 August 1846, Colliton was arraigned in Nenagh, Co. Tipperary. His trial was reported as follows:

> Patrick Colliton was given in charge for threatening Jeremiah Wixtead to quit his habitation.
>
> Jeremiah Wixtead examined by Mr Sauase ... I took land from a man named Wm Kelly a year and a half ago: I gave him 50l, for his good will of it; the prisoner is a father in law [sic] of Kelly's; on the 29th of April last I heard a rap at the door and I desired it to be opened; I am married; my wife's name is Biddy Brien (laughter); when the door was opened the men came into the room: one of them had a pistol, and another a gun; I am unable to identify the prisoner as one of the party; the men desired me to give up the land I had taken or they would have my life.
>
> John Wade (a little boy about 12 years old) was examined by Mr Scott and corroborated the foregoing witness; after considerable pressing by Mr Scott, and some hesitation on the part of the witness, he identified the prisoner as one of the men.
>
> To Mr Bolleston – My mother said to me if the prisoner was transported she would not fear anything.
>
> To a Juror – It is in consequence of what my mother said, that I swore to day against the prisoner; I am not sure the prisoner is one of the men that was at the house.
>
> To Mr Scott [sic] – Were you told not to identify the prisoner?

Witness – No, Sir.

Margaret Wade (sister to the last witness) was examined, and identified the prisoner as one of the men.

To the Judge – My mother desired me not to swear against the prisoner if I was not certain that he was the man.

Eliza Wixtead said, she never desired her son, John Wade, to swear against the prisoner.

John Wade was here confronted with his mother and told by the Judge, if he did not tell the truth he would be committed to prison; in answer to the judge he admitted that his mother did not tell him to prosecute the prisoner.

Constable Walsh deposed to seeing Elizabeth Wade identify the prisoner amongst a number of men.

Mr O Dell, 81, deposed to the neighbourhood in which the outrage was committed, having been in a disturbed state at the time.

The Jury without leaving the box, returned a verdict of guilty. The prisoner is quite a young fellow not being more than 19 years of age.[9]

While the newspaper account of Colliton's trial is somewhat confusing, it is quite clear that the 12-year-old John Wade was reluctant to identify Colliton and that the boy's mother had considered what may become of her family after the trial. She had hoped that Colliton would be transported overseas and he was, though only as far as Spike Island.

So it was that Spike Island's initial role in the criminal justice system was written. It would accommodate serious offenders, but not as serious as those who remained in Dublin awaiting transportation.

---

9 *Tipperary Free Press*, 8 August 1846.

In time, this would change as the Spike Island depot expanded to accommodate all sorts of convicts, with all sorts of sentences. Indeed, the island had already been modified significantly in advance of the arrival of Colliton and his fellow prisoners.

3. The Geography of a Prison

Once all were disembarked on the island's pier, the convicts were marched up a steep, meandering track. As they crested the hill they probably noted the town of Cove[1] across the deep-water channel on their left-hand side. Ahead of them, the foreboding grey limestone walls of Fort Westmoreland contrasted starkly with the prettiness of the surrounding harbour. Soon they were passing through the arched entrance, flanked by two of Fort Westmoreland's six bastions.

Emerging into the daylight on the darker side of Westmoreland's walls, the prisoners were inside a large, star-shaped artillery fort. The scale of this facility dwarfed even the largest of the county gaols. This was not at all apparent to them, however, because about 50ft (15.2m) in front of them a 20ft high (6.1m) stockade inhibited their view of anything beyond it. They had just passed through a set of casemates (vaulted chambers built into the ramparts between the fort's projecting bastions), which housed the fort's small garrison now that the barracks buildings had been given over to the prison, and they were standing in the barrack yard. The stockade was all that would separate their convict establishment from their military neighbours. Soon the convicts were marching through a gate at the centre of the stockade and into the interior of the fortress.[2]

The inside of the fort was a wilderness. Large outcrops of rock and dense thickets of undergrowth dominated the spaces between the few buildings, often obscuring the line of vision from one side of the

---

1 Originally called the Cove of Cork, Cove was renamed Queenstown after Queen Victoria's visit in August 1849. The name of the town was changed to Cobh after the creation of the Irish Free State.
2 NAI, CSORP/1847/G8814. The stockade was erected in front of the casemates in anticipation of their future conversion to another convict prison.

fort to the other. The Inspector General of Prisons described it thus:

> ...the whole of the interior of the fort was found by us in a state of nature, i.e. that no steps had been taken to level the ground within the walls; the whole was rough, and in many places blocks of solid rock of great height intercepted communication.[3]

Minerva's men and other convicts would soon begin to tame this wilderness, gradually transforming it into a modern barrack square.

In the months before their arrival, the Board of Ordnance, in partnership with the Inspector General of Prisons, had toiled feverishly to transform the military base into an acceptable prison. The work was overseen by the Inspector General of Prisons, Major Edward Cottingham, whose difficult brief was one that overshadowed and inhibited the early years of the prison's development. Cottingham was unable to go about the construction of a convict prison, but rather had to ensure that the depot was only of a temporary nature. As he explained in a letter to the Lord Lieutenant:

> I beg to observe that I have in all the alterations that suggested themselves to me strictly kept in view the instructions contained in the letter from the Home Office that this measure is only a temporary one and that at any time the arrangements consequent upon making it a convict prison can be removed and the buildings restored to their original purpose.[4]

The Home Office in London had made it clear that Fort

---

3 HMSO, *Prisons of Ireland Report 1847.*
4 NAI, CSORP/1847/G8814.

Westmoreland would remain key to its coastal defence plans and insisted that it could be converted back into a military installation within one week. Nonetheless, Cottingham had made some considerable alterations to the fort before the convicts walked through its gate.

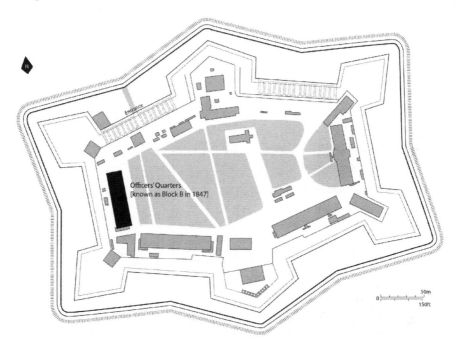

Figure 3.1 Location of Block B. This building was originally known as the Officers' Quarters and was later called the 1916 Building as it was burned accidentally that year. (Image © courtesy of Department of Archaeology, UCC)

Inside the fort, the men were marched toward the rear, or southern, wall. They passed a large rocky outcrop on their left and an imposing two-storey block on their right. With its limestone façade and red-brick trim, this building was known as Block B and, until Cottingham's alterations, had housed the officers of Spike Island's garrison (Fig. 3.1 and Fig. 3.2). For a time, the new governor could not take up the residence provided for him in the upper storey of Block B. The difficulty occurred as a result of a quirk in the administrative system. Nobody in the convict service had the authority to order the military out of the block and so an application had to be made to the military to issue such an order. Although the order was eventually issued, the governor and his staff had been absent from the island during the crucial period of its transition from military base to convict depot, resulting in further delays to the completion of the project. However, by the time of the convicts' arrival, the governor and his officers had been installed.[5]

Figure 3.2 Block B (originally Officers' Quarters) today, viewed from the east. (Image © authors)

Another 20ft tall (6.1m) stockade obscured most of their view of Block B as they passed it by. By now they could probably see Block A, ahead of them (Fig. 3.3 and Fig. 3.4). This was a slightly larger structure than Block B and its two storeys ran the length of the seaward wall of the fort between No.2 Bastion and No.3 Bastion.

---

5 NAI, GPO/XB/3/178.

It had been built some 30 years previously and had originally accommodated the ordinary soldiers in its 22 barrack rooms. In the months before the convicts' arrival, Block A was completely refurbished so that it could now provide secure lodgings for its convict detainees. A 20ft high (6.1m) stockade was erected 32.5ft (10m) in front of the façade of Block A. The stockade extended for 20ft (6.1m) beyond each gable and was joined to the fort's rampart wall at the rear. The wall of the fort was adorned with 3ft long (0.9m) iron bars pointing downward, the 19th century's answer to razor-wire. In front, the stockade was further divided internally by 10ft tall (3.1m) palisades, creating a series of separate yards that were considered essential to the segregation of prisoners. Similar palisades divided the corridor between the rear of Block A and the wall of the fort, creating a number of separate yards in that space. In total, the block had 10 airing yards, with privies, washing troughs and sheds in each one. The men lodged on the block's ground-floor used the yards at the front of the building, entering them directly through the doors on that side. The occupants of the upper floor used the yards between the rear of the block and the fort wall. Those yards were accessed via a corridor to the rear of the 11 dormitories along the length of the upper floor. Four rooms at either end exited via stairs constructed at either gable, while the three middle dormitories exited via a central staircase.

The interior of Block A had also received a significant overhaul. Indeed, it seems that 'everything had to be constructed as *de novo* except the absolute walls of the barracks'.[6] The block contained 11 dormitories on its ground floor, each one measuring 48ft by 18ft (14.6m x 5.5m), and 11 smaller dormitories upstairs, each one measuring 40ft by 18ft (12.2m x 5.5m). It was intended by the prison

---

6 HMSO, *Prisons of Ireland Report 1847.*

authorities that each of these dormitories would sleep up to 30 men, thus the block could accommodate 660 inmates. By the end of 1847, less than three months after the arrival of the first convicts, 608 were lodged there. The men who arrived on the *Minerva* first slept on soldiers' 'billet beds', which were procured from the naval stores on nearby Haulbowline Island. These beds were later replaced by suspended cots (hammocks), which allowed room for the necessary table to be installed in each dormitory. This table was used for eating and for indoor work. Meals were initially carried on specially fitted hand-trucks that carried mess trays from the kitchen, situated in the uncompleted barracks building to the east of Block A.[7]

Figure 3.3 The façade of Block A today, from the northeast. (Image © courtesy of S.H. Bean)

The authorities had encountered significant difficulty in providing the sewers for Block A. Curiously, the military personnel had not been provided with comparable measures of hygiene and a sewer

---

7 Ibid. & NAI, CSORP/1847/G8814. It should be noted that the prison's kitchen later changed its location.

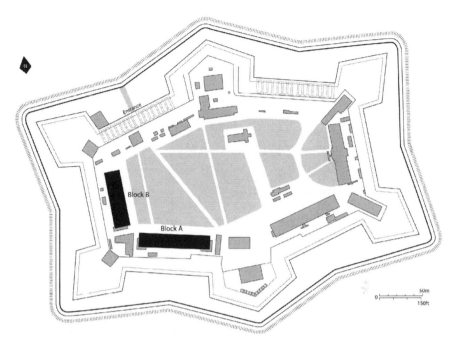

Figure 3.4 Block A's location. Blocks A and B were the only barracks buildings completed before the fort-building project was suspended in 1820. (Image © courtesy of Department of Archaeology, UCC)

had to be blasted from the solid rock beneath the prison yards.[8] The sewer was considered a potential escape route, so iron grilles were placed on either end and wooden sentry box-type latrines were built on its course in each of the rear yards. It joined an older sewer that ran from the rear of Block A, through the sally port, before then joining another one that had emptied the soldiers' privies in No.3 Bastion. These latter were the latrines that were now converted into cells for solitary confinement (Fig. 3.5 and Fig. 3.6).[9]

    The conversion of a military base to a secure convict depot was a complex task. It was further complicated in that all of the works outlined above had to be completed in less than four months. On 7

8 HMSO, *Prisons of Ireland Report 1847*.
9 NAI, CSORP/1847/G8814.

31

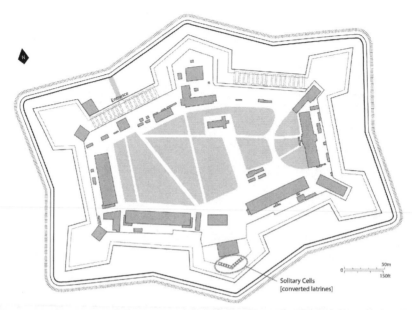

Figure 3.5 Location of the original latrines, some of which were converted to cells for solitary confinement in 1847. (Image © courtesy of Department of Archaeology, UCC)

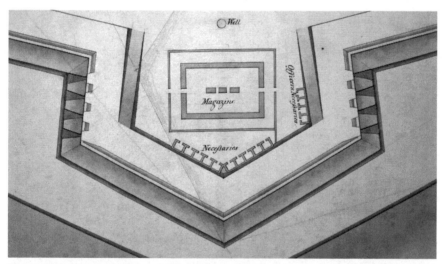

Figure 3.6 Original plan of the latrines, labelled *Necessaries* on this drawing from the 1820s. By 1847, 17 'necessaries' (or spaces for same) ran the length of the southern wall extending west and east from the central 10 marked on this diagram. The Officers' Necessaries had been removed. (Image © PRO: MPH1/188)

August 1847, under pressure from the governors of crowded county gaols and from the Home Secretary, Sir George Grey, the Lord Lieutenant's Office addressed the following enquiry to the Inspector General of Prisons:

> I am directed by the Lord Lieutenant to acquaint that a further communication has been received from Sir George Grey, requesting to be informed in what state the arrangements at Spike Island are, and what has occasioned the delay in completing the plan originally decided on for the reception of convicts there. I am to request that you will immediately furnish me with the information requested by Sir George Grey and he would like to know at the same time whether there is any other point connected with the matter which it would be desirable to have brought under Sir George Grey's notice, in order to complete the undertaking in the most expeditious and satisfactory manner.[10]

The reply informed the Lord Lieutenant that some difficulty had been encountered 'in consequence of the contractor ... not having forwarded his works as expeditiously as he ought to have done'. Nonetheless, Captain Cole of the Royal Engineers had intervened and promised to keep the 254 men employed on the works moving ahead as rapidly as possible.[11] The letter did not inform the Lord Lieutenant that Major Cottingham was ailing under the pressure of the task. A committed Orangeman, Cottingham was a veteran of the peninsular campaign. He retired from the army after sustaining severe wounds at the Battle of Albuera in 1811. In his role as Inspector General of

---

10 NAI, CSORP/1847/G8783.
11 NAI, CSORP/1847/G8911.

Prisons, Cottingham was a very diligent and determined character, and his colleague later recalled the Major's demise:

> From July to October, Major Cottingham, with little interval, resided almost constantly at Cove, and, I believe of those who met him there, none will deny that few could have equalled him in the quickness and intelligence with which he carried out the arrangements; and none could have exceeded him in anxiety and constancy of exertion. The last, however, combined with exposure to severe weather, proved too much for an enfeebled constitution; and shortly after the completion of his undertaking, and his return to Dublin, he was taken seriously ill, never rallied, and died at the beginning of the year.[12]

Cottingham may have been one of the first victims of Spike Island's convict prison, but he certainly wasn't the last. Having received its first inmates on 9 October 1847, before the end of that year seven convicts had died. Unlike Cottingham, they were not in receipt of any posthumous tributes and their names survive only in the Coroner's requests for expenses for attending their inquests.[13] Indeed, records of the early years of Spike Island's convict prison are very incomplete.

In the days following the *Minerva*'s arrival her convicts were joined by others from counties Waterford, Tipperary and Kerry. Shortly after, other ships ferried more offenders from Dublin.[14] It is likely that Thomas O'Neill spent those days hidden away in a solitary cell at

---

12 HMSO, *Prisons of Ireland Report 1847.*
13 NAI, CSORP/1849/G2637.
14 *Southern Reporter and Cork Commercial Courier,* 9 October 1847, *The Cork Examiner,* 11 & 20 October 1847, *Tipperary Free Press,* 16 October 1847, *Kerry Examiner and Munster General Observer,* 29 October 1847, *Limerick and Clare Examiner,* 13 October 1847. See also: NAI, CON/LB/3/October 1847. Some convicts sent to Cork from Tipperary, Waterford and Kerry were forwarded to Dublin. It is also worth noting that military convicts initially lodged on Spike Island were subsequently dispatched/returned to Dublin.

the rear of No.3 Bastion. There is no way of knowing what happened to him after the *Minerva* thefts. We can say that there is no record of his ever leaving, but neither is there a record of his death on the island. Just over 1,200 convicts were to die on the island during the 36 years of the prison's operation; the names of about 80% of these are known. While the death rate on Spike Island was very high in its early years, the overwhelming majority of the prisoners served their time and were released. It is likely that O'Neill did likewise. He was probably there to see, or may even have participated in, the island's first attempted breakout on 1 December 1847. That escape attempt was led by Michael Power and was uncovered when the military sentry heard the bricks being removed from one of the bricked-up windows at the rear of Block A.[15]

James Cleary left Spike Island in September 1848. He was shipped back to Dublin and days later he departed Ireland, bound for Australia aboard the convict ship *Pestonjee Bomanjee*. During the voyage he was treated by the ship's surgeon for diarrhoea and ophthalmia, but he eventually arrived in Van Diemen's Land on 2 January 1849.[16] By March of that year he was convicted of burglary in Hobart. While the offence was placed on his record, he was not punished. Cleary eventually left the convict system in November 1853. Curiously, there is no record of his being married a third time and his name passed quietly from all Australian records.[17]

Patrick Colliton probably served his seven-year sentence on

---

15 NAI, GPO/LB/1/202 and GPO/XB/3/242. There were several prisoners of that name who might have been imprisoned on the island in late 1847. Indeed, it seems that Grace was admonished for not being clearer about which of these men he referred to when writing to the Inspector General. (See NAI, TR 6, p.202, p.187, TR7, p.35. See also: NAI, CRF/1847/ P8.)

16 PRO Admiralty (ADM) 101/59/3.

17 AOT, CON/14/1/39 and CON/33/1/92.

Spike Island. There is no record of his ever having left the island after any appeal or otherwise. Although a man of the same name and age was accused of assault in Nenagh in 1849, a slight difference in height and description of complexion means that it is quite likely a different person. However, the fact that this Patrick Collison [sic] stood accused of assaulting a man named Brien suggests that he may have been a relative of the man incarcerated on Spike Island after the testimony of Biddy Brien's husband.[18]

While it appears that Colliton and O'Neill remained on the island after Cleary had been shipped out, they did not pass their days in idleness. From the beginning, the Spike Island convict prison was expected to extract the maximum productivity from its convict workforce. In spite of the initial edict to ensure it remained a temporary depot, Spike Island would be changed and reordered considerably over the course of its lifetime as a holding centre for convicts.

---

18 NAI, Nenagh Prison Register 1848-50, 1/30/3.

4. In Mitchel's Time

The Anglo-Irish Treaty of December 1921 created the Irish Free State but left control of the Cork harbour forts with Britain. This was a source of irritation to Irish nationalists until the facilities were handed over to Irish control in July 1938. Some years later the new Irish administration renamed Fort Westmoreland. Perhaps not surprisingly, the fort was named after the author of one of the influential texts of Irish nationalism, who was also the best-known inmate of the prison. Spike Island's fort would now be known as 'Fort Mitchel,' in honour of John Mitchel, a leader of the mid-19th-century nationalist Young Ireland movement (Fig. 4.1). Mitchel had spent all of four nights on the island before being transported to Bermuda aboard HMS *Scourge*.

Figure 4.1 John Mitchel (1815–1875) as a younger adult. Mitchel was 32 years old at the time of his captivity on Spike Island. (Image © National Library of Ireland)

Amid growing dissatisfaction with the British government response during the appalling famine, the Irish separatist movement was flexing its militant muscles in the latter half of the 1840s. John Mitchel had come to the attention of the authorities through his contributions to two Irish nationalist newspapers, *The Nation* and *The United Irishman*. By 1848 this well-known nationalist was publicly advocating an armed rebellion against British rule in Ireland. This led to his arrest and subsequent conviction for 'Treason Felony'. He was sentenced to 14 years' transportation and was dispatched to

Spike Island. John Mitchel arrived in Cork harbour on 28 May 1848.

On his first sighting of Spike Island, Mitchel thought it 'a rueful looking place'.[1] He was rowed to the pier and escorted from there to the interior of the fort. On entering Fort Westmoreland, Mitchel later described being escorted 'past several sentries, through several gratings, and at last into a small square court'. He went on to describe the 'vaulted room' that served as his cell and was accessed via a door from this court. Over a century after his departure, it had become a common but erroneous assumption that the courtyard Mitchel referred to was the one on the west side of what came to be called the Mitchel Gaol – containing the solitary cells – and that the vaulted room was one of the cells within. However, the so-called Mitchel Gaol, now known as the Punishment Block (see Chapter 11), was not built until over a decade after Mitchel's incarceration on the island.[2] This created some confusion as to where the fort's namesake actually spent his few nights on the island. However, the key might lie in another passage from his famous *Jail Journal*:

> There is a door in the high wall leading into another inclosure [sic] and as I was taking a turn through my territory today,

---

1 Mitchel, p.9.

2 The '*Mitchel Gaol*' is so called because it is purported to be the location where John Mitchel was held while on Spike Island. This is not possible given the details presented in Mitchel's own account and the fact that the structure was built between 1859 and 1860 as a means of providing cellular accommodation for prisoners (see pp.172–6). In 1860, a German visitor to the prison noted that 'Separate cells have lately been commenced on the island to enforce cellular imprisonment when required as a disciplinary punishment for bad conduct, and to prevent the necessity of sending such prisoners to the distant prison at Mountjoy' (von Holtzendorff, F. 1860. *The Irish Convict System: More Especially Intermediate Prisons.* UK: University of Liverpool, Knowsley Pamphlet Collection, pp.72–3). The building is described as complete in the prison governor's report of February 1861. In addition, the building is not marked in the first edition OSI map, which was completed before 1846. Neither was it marked on the Arthur Roberts's map from June 1848 (CSORP/1849/Box 3/621/7).

the turnkey was near that door, and he said to me in a low voice – "This way sir if you please"; he held the door open, I passed through...[3]

His description of a 'high wall' is interesting, especially when coupled with the fact that a door in that wall opened into another enclosure within the fort. This means that Mitchel was certainly located behind a stockade, indicating that he was located in Block A, Block B or in the northwest casemates of the barracks. Mitchel's room adjoined a courtyard and therefore had to be on the ground floor. He also described it as large and 'vaulted'. The casemates were then occupied by the military, the magazines were each serving different functions, and the only remaining 'vaulted' rooms on the ground floor were those on the bottom storey of Block B (Fig. 4.2; see also Figs 3.1 and 3.2).[4] That location would also have placed him directly under the watchful eyes of the prison's senior staff, who were located on the upper storey. The Block's top floor also provided office accommodation and one of the rooms housed a Protestant chapel. By March 1848, with the convict population now standing at 608, the bottom floor of Block B was given over to convict accommodation. The party walls were removed from seven of its ground-floor vaulted rooms and the large wards created were each kitted out for 30 convicts. The remaining two ground-floor vaulted bays retained their party walls, creating an additional four rooms. It seems that, for a few days, Mitchel had one of those four rooms to himself.[5]

---

3 Mitchel, p.11.

4 There were 'large vaulted' rooms in the magazines in No.3 Bastion and No.6 Bastion, but each of these was serving another function at the time of Mitchel's imprisonment and neither was surrounded by a stockade.

5 HMSO, *Prisons of Ireland Report 1847*. Although it is not possible to say exactly when Block B was opened, it must have occurred before 1 March 1848. Block A was incapable of

Figure 4.2 Block B: Mitchel was probably incarcerated in one of the ground-floor rooms. (Image © authors)

Mitchel's few days on Spike Island were passed in relative comfort and it seems that his 'gentleman' status permitted indulgences denied to other convicts. A Cove-based solicitor was even granted an interview with Mitchel; such requests were usually refused.[6] The Medical Superintendent, Dr Robert Calvert, declared Mitchel to be in a delicate state of health and that not only was he unfit for manual

---

accommodating the number confined on that date. However, the 1848 Report makes it clear that Block B was functioning by the end of that year and could have provided the additional capacity. The 1848 Report also indicates that Block B had a total of 29 rooms. This indicates that the upper floor maintained its subdivided structure per the plans of 1833 (PRO, MPH 1/790), and that the lower floor maintained the subdivision of the rooms not used by convicts. Given Mitchel's description of a 'small Square court', it is almost certain that he was detained at the rear of Block B, where the four central rooms were the only ones that had doors opening on to what might be described as 'square courts'. If one assumes that the guardroom was located at the rear of the most central casemate, then it is likely that Mitchel (who describes a guard patrolling his yard) was located next to it. Though far from certain, the most likely location of John Mitchel's cell is four doors down from the southern end of Block B (now called the Officers' Quarters).

6 NAI, CON/LB/3/May and June 1848. See also: *Northern Whig*, 8 June 1848.

labour but should be provided with a special diet.[7] While Mitchel sat in comparative comfort before his transportation to Bermuda, and later Van Diemen's Land (he received preferential treatment in those locations, too, on account of his class), the remainder of the prison was coming under increasing pressure from overcrowding. By the end of 1848, the island's convict population had doubled once again, with more than 1,200 men now confined there. A third block was urgently required. That block came in the form of a unique prefabricated structure known as 'the Timber Prison'.

On 16 August 1848, a report by Inspector General Clement Johnson suggested that 'no difficulty can exist in erecting a moveable wooden prison ... within the walls of the fort of Spike Island, as a very large space of ground, amply sufficient for the purpose has already been levelled by the labour of the convicts'.[8] It seems that the space of ground to which Johnson referred was 'between the present range of wards and the unfinished barrack containing the cook room and stores'.[9] This indicates that the Timber Prison was located immediately to the north of No.3 Bastion, between Block A and the unfinished building to the east of it (Fig. 4.3). This was seen as an advantageous location as it placed the new prison near the tanks and the main store and made it a 'convenient place for supervision'.[10]

---

7 PRO, CO 37/125/139.
8 NAI, CSORP/1848/G8019.
9 NAI, CSORP/1848/G9731.
10 Ibid.

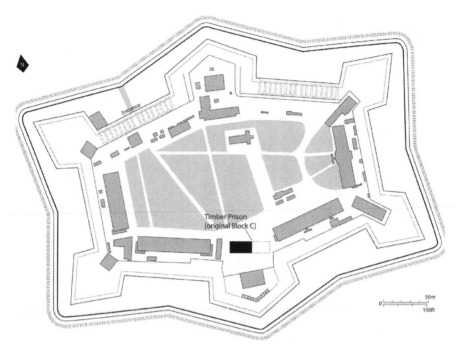

Figure 4.3 The location of the Timber Prison, Block C. The building shown was still in place in 1879 and may be the western half of the Timber Prison, the eastern half having been removed in the early 1870s to facilitate the installation of new ordnance on No.3 Bastion. The remains of the Timber Prison were demolished in the early 20th century. (Image © courtesy of Department of Archaeology, UCC)

The Timber Prison was originally intended for use on Boaz Island in the Bermuda penal colony, where it was intended to house about 200 men. Spike Island's overcrowding problems resulted in an order that it be sent to Cork harbour instead; a stone building was eventually erected on Boaz Island. The Timber Prison was assembled in Deptford, in London, by the same contractors that had constructed similar units on Portland Island in Dorset.[11] It was shipped to Cork in September 1848. The same ship probably transported the cots that the inmates of HMP Pentonville had constructed for the inmates of Spike Island.

---

11 PRO, CO 37/125.

These cots were a significant improvement on the hammocks of Blocks A and B.[12] Even after the Timber Prison reached Spike Island, there appears to have been a substantial delay in getting it ready to house convicts. It still hadn't come into use by the end of 1848. However, in February 1849 Johnson again wrote to Dublin Castle, informing the executive that the new prison could accommodate up to 400 prisoners and that:

> Whatever may be the objection to the principle of placing so many prisoners into a building of such a nature, still as the whole plan must be considered as merely of a temporary nature, all other considerations should be married to the advantage of making room for the greatest possible number.[13]

The Timber Prison received its first convicts in the latter half of March 1849. From the beginning, security concerns were expressed regarding its site and construction.[14] While individual cells were seen as the ideal form of incarceration, the Timber Prison consisted of two large rooms separated by a guard room.[15] By the time that Denis Nelligan arrived on Spike Island in 1849, the Timber Prison was already overcrowded.

Nelligan's arrival was symbolic of a departure from the initial intention of imprisoning on Spike Island only those convicts sentenced to seven years' transportation. Nelligan was sentenced to life, and apart from those sentenced to execution, there was no offender

---

12 NAI, CSORP/1848/G9431. It is clear from this correspondence that Blocks A and B were fitted with hammocks by August 1848.

13 NAI, CSORP/1849/G1535.

14 NAI, GPO/LB/2.

15 PRO CO 37/125/183.

considered more dangerous than a 'Lifer'. At 40 years of age, Nelligan stood 5ft 9 in. tall (1.75m) and his sallow complexion was offset by his blue eyes. Like most sexual predators, there was nothing distinctive about his physical appearance.

Ellen Corbett was a 30-year-old servant who had recently been dismissed from her position at the house of a 'gentleman farmer'. On 25 March 1845, down on her luck, she had travelled to Limerick to do some shopping on behalf of a cousin. It was on her return to Bohermore, on the outskirts of the city, that Corbett made the fateful decision to enter a public house near the Pike. Several men were in the public house and it seems that Corbett certainly interacted with some of them. Whether or not she was intoxicated at the time was the subject of some debate. Drunk or sober, Corbett left the public house and continued on the road towards Bohermore. Shortly afterwards she was accosted by Denis Nelligan and three other men. She recognised two of them as her companions in the public house. Other men may have offered to accompany the woman on her journey in the hope of initiating some form of courtship. These men, however, had decided that courtship was an unnecessary ritual. They could take what they wanted by force. They dragged her over the ditch, into a field, where she was raped at gunpoint by the four assailants.

When her ordeal was over, Corbett made her way to the nearby house of Mary McCarthy in search of lodgings. McCarthy told the court that Nelligan and another man had brazenly followed their victim to her house. Corbett immediately 'told them to go away with themselves, that she would go no farther with them'. She then went to bed sick and trembling, and later confessed to McCarthy that she had been raped.

Ellen Corbett reported her ordeal to the police the following morning. They rounded up three of the suspects immediately, but Denis Nelligan had vanished. A previous conviction for manslaughter was probably his main motivation for fleeing to London, where he was arrested by the Metropolitan Police some time later. This convicted killer was returned to Ireland and found guilty of rape almost 12 months after the crime had occurred. The *Limerick Chronicle* did not record a graphic description of Nelligan's crime, instead simply commenting that 'the details were revolting'. The judge was equally appalled, and charged the jury as follows:

> His Lordship it [sic] his charge said, that it would not be necessary for him to enter into any lengthened detail of the case. Charges of such a nature had often been made against innocent men, and in many cases of the kind the offence had not actually been committed, it was a most serious offence, and aggravated in a very great degree when more than one man was concerned in the perpetration of it. If the prosecutrix had told the truth, she was the subject of a most dreadful outrage indeed – one of the most atrocious and disgusting, said his Lordship, that I have ever heard brought forward in a court of justice. The very heniousness [sic] of this charge made it a case demanding the most careful consideration of the jury...[16]

Denis Nelligan was found guilty and sentenced to transportation for life. By August 1849, he had been transferred to Spike Island. Nelligan appealed his sentence in 1853 and again in 1854. Local police later gave some credence to reports that the victim had mistaken Denis for his brother, John, and that the wrong man may have been

---

16 *Limerick Chronicle,* 11 March 1846.

detained on Spike Island. The Nelligan family, generally described as 'riotous and violent', had left the country by August 1854. In the absence of a confession from his brother, Denis Nelligan's conviction stood. By the age of 45, he was completely unfit for labour. This could not be used as justification for his release, however, as 'such must be the case with all men sentenced for life sooner or later'. [17]

Nelligan shared the island with Patrick Hanlon and Michael Leahy. They had arrived on the same day as him and had been convicted of a similar crime after they raped and robbed Mary Allen in Cork on 8 October 1845. These men had also tried to abscond when they stowed away aboard the *Bride*. After their capture they were sentenced to transportation for life. In reality, this meant more than a decade of hard labour on Spike Island.

From the beginning, the authorities on Spike Island were anxious to ensure that all convicts were constantly employed. Employment was considered useful not only in terms of associated productivity but also as a method by which discipline could be maintained and insubordination might be minimised. When the island was due to take in its first prisoners in 1847, the Inspector General of Prisons, Clement Johnson, wrote to Spike Island's governor, Richard Grace. Inspector Johnson was anxious that the convicts be worked until they were fit only for sleep:

> During the day time, the principal object must be to keep the convicts constantly employed and under strict instruction. Exercise within their yards, making and repairing the prison

---

17 NAI, CRF/1853/N6 & CRF/1854/N17. While the Medical Officer certified that Nelligan was infirm and unfit for labour, he also stated that he was 'not of the opinion that his life is in immediate danger'. It is likely that Nelligan was transferred to the new depot for infirm convicts at Philipstown.

clothing, attending to the instruction of the schoolmaster and his assistants are obvious modes of employment; but it will also be your duty to put yourself in communication with the Officers of Engineers so as to ascertain what works of manual labour connected with the fortifications and buildings it may be advantageous and safe to employ the prisoners in completing for the public benefit...the labour exacted from them must be continuous and severe. This I consider imperative for two reasons: in the first place, constant occupation during the day will be necessary to prevent plotting and scheming to escape; while in the second, as great numbers must of necessity be left together during the night, it is desirable that the prisoners should go to bed to sleep, and not to converse or cabal, from which practice the greatest mischief might arise. To effect this purpose a certain degree of fatigue is most desirable, and that is most easily induced by labour in the open air.[18]

There was no time for the convicts to receive visits from the outside world. Indeed, it was considered that 'such indulgences should only be conceded under very urgent circumstances'.[19] Even within the prison, the inhibition of communication ensured that the prisoners' existence was as joyless as possible:

During these periods of employment the very strictest discipline will be necessary; and all verbal communication, except for the purpose of carrying on the works, must be restrained as much as possible. I am of opinion both from observation and reading, that any attempt to enforce *perfect silence* amongst bodies of prisoners employed together, produces an

18 HMSO, *Prisons of Ireland Report 1847*.
19 NAI, GPO/XB/3/311.

evil effect. In the first place, as the prisoners *will* attempt to communicate with each other, the number of offences against discipline and consequent punishment is aggravated far beyond the proportion of any benefit which would possibly be derived from the most complete success. Any communication between the prisoners likely to produce evil, can be easily held in check by keeping the prisoners as far apart from each other as is consistent with the space in which they are employed, and strictly requiring that any address from one prisoner to another should be made in a voice audible to the officer in charge.[20]

These near-silent labourers were first employed in a variety of tasks associated with the improvement and upkeep of the fort. They cleared the Parade Ground by quarrying the remaining rock and filled the ramparts with much of the material they extracted. They made several roads and yards, deepened old sewers and created new ones. Convict tailors were employed in making and repairing convict and officer clothing. Convict plumbers, masons, glaziers, tin smiths, chimney sweeps, painters and wire-workers were all gainfully employed. Some were charged with the task of making coffins for the prisoners who died and were buried on the island.

Within a month of the convicts' arrival the island's wells were occasionally pumped dry, and so forcing pumps were fitted to them in early 1848.[21] These wells also supplied water to the military in the casemate barracks, and the convicts were expected to keep that supply intact.[22] By the middle of 1848 there was concern that the increasing

---

20 HMSO, *Prisons of Ireland Report 1847*.
21 NAI, CSORP/1849/Box 3/621/7. See also: NAI, GPO/LB/1/163 and GPO/XB/3/239. Indeed, the lack of fresh water had threatened the occupation of Block B.
22 NAI, CSORP/1847/G8814.

numbers of convicts could create a catastrophic drought during a dry season. With that in mind, convicts were dispatched to draw sea-water from the shore in order to clean the sewers. In addition, two large water tanks located in the ramparts of the fort underwent repair. But the solution to Spike's water shortage was the excavation of two gigantic storage tanks in the centre of the fort, and the channelling of run-off rainwater into those tanks via a series of drainage pipes.[23]

The use of the convicts to draw water to clean the sewers may be the origin of a story still circulating on the mainland in the 20th century that prisoners were kept busy with pointless tasks, such as carrying buckets of water from one side of the island to the other. Spike Island was a public works prison: forced labour was an integral part of the punishment regime and it was understood to have a rehabilitative effect on the convicts. Tasks ranged from the productive to unproductive busy work. As in every prison of the age, many unskilled convicts were tasked with 'picking oakum'. In those days oakum was produced by deconstructing old oily ropes and it was often used for caulking the timber joints of ships. In all, the first full year of convict labour on the island was valued at £3,170.[24] If that figure is adjusted to today's value using average inflation rates, it comes to almost half a million euro.[25]

Although the island was reasonably productive, the authorities always sought to extract more productivity from their charges. They were also anxious that convict labour be used to the advantage of society and not just the prisoners themselves. To that end, the convict

---

23 NAI, CSORP/1848/G8019. See also: NAI, GPO/XB/3/239, 249 and 356. This system was certainly effective, but water shortages and water supply issues created periodic problems throughout the lifetime of the prison.

24 HMSO, *Prisons of Ireland Report 1848*.

25 This value, and any subsequent contemporary valuations, are calculated by use of Bank of England's inflation calculator available at www.BankofEngland.co.uk.

department instructed Governor Grace to allow the convicts to labour off the island, if necessary, and to 'place at the disposal of the Officer of the Engineers ... those convicts who are best adapted to this service at the same time taking care that they are distributed in gangs in such a manner and with such a guard as in his [Grace's] opinion will form a complete security against any danger of escape or violence'.[26] In addition to the levelling of the fort's interior, one of the first major projects undertaken on behalf of the military was the construction of a breakwater on the eastern shore of nearby Haulbowline Island.[27]

One of the primary difficulties perceived by the authorities in using the labour of Irish convicts was their lack of skills when compared to their peers from the industrialised heartlands of Britain. In June 1849, it was estimated that only one-quarter (159 in all) of Spike's prisoners were skilled labourers.[28] Work for unskilled labourers was to be provided by the establishment of an agrarian depot on the island. However, the 'rental and particulars' of the land outside the fort was owned by Mr William Sealy and he had rented much of it on fixed-term leases that weren't due to terminate until 1851.[29] By 1853 the island's lands had been 'transferred to the Irish Government',[30] but Sealy's rights to those lands were still the subject of a legal review. He was one of the many landowners whose estates became insolvent as their tenants died and emigrated during the famine. The Encumbered Estates Acts (1848 & 1849) were passed in order that such estates could be sold and their creditors reimbursed. This

---

26 NAI, GPO/LB/12/1.
27 NAI, CSORP/1849/G1434. The necessary tools were provided by the convict department at no additional expense to the Board of Ordnance.
28 NAI, CSORP/1849/G4696.
29 NAI, *Encumbered Estates Court Rentals, Sealy, Jan-Jun 1859, Vol 55*. See also: NAI, GPO/LB/2/130.
30 NAI, GPO/LB/3/218.

process often involved lengthy legal procedures. Eventually, in 1859 the Landed Estates Court sold Sealy's nominal rights to Spike Island's land to Lieutenant Colonel JP Beamish.[31] The legal wrangling as to who owned the rights to the island's land may have been the reason that the authorities' grandiose plans to grow and process flax and hemp never came to fruition.[32]

If the lack of skilled labour and arable land weren't enough to limit the productivity of Spike Island, the ill-health of many of its prisoners also took its toll. As the only Irish convict depot equipped with a hospital, it very quickly became a home for infirm prisoners. The convict hospital had been created in time for the opening of the prison in October 1847 by converting an ammunition store in No.6 Bastion (Fig. 4.4). In 1852, the Inspector of Government Prisons described the situation as follows:

> Serious complaints are made, however, of the limited number of prisoners appropriated to these works and the ineffectiveness [sic] of their labours. Under existing circumstances I am unable to devise any plan which will rectify these matters, for only about 45 to 50 per cent of the convicts are properly available for public works: a state of things necessarily resulting from the appropriation of Spike Island as a general depot for the convict service in Ireland, instead of to the exclusive object of public works; while the almost entire absence of hospital accommodation in the other Government prisons, has rendered this rather an hospital for con-

---

31 *The Cork Examiner*, 19 January 1859. Beamish was later involved in a legal squabble regarding police jurisdiction on Spike Island (NAI, GPO/LB/31/195).

32 NAI, CSORP/1849/G4696. The ambitious plan was detailed by the Royal Engineers in 1849, and the scheme was not ruled out by the Lord Lieutenant. However, the Governor's Reports never referred to the production of these crops.

victs, than, as it ought, and is supposed to be, a prison for hard labour.

Upwards of 600 prisoners are either in hospital or convalescent wards, chronic patients, aged, or infirm...the physical debasement of the Irish convicts, arising from the late famine, still continues; and they are absolutely disqualified (however well disposed) from performing a good day's work.[33]

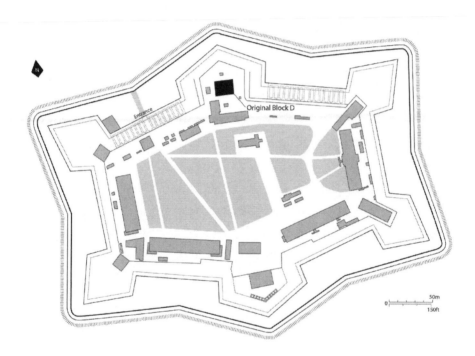

Figure 4.4 Location of the hospital in what had been the North Magazine in No.6 Bastion. Built for the storage of gunpowder and ammunition, this became the first convict hospital in 1847, but quickly proved too small and was converted to prisoner accommodation in 1849 and called Block D. (Image © courtesy of Department of Archaeology, UCC)

33 HMSO, *Prisons of Ireland Report 1851.*

A year later he continued:

Nominally 2,300 prisoners are detained here; but out of this large number, the average at the disposal of the Royal Engineer Department rarely exceed [sic] 900: of the residue, a part consists of invalid convicts, old and impotent men, or chronic patients, while the hospital and convalescent wards are crowded with the removals from other depots, in which the hospital accommodation is deficient. The number of these useless persons seldom falls below 700 to 800.[34]

In the aftermath of one of the worst famines in global history, Spike Island had become a spill-over convalescent ward for the ill and infirm of the crowded Dublin depots. While the guarantee of food, and rudimentary medical attention, almost certainly increased the life expectancy of many of the island's early convicts, it wasn't enough to guarantee the recovery of their health. Many of the older and infirm convicts took up space in Spike Island's hospital wards but were fit for little else. One of the means the prison authorities had at their disposal to reduce numbers was to transport convicts overseas. This involved a selection process whereby the unhealthy were generally deemed unfit for transportation.

Patrick Hanlon and Michael Leahy remained on Spike Island until 1851, when they were transported to Bermuda aboard the *Bride*.[35] The health of both men was compromised and on 9 May 1855, less than 10 years after their brutal attack on Mary Allen, Patrick Hanlon and Michael Leahy were freed after being declared 'unfit'.[36] By

---

34 HMSO, *Prisons of Ireland Report 1852.*
35 PRO, CO 37/143.
36 NAI, TR6, p.33, CRF/1846/H8, CRF/1846/L8.

that time Denis Nelligan had been transferred to Smithfield in Dublin, from where he was released a few days later.[37]

During his brief period of incarceration on Spike Island, John Mitchel was completely isolated from men like Hanlon, Leahy and Nelligan. Indeed his account of his stay in the prison lacks any description of any convict he may have encountered. Not only did Mitchel not describe any sight of his fellow convicts but neither did he describe any sounds. Whether this was as a result of the near-silence in which the convicts existed, or Mitchel's lack of interest in their existence, we cannot say. Not all of Spike Island's gentlemen were given the privileges that Mitchel was afforded. Just a year after Mitchel's departure, John Lynch, the former manager of Tralee's Savings Bank, served his sentence for fraud among Spike Island's general population. Another gentleman who served time with Lynch and the rest of Spike's convicts was the former mayor of Kilkenny, Robert Cane, who, like Mitchel, was imprisoned for his associations with the Young Ireland movement.[38] Mitchel's experience of Spike Island was far from typical, yet his account of it remains a valuable source from the perspective of a prisoner and from which key information can be extracted.

---

37 NAI, TR6, p.128, CRF/1853/N6, CRF/1854/N17.
38 NAI, OP/1849/38.

5. The Prison Staff

On the day that convicts Nelligan, Hanlon and Leahy had entered Fort Westmoreland and first encountered the penal regime that would punish them for their crimes, another man was contemplating leaving the island. That man would one day enter the annals of American history as one of its most famous generals. His name was Patrick Ronayne Cleburne and he had been part of Spike Island's military garrison since the spring of 1849.[1]

Patrick Ronayne Cleburne was born in Ovens, Co. Cork, a rural area west of Cork city and approximately 40 kilometres from Spike Island. He was the son of a wealthy Protestant landowner and was baptised in the Church of Ireland at Athnowen, near Ovens. In an Ireland undergoing rapid political and social transition, Cleburne's family was known to be among the more liberal of their social class and in the 1820s had even voted for candidates who had called for Catholic Emancipation. There is no evidence to suggest that the Cleburne family remained anything other than loyal subjects of the British crown and supporters of the Union of Great Britain and Ireland. In his youth, Cleburne served as an apprentice physician in Mallow, Co. Cork. The apprenticeship is worth noting because during Cleburne's stay in the town, Mallow was a hotbed of Irish nationalist activity, with Thomas Davis resident there and Daniel O'Connell using it as a venue for political rallies. If Cleburne's stay in Mallow sowed the seeds of doubt about British rule in Ireland, the seeds did not instantly bear fruit. In 1846, Cleburne failed his second entrance exam for the Apothecaries' Hall medical college in Dublin. He did not

---

1 PRO, WO/5446.

wish to return to his family in Cork as a failure and instead enlisted in the British Army. Cleburne concealed his privileged background from his superiors and began his military career as a common soldier. He enjoyed the military lifestyle and formed a lifelong attachment to military drill, tidiness of uniform and the general discipline of military life. However, the Great Famine and the military duties related to it also left a profound mark on the young Cleburne. His regiment was moved around between various Irish barracks during those bleak years and death greeted them at every port of call.[2]

Nowhere would the ravages of the famine have been more apparent to Cleburne than on Spike Island, when he arrived there in early 1849. While the suffering of the poorer classes was very visible to the young Cleburne, his family's circumstances would have meant that he was also conscious of the impact on his own class. Large lessees like the Cleburnes faced severe economic hardship. The government had extracted additional taxes from them in order to pay for the limited public relief that was provided. This tax came at a time when prices were falling and the quality of produce diminishing. Eventually, Cleburne's mother proposed that the family emigrate to the United States. From Spike Island, Cleburne wrote to his half-sister:

> I think if Mamma has made up her mind to go the best plan would be to go as soon as possible, but not without sending some of us in advance so as not to be wholly ignorant of the manner of business in that country. All I can say at present is this: that if we should go & our hopes of prosperity be fulfilled I will be happy in the happiness of all; or if on the contrary disappointment and advirsity [sic] await us, I will

2 Phillips Joslyn, M. (ed.) 2000. *A Meteor Shining Brightly: Essays on Major General Patrick R. Cleburne*. Georgia: Mercer University Press, pp.1–17.

endeavour by every means in my power to aleviate [sic] it...
still I will say the prospects in this country are anything but
good; and experiance [sic] goes very far to prove that they
will not be better.[3]

Nonetheless, the island provided him with what he later
proclaimed his proudest moment in a most illustrious military career
when, three days after he wrote the above, he was promoted to the
rank of corporal.[4] A little over a month later, on 2 August 1849,
Cleburne had his first encounter with the pomp and ceremony of a
royal visit as Spike Island's guns roared across the harbour to welcome
Queen Victoria to Cork. The harbour buzzed with activity, but the late
evening arrival of the royal yacht probably meant that the convicts
could only listen from their wards. Perhaps Cleburne saw the drama
unfold:

> About the hour of nine o'clock, amidst the anxiety of the in-
> habitants of Cove, and the persons on board the vessels in the
> bay, which were crowded with eager spectators, the Royal
> yacht was seen coming in the harbour. The cannon on board
> the war ships in the harbour and the batteries on the islands,
> thundered forth a greeting which was the signal for the bon-
> fires on the hills and rockets and other fireworks from the
> ships and town. In an instant the hills were covered with blaz-
> ing bonfires; innumerable rockets shed a vivid but tempo-
> rary brilliancy; blue lights were shown from the Ganges, La
> Hogue, and the other ships of her MAJESTY'S escort – and
> amidst the roar of the cannon and the sustained brilliancy of

3 Purdue, E. & H. 1973. *Patrick Cleburne: Confederate General.* Texas: Hill Jr College
Press, pp.12–13.
4 Ibid., p.13. See also: PRO, WO12/ 5443, 5444, 5445 & 5446.

the fire works, the Royal yacht steamed alongside the Ganges – the lateness of the hour rendering it unadvisable to anchor in the place appointed...

Until a late period of the night bonfires continued to blaze with undiminished brilliancy – particularly on Spike Island; at Hoddersfield, the residence of Colonel HODDER; at Trabolgan the residence of E.B. ROCHE Esq., MP.; and the various commanding eminences around the harbour.[5]

Cleburne may well have stoked the island's fires on the night in question. The following day, he and the convicts with whom he shared the island undoubtedly heard the cannon on Forts Camden and Carlisle salute Queen Victoria as she toured the harbour. As they went about their daily labours they surely noted the brightly decorated ships with all of their yards fully manned. That day Cove changed its name to Queenstown, a designation which lasted some eight decades. It all did little to change Cleburne's mind on the prospects for his country, however, and just seven weeks later he purchased his discharge from the British Army. On 5 November 1849, he sailed past Spike Island aboard the *Bridgetown* at the start of his passage to America.[6]

Cleburne went on to become one of the most famous and respected generals of the American Civil War. As he initially settled in Arkansas, he fought for the Confederacy, rising to the rank of major general and taking command of a division. Cleburne's troops were to the forefront of famous Confederate actions in the Western Theatre at Shiloh, Perryville, Stones River, Chickamauga and Ringgold Gap. He and his division stood out as an exceptional body of men. When others

---

5 *The Cork Examiner*, 3 August 1849.
6 The final entry for Cleburne's location is left blank on his unit's Muster Roll. This seems to be normal practice if the man has not been transferred in the previous quarter. Thus, Cleburne does not appear to have transferred from Spike Island after his promotion.

retreated, they held firm. When other attacks faltered, Cleburne's men broke through. The Irishman eventually earned the *nom de guerre* 'Stonewall of the West'.[7] His units were rigidly disciplined and exceptionally well trained and drilled. A British lieutenant colonel who met with Cleburne during the American Civil War recorded that the Irishman had told him:

> ...that he ascribed his advancement mainly to the useful lessons which he had learnt in the ranks of the British Army, and he pointed with a laugh to his general's white facings, which he said his 41st experience enabled him to keep cleaner than any other Confederate General.[8]

Figure 5.1 Major General Patrick Ronayne Cleburne (1828–1864), photographed in 1861 in the uniform of the Confederacy. (Image © Library of Congress)

Many of the characteristics that distinguished Cleburne's command were first taught to him while he soldiered in the British Army, on Spike Island and elsewhere.

In early 1864 the Irishman halted any further prospects for career advancement with a dramatic and blunt proposal. Tired of fighting against overwhelmingly superior numbers of Union troops and watching the Confederate resources dwindle by the day, Cleburne proposed what many

7 McCarthy, C. 2009. *Green, Blue and Grey: The Irish in the American Civil War.* Cork: Collins Press, pp.38-43.
8 Purdue, p.13.

Southerners considered unthinkable. The Irishman wanted southern slaves to fight for the Confederacy in exchange for their post-war freedom. His suggestion met with quiet disapproval and his military career seemed to stall. Major General Patrick Ronayne Cleburne died leading a charge at the Battle of Franklin on 30 November 1864, a little over 15 years after his departure from Spike Island. Counties are named for him in Alabama and Arkansas, while a Texan lake and a Texan city also bear his name. Cleburne wasn't the only soldier of the American Civil War who had spent some time on Spike Island. At least one Confederate private claimed to have been a warder on the island, while one Union war hero had allegedly been imprisoned there. Indeed, it was said that many of Spike Island's former prisoners often returned as part of the military garrison.[9] They may well have encountered another of the island's war heroes, Richard William Croker, who arrived on Spike Island not long after Cleburne had departed.

Croker was a veteran of the First Anglo-Burmese War (1824–1826). He was wounded when a musket ball was lodged in his leg during the Battle of Yangon on 1 December 1824. All attempts to remove the ball failed and he carried it in his leg for more than a quarter century. Then in late 1850, the Irish Surgeon General performed two operations that removed the lead from Croker's leg. Shortly afterwards he was appointed a third-class turnkey (prison guard) on Spike Island.[10] Croker still suffered from the effects of his wound, however,

---

9 Gibson, Rev. Charles Bernard. 1864. *An Irish Convict in the Federal Army.* In: *Once a Week,* 27 August 1864. And *Face to Face with the Fenians: Mugshots of American Civil War Veterans, Part 1* @ *irishamericancivilwar.com.* See also: Kane, Michael H. 2002. *American Soldiers in Ireland 1865-67.* In: *The Irish Sword: The Journal of the Military History Society of Ireland,* Vol. 23, No. 91.

10 NAI, CSORP/1851/G6044. Croker was not among the first staff appointed to the Spike Island depot (NAI, CSORP/1847/G8480), therefore he could have arrived on the island at any time between 1847 and 1851. However, the 1851 memorial states that he applied for a

and because of 'his unfitness for that [turnkey] duty and in defer-ence to his former condition, he was placed in the Store Department'.[11] Croker was decorated by the War Office in September 1851. Perhaps inspired by this honour, he petitioned the Lord Lieutenant for a pro-motion. His salary in the Store Department of the prison amounted to £35 per annum, increasing to £45 per annum in increments. As a turnkey he had received at least £40, with the potential to earn £52, per annum. Croker was aggrieved at the expense he incurred travel-ling to and from the island by ferry and paying rent at Queenstown, while some of the turnkeys were accommodated on the island. On re-viewing his complaints, the Inspector of Government Prisons felt that the State's charity had been extended far enough in relation to Croker. The Inspector informed his superiors that:

> With every disposition to serve Mr Croker, it is my duty to state that he is almost useless in the prison and that he does not appear suited to the convict service.
>
> As to giving him an increase in salary from the prison funds, I submit that it could not be done without injustice to other officers who have been appointed before Mr Croker joined.[12]

Whatever service Croker had given the Empire, it was not considered worthy of the raise requested. But it was agreed that he could reside with the other officers on the island, if he so wished.

---

position at Royal Hospital in Kilmainham whilst recovering from surgical procedures. One of those who petitioned for employment on his behalf was the surgeon who had removed the musket ball. He failed to obtain a position in the Royal Hospital, but was appointed turnkey on Spike Island soon afterwards. Thus, he did not arrive on Spike Island until after the procedure was carried out.

11 NAI, CSORP/1851/G6044.

12 NAI, CSORP/1851/G6044. See also: NAI, CSORP/1847/G11077.

Indeed, his residing away from the island had been considered an indulgence. Although he didn't get the money he had requested, Croker could consider himself fortunate that the State felt an obligation to a man described as 'useless'. Yet he seemed somewhat disgruntled and his relationship with his superiors remained a frosty one. In December 1851 he was suspended from duty for refusing orders from the governor.[13] However, in comparison to many of his colleagues, this useless old soldier was a shining beacon of productivity.

Spike Island's first members of staff were appointed on 28 July 1847. They comprised 25 turnkeys overseen by a governor, a sub-governor and a local inspector, while a clerk was also appointed. The island's first governor was Richard Grace. Governor Grace was a former governor of Cork County Gaol, located at Gaol Cross on what was then the western edge of Cork city, and whilst in that position was roundly praised for his 'habits of steady discipline united with kind treatment to the prisoners'. Indeed, in 1838 his superiors reported that he was 'a person highly qualified to conduct an extensive gaol on the best principles'.[14] Grace was to be assisted by John Donnelly, the former sub-governor of Omagh Gaol. Donnelly was the government's second choice for the sub-governor role and was only appointed when a John Temple refused the position.[15] Donnelly did not take the post either. The deputy governor at Smithfield was ordered to temporarily fulfil that role on Spike Island and a twenty-sixth turnkey was appointed and placed on probation for the position of deputy governor.[16] That turnkey was George Downes, a former policeman who had served as transit officer aboard the *Essex* hulk in Kingstown. Downes

---

13 NAI, GPO/LB/2/401.
14 HMSO, *Prisons of Ireland Report 1837.*
15 NAI, CSORP/1847/G8730.
16 NAI, CSORP/1849/G10267 & CSORP/1847/G10795.

was appointed deputy governor and master of works in December.[17] The conduit between Grace and his superiors in Dublin was the 'Local Inspector', Captain Robert Atkins.

Spike Island's turnkeys were entirely new to the convict service and had been trained into their job at various Dublin prisons by the governor of Smithfield. Grace had met them when he visited them in August.[18] However, a brief stint under the supervision of the governor at Smithfield was no substitute for experience. In addition to the theft aboard *Minerva*, the lack of experience of some of Spike Island's turnkeys, coupled with their unsuitability for the service, caused some significant teething problems.

The position of Head Turnkey was filled by Robert Ares, a former Colour Sergeant from the 60th Rifles regiment.[19] Unfortunately for Ares, his career ended in bitter recrimination when he accused Deputy Governor Downes of 'frauds, drunkenness etc.'. It appears that Ares was then forced to relinquish his keys while on the public parade and demoted to take charge of another convict class. Ares refused the demotion and wrote a rather hasty and forthright letter of resignation. In the letter he referred to the deputy governor being 'under the protection of certain parties, whose interest alone saved him from disgrace'. Although Ares subsequently petitioned the Lord Lieutenant to reappoint him to the position from which he had resigned, the reappointment was refused. The man to whom Ares had surrendered his keys was another old soldier, Sergeant Robert Hurst. It was Hurst who replaced Ares as Head Turnkey.[20]

---

17 NAI, CSORP/1855/10967. See also: NAI, GPO/XB/3/210 & 249.
18 NAI, CSORP/1847/G8911. See also: NAI, GPO/XB/3/178.
19 NAI, GPO/XB/3/249.
20 NAI, CSORP/1849/G10267, NAI, GPO/LB/1/273–278.

If Hurst was one of the 'certain parties' whose interests had aligned with Ares's dismissal, he failed to capitalise on his former superior's misfortune. He served as Head Turnkey for two years before his career also ended in ignominy. In 1851, the sergeant was dismissed when he absented himself from the island without permission. As if to compound that offence, he then took to drinking with some other members of Spike Island's staff in Queenstown before returning to the island and providing his colleagues with the password they needed to re-enter the fort. Although he pleaded with the authorities to reinstate him, his appeal was dealt a blow when his superiors explained that:

> In his examination he denied having <u>seen</u> the parties in question on this evening while it was clearly proved that he had crossed in the same boat from the island, had been drinking with them in a public house there, and had returned also with them – and this denial he proposed to <u>substantiate on oath</u>.[21]

Hurst's brazen lie was his undoing and the Lord Lieutenant instructed his secretary to 'acquaint Sergeant Hurst that the order for his removal cannot be revoked'.[22] Hurst was still in receipt of a pension from the army and thus wasn't entirely without means.

The dismissal of the island's most senior turnkeys, on two separate occasions, was symptomatic of a wider problem. The staff of the convict depot frequently lived by their own rules. Like some of their charges, some of the turnkeys weren't above resorting to theft in order to better their own situation. Indeed, a peculiarity of the prison's administration was a requirement for the governor to provide personal

---

21 NAI, CSORP/1851/G5726.
22 Ibid.

security for the prison's stores.[23] Ironically, dishonesty was a common characteristic among the staff employed to confine thieves, and none was more dishonest than Matthew Humphreys.

Humphreys was a veteran of the Grenadier Guards and had worked as the cook in Kilmainham Gaol for a little more than four-and-a-half years. He applied for the situation of cook in the Spike Island depot in December 1847 and was duly appointed. Upon taking over the kitchen duties, Humphreys instituted a practice that he claimed was common in every such establishment. He began seeking payment from his suppliers. Humphreys asked the meal supplier for money, which he referred to as 'sackage'. He then issued similar requests to the suppliers of meat and vegetables. When his superiors discovered that he had sought such payments, Humphreys was dismissed from his post. He appealed the decision, citing his argument that such practice was quite common in similar establishments. He even informed his superiors that Spike Island's baker had received 'sackage' from the meal supplier. He also appealed to be appointed to another prison. Curiously, Humphreys could only say that he was 'almost certain' that he had committed no crime. He wasn't certain enough, and his appeals fell on deaf ears.[24] The 'large family' that depended on Humphreys's income was not sufficient reason to grant any mercy to the wrongdoer. Officialdom didn't hesitate to set an example, even when it came at the expense of an innocent family.

Perhaps the harshest example they set in disciplining a member of staff came with the dismissal of Thomas Whitehead, who was appointed a third-class turnkey on 9 March 1851. Frequent complaints were made regarding his behaviour whilst in the post, even before

---

23 NAI, GPO/19/597.
24 NAI, CSORP/1848/G10649.

he placed himself on the sick list and absented himself from duty around the middle of June in the same year. Thirty-three days later, on 11 July, Local Inspector Captain Robert Atkins found Whitehead 'drunk on the streets of Queenstown'. The turnkey was immediately suspended and his case reported to the authorities in Dublin, with a recommendation that he be permanently dismissed. The Chief Secretary agreed and Whitehead's absence and drinking spree cost him his job. Interestingly, it was not Whitehead himself who appealed the decision, but his young wife. On 23 August 1851, she wrote the following plea:

> The Daughter of an old public officer, Mr McCartney, Chief Constable of Drogheda, presumes to plead the case of her unfortunate husband, Thomas Whitehead, lately removed from the Situation of Turnkey at Spike Island for having been intoxicated at Queenstown.
>
> Sir, I do not attempt to excuse his offence, nor to com plain of the justice of his dismissal, but humbly and earnestly to approach your compassionate sympathy for myself, who through the indiscretion of my husband, must with two unoffending children be thrown helplessly upon the world, without home, protection, or any means of support.
>
> I humbly crave Sir, that you will be graciously pleased to recommend the re-instatement of Mr Whitehead to the situation even of watchman in some of the Dublin prisons. He has learned a severe lesson and if he should again offend, I shall be contented to suffer in silence, nor ask to remind you of my destitution.[25]

---

25 NAI, CSORP/1851/G5084.

The Inspector of Government Prisons noted that Mrs White-head was 'a very respectable young woman' who had 'complained of his [Whitehead's] total neglect of her'. Nonetheless, he felt that he could not recommend any mercy be granted to Whitehead lest 'similar indulgences must be awarded to others who have been dismissed for that offence'.[26] One of the 'others' of whom he wrote was the former trade instructor of smiths, James Dunne. In November 1849, Dunne was dismissed for returning to the prison in a state of intoxication, even though this was his first blemish on an otherwise clean record.[27]

From the beginning, the inexperience of Spike Island's staff was a cause for concern.[28] And it seems that some of them certainly had a tendency to bend or break the rules of their employment. In 1849 an enquiry was made 'into the conduct and efficiency of the officers connected with the convict depot' on Spike Island.[29] It was little wonder that such was the case. On at least one occasion, a turn-key was transferred 'from Mountjoy to Spike, on account of miscon-duct'.[30] Spike Island seems to have become a convenient source of employment for old soldiers and for the most unfit and infirm individuals in the convict service.

At 8.30pm on 30 April 1849, the inexperienced staff was test-ed to the limits of its ability when a riot erupted in the Timber Prison, which had only received its first convicts in the previous month. A 'premeditated fight' among the convicts broke out and soon most of the men in the Timber Prison were involved, with convicts even man-aging to scramble over the roof of the warder's quarters that sat in be-

---

26 NAI, CSORP/1851/G5160.
27 NAI, CSORP/1849/G9306.
28 HMSO, *Prisons of Ireland Report 1849.*
29 NAI, CSORP/1849/G2829.
30 NAI, CSORP/1849/G6827.

tween the prison's two wards, in order to enter the fray. The military were called into action and they sealed off the whole fort while the warders sought to bring the situation under control. Within two hours the main culprits were locked in the solitary cells in No.3 Bastion.[31]

Spike Island's inexperienced staff was soon to preside over a prison the size and scale of which were unprecedented. While war heroes like Cleburne and Croker came and went from the island as their duties demanded, and men like Whitehead and Hurst actively destroyed their careers, the prison continued to expand and require more staff. By the end of 1852, Spike Island had the largest prisoner numbers in the United Kingdom, as it was then constituted, and it imprisoned some very interesting criminals, who had some very interesting ideas as to how to end their incarceration prematurely.

---

31 NAI, OP/1849/38.

6. Expansion and Escapes

Twenty-five-year-old William Watson was convicted of the theft of three heifers in October 1848.[1] Watson stole the animals near Celbridge, Co. Kildare, and then brazenly drove them through the night to Smithfield market in Dublin. On questioning, he swore that he had bought the animals in Tullamore eight months previously. Watson was suspected of having committed a similar theft near Kildare the previous month and was convicted of the Tullamore theft on 24 October 1848. He was lodged in Dublin's Newgate Gaol for a time, and even attempted an escape, before he was dispatched to Spike Island in February 1849.[2]

Soon after his arrival at the island depot, Watson was lodged in the newly opened Timber Prison, or Block C (see Fig. 4.3). There, he was joined by John Byrne who had been convicted of the theft of a case of surgical instruments in Co. Armagh. These two men evidently struck up a friendship and trusted each other enough to begin planning their escape. In the early hours of Friday, 5 October 1849, they put that plan into action. *The Cork Examiner* later described the daring feat of Spike Island's first recorded escapees:

> The officers of the Convict Depot at Spike Island were thrown into much consternation at an early hour this morning on discovering that two convicts ... who had been undergoing their periods of transportation – had effected their escape from the

---

1 NAI, Newgate Prison Register and NAI Ireland-Australia Transportation Database. Although these sources disagree on the trial date (the register recorded the date as 21 October, the database as 24 October), the difference would appear to be the result of a simple error in transcription. No other William Watson recorded in any extant prison register comes close to matching the records of the prisoner who subsequently escaped from Spike Island.
2 NAI, CRF/1849/W10.

prison and island ... The convicts had been located in that part of the depot called the "model prison," the windows of which, it appears, are not of the most secure description; as, on examination, it was evident that the escape was effected by the removal of the window sash. On quitting their cell they succeeded in getting over several walls, notwithstanding that the sentinels were on patrol; and, on getting clear of the prison, they were so fortunate as to find a boat moored by the shore which they managed to work, without oars, across the little bay that separates Spike Island from Ringaskiddy, where they hauled the boat ashore and decamped. As yet no clue has been discovered to their track; but there is scarce a doubt of their capture, as they are habited in the prison cloth-ing.[3]

The escape was indeed a daring one. However, daring alone cannot explain the escapees' good fortune. It is difficult to explain precisely how two men climbed from a prison window and then walked freely through the only entrance to a military fort. Perhaps the key was the location of the Timber Prison and the lack of security that prevailed on that site. In addition, it seems that the men had the good fortune of being under the guard of an inexperienced turnkey called McGrath. When Warder McGrath left his post at the Timber Prison in order to inspect the solitary cells located in the bastion to the rear of the building, Watson and Byrne simply removed part of the window and climbed out of the prison.[4] The governor later explained that the Timber Prison was overcrowded and was not surrounded by a stock-ade.[5] So as soon as the men dropped from the window, they didn't

3 *The Cork Examiner*, 5 October 1849.
4 NAI, GPO/LB/2/74.
5 HMSO, *Prisons of Ireland Report 1849*.

have to make their way out of a high-walled compound, although they were still contained within the fort. It is highly unlikely that the two men would have been able to scale the walls of the fort and drop into the moat without risking severe injury or death. A more likely route seems to have been through the military barracks that still occupied the casemated rooms on either side of the entrance and then out the front gate of the fort. But how could such a bold move go unnoticed? The answer may lie in the following letter, written more than a year before their escape. In it, Major General Charles Turner complained of the unrestricted access that prevailed between the military barracks and the convict depot:

> I have to report that two out of 16 casemates within the fort are given up for a canteen. This arrangement not only occupies a space most necessary for the troops, who ought all to be close at hand, for the suppression of possible outbreak amongst the 800 convicts, whom they guard, but also, as I would submit, such an establishment with its necessary requirements lies open to the following serious objections. The inner iron rail gate at the fort entrance is supposed to be kept shut, but as there is a high stockade between the casemates and the part occupied by the convicts, any person requiring to go to the canteen, civil or military, is allowed to come so far within the fort, and I confess I was astonished while I was there at the number of persons I saw passing in and out. This cannot be but disadvantageous to the military and I do not see that I am authorised to alter it especially as the civil labourers within, Turnkeys and their wives have a power of entrance beyond my control. It may perhaps be within my duty to submit that this seems also to afford possible opportunities of communications which might lead to the escape of convicts,

71

where money for tampering could be provided. Before dismissing this part of my report I beg leave to point attention to
my assertion that I found the <u>wives</u> of the Turnkeys pass in
and out: to cook their husbands' meals every day. I conclude
that such measure is not deemed objectionable though plots
and tampering might be carried on through their agency. I
therefore most earnestly recommend the <u>removal</u> of the can-
teen from <u>within</u> the <u>fort</u>.[6]

Turner was almost indignant in his underlining. He was
shocked that wives were allowed within a military barracks. What
may have been more prophetic, however, was his assertion that this
breach of the outer perimeter created a security risk for the convict
depot. Civilians and military were simply allowed to come and go
from the barracks as they pleased. The gate was left open to permit
them access. So when Watson and Byrne escaped from Block C, they
didn't have to breach the 20ft high (6.1m) stockades that surrounded the other two prisoner accommodation blocks; and if they could
somehow find their way into the barracks via the gate in the stockade
that surrounded it, they were quite likely able to walk out the front
gate of the fort. Turner had alluded to the co-operation that convicts
might receive from sympathetic or financially motivated civilians. It
is possible that one such civilian, or soldier, opened the stockade gate
for Watson and Byrne.

Unfortunately for William Watson, his escape was not as
permanent as he would have desired. Like so many escaped prisoners,
in every age, he was unable to leave his life of crime behind him. A
little more than three months later he was arrested for burglary and

6 NAI, CSORP/1848/6246.

returned to prison. The *Freeman's Journal* gave the following account:

> In our police intelligence of yesterday the details were given of the arrest of a burglar, who had been stopped by the police in the neighbourhood of Beggars Bush Barracks with a sack full of groceries, supposed to have been stolen.
>
> On the committal of the prisoner to Newgate he was at once identified by Mr Bourne, the deputy governor, as a convict who had been sentenced to ten years transportation, but who, together with an accomplice, had succeeded in effecting his escape from the convict depot at Spike Island. The prisoner, whose name is William Watson, is a native of Dublin. He has proved himself a most daring and determined character. He effected his own escape and that of his accomplice by removing the window frame of their cell. Watson swam, ironed as he was, from Spike Island, and succeeded, notwithstanding a strong tide setting out of the harbour, in reaching the buoy, whence he was picked up by a fishing boat. He has subsisted by plunder since his escape.
>
> Much credit is due to Inspector Finnsmore, who captured the daring burglar, who, it has been ascertained, had broken into Beggars Bush Barracks. His recognition at Newgate by the deputy governor also shows the close attention to his duty of that functionary.[7]

It seems that the newspaper was incorrect on at least one detail. Official records indicate that Watson was detained at Kilmainham, and not at Newgate. In any event, he was convicted of both burglary and escape and returned to Spike Island on 27 September 1850, nearly a year after his daring departure. This time his sentence was transpor-

---

7 *Freeman's Journal*, 19 December 1849.

tation for life. His wife, Catherine, appealed his conviction, claiming that she and Watson's only child would be destitute if the sentence were not mitigated. She also claimed that Watson's escape from Spike Island came about as a result of his anxiety regarding the welfare of his family. Her appeal was ignored. Indeed, the Dublin Metropolitan Police informed the Chief Secretary's Office of its suspicion that his wife had smuggled a crowbar into Newgate to facilitate Watson in his previous escape from that prison.[8] William Watson was eventually transported to Bermuda aboard the *Bride* convict ship in May 1851.[9]

It also seems that the newspaper accounts were contradictory in reporting the method by which Watson and Byrne left the island. The earlier, and local, account of their leaving by boat to Ringaskiddy seems more likely than their swimming to some unknown buoy at some unknown location. While officials remained tight-lipped on how the escapees left the island, and indeed the fort, in the aftermath of this event they seemed much more concerned with civilian access to the island than was previously the case. As far back as July 1848, the Inspector General of Prisons had expressed concern regarding convicts who laboured outside of the fort coming into contact with the island's small civilian population.[10] He recommended:

> ...strict regulation with regard to the number and character of
> the persons allowed to reside upon the island. The objection
> which I have always made to the employment of Irish con-
> victs upon public works of course only applies to works upon

---

8 NAI, CRF/1849/W10.
9 NAI, TR10, p.79.
10 It should be noted that this small civilian population appears to have pre-dated the establishment of the depot. It is likely that it consisted of people connected to or descended from military personnel who had been garrisoned on the island. However, it seems that an undetermined number of people came and went from the island as they pleased.

the mainland or in a position where they would of necessity be placed in contact with a numerous population who might be expected to sympathise with them and aid in their attempt to escape.[11]

Watson and Byrne's escape highlighted a problem whereby potential contact with members of the public compromised the security of a very large prison. It wasn't a problem that could be easily addressed. As Spike Island had been established as a temporary facility, the necessary warrant to declare the whole island a convict depot, and thereby exclude civilians from it, had never been made.[12] Just a few months before the men escaped, Local Inspector Atkins had also expressed his concerns about local civilians landing on, and living on, the island. He too suspected that they could assist convicts wishing to escape and asked that 'measures be taken by Government ... to clear the island of all persons not under military control'.[13]

It took almost two years for the government to act. In July 1851 a warrant was finally issued declaring 'Spike Island and its lands to be a depot for the reception of convicts under rule of transportation'.[14] The military were asked to assist the prison office in enforcing this new exclusion zone and on 21 July 1851, General Turner was instructed to 'carry the wishes of the Irish Government into effect with regard to the exclusion of strangers from the Convict Depot and grounds at Spike Island'.[15] Throughout the subsequent three-and-a-half decades of the convict prison's existence, substantial civilian

11 NAI, CSORP/1848/6246.
12 It should be noted that Cottingham had expressed the desire that such a warrant be issued as early as 1847, although it appears that he specifically referred to the fort and not the entire island (NAI, GPO/XB/3/197).
13 NAI, CSORP/1849/G9496.
14 NAI, CSORP/1848/G4328. See also: NAI, GPO/LB/2/305.
15 Ibid.

populations remained resident on the island, but these civilians were the families of prison employees or military personnel.[16] All other civilians were now excluded. These measures were too late to prevent the escape of John Byrne, who does not appear to have been recaptured.[17]

Watson and Byrne had escaped from a very different prison from the one that *Minerva* had visited back in 1847. In the first five years of the convict depot's existence, it had expanded at an exponential rate. After the erection of the Timber Prison (Block C; see Fig. 4.3), the depot's capacity was further increased in 1849 when the hospital located in the former shell store (the North Magazine) in No.6 Bastion was transformed into prisoner accommodation, known as Block D (see Fig. 4.4). The new hospital, with capacity for 150 patients, was located in part of Block F, the recently finished cookhouse building in the southeast corner of the fort, which had been left in 1820 with only the first storey completed (Fig. 6.1).[18] With the hospital removed, the four rooms in Block D provided accommodation

---

16 NAI, GPO/LB/31/195.

17 John Byrne may have changed his name and may have appeared in subsequent prison records. There is a vague possibility that he may later have become an infamous New Zealand outlaw who went by the name of Isaac Robinson. The authorities in New Zealand suspected that Robinson had escaped from Spike Island around 1851, and had killed a guard during that escape (NAI, CSORP/1867/12313). However, Robinson appears to have been at least 10 years younger than Byrne. Our research has been unable to uncover any definitive trace of the man who, with William Watson, vanished into the blackness of the Ringaskiddy night on 5 October 1849.

18 The hospital was moved in 1849 (see: Grace in HMSO, *Prisons of Ireland Report 1849*). Although the governor refers to the hospital being 'built', it is assumed that he was referring to the kitting-out of the building in the southeast corner of the fort. That building did not exist in 1844 (see: PRO, MFQ 1/1335), but was clearly marked as consisting of only the walls and ground-floor in the Cottingham report of 1847, when it was proposed to house the kitchens in the completed ground-floor at the western end of the range (see: NAI, CSORP/1847/G8814). In addition, all but one of the buildings within Fort Westmoreland, as marked on the first edition OS map dating from 1846, were in use by 1849. The only building for which other documentation does not specify a use was the long soldiers' barracks just east of No.3 Bastion.

for a further 100 convicts (Fig. 6.2). Soon, the governor decided that this block should be appropriated for the exclusive use of the juvenile class, prisoners who were under 16 years of age. By the end of 1849, Fort Westmoreland was home to 1,455 convicts. Even so, the expansion was just beginning.

Throughout 1850, the relentless reorganisation and ceaseless growth continued apace. The South Magazine in No.6 Bastion, which had previously accommodated the gas house and coal store, became Block E and provided lodgings for 100 more convicts (Fig. 6.3). Immediately east of Block E, the other half of the kitchen/hospital building, Block F, provided accommodation for 153 men (Fig. 6.1).[19] Meanwhile, construction of a new prison building began 'on the east side of the square'.[20] But the most significant expansion of the Spike Island depot came in July 1850, when two more of Cork harbour's forts were added to it.

---

19 HMSO, *Prisons of Ireland Report 1850*. Although the building which became Block F, and the hospital, was initially subdivided into 11 compartments (see: NAI, OP/1847/107, Cottingham Map), it seems that by 1850 its design was altered to provide six hospital wards, and six convict wards. It seems that five of these compartments later accommodated six hospital wards along with a general store and turnkeys' quarters (see p.91). The governor also considered expanding hospital accommodations by 'throwing some of the wards of F Prison into it on the upper range' (see: Grace in *Prisons of Ireland Report 1850*). This indicates the proximity of the hospital and Block F in the building described.
20 Ibid., p.18.

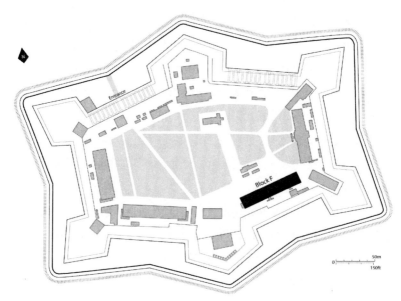

Figure 6.1 Location of Block F. Like many of the prison buildings, the name of this block changed as the prison was reorganised. This was renamed B Prison when the original Block B was converted to Prison Officers' Quarters. In the 20th-/21st-century prison (1985–2004), this building was known as Block B. (Image © courtesy of Department of Archaeology, UCC)

Figure 6.2 North Magazine in No.6 Bastion: the original Block D served as the prison hospital from 1847 to 1849 before being converted to accommodation for 100 juvenile convicts, i.e. prisoners under 16 years of age. (Image © authors)

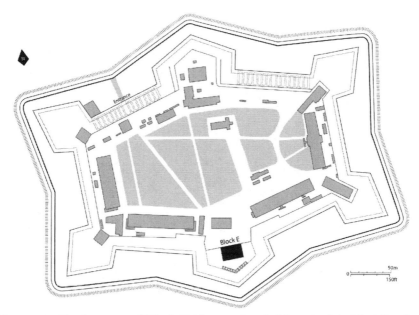

Figure 6.3 The location of Block E (former South Magazine) in No.3 Bastion. Originally a free-standing gunpowder store mirroring the North Magazine in No.6 Bastion, in the 1870s the rectangular structure was incorporated into a concrete platform covering all of No.3 Bastion. This concrete structure was to provide new gun emplacements on top of the bastion. The cut limestone of the north wall of Block E is still visible from the Parade Ground, while the building remains intact but covered and surrounded by the bunker. (Image © courtesy of Department of Archaeology, UCC)

Forts Camden and Carlisle were sited almost directly opposite each other on two prominent headlands forming the narrow channel that opened out into the lower harbour of Cork on one side and the open sea on the other (Fig. 6.4). Any unwelcome vessel attempting to enter the harbour would have had to sail between the guns of Camden, to port, and Carlisle, to starboard, while staring down the guns of Spike Island immediately ahead of it. However, like Fort Westmoreland, Forts Camden and Carlisle were in a state of disrepair. Given that there was an ideal source of free labour located across a short stretch of water from these two military establishments, it was decided that small numbers of Spike Island's convicts would be relocated to the outer forts. On 30 July 1850, 50 convicts were moved to each fort.[21] The operation of the outer forts was placed under Local Inspector Atkins. In his report for 1850, Atkins explained how the outer prisons had come into being and how it was intended that they should operate:

> First, from the crowded state of Spike Island Government prison, from the unparalleled increase in crime; and, secondly, to take advantage of the convict labour, under the superintendence of the Royal Engineer Department, in forming bastions removing old ruins, levelling and making the glacis, the entire of which was unformed, and in an extremely rude state.
> ...The hours of labour are from 7am until 9, then one hour is allowed for breakfast; then from 10 until 2; one hour for dinner, then work is again resumed until 6 in the summer and 4 in the winter.[22]

Where Spike had become a home for hundreds of sick and infirm prisoners, Forts Camden and Carlisle had siphoned off the healthiest convicts in order to carve modern ordnance forts from the rockface above Cork harbour. Like their parent depot on Spike Island, the prisons in the outer forts were supposed to be temporary; they were initially appropriated for the use of the convict service for two years. The military provided a garrison of 78 officers and men at each fort in order to enhance security at these peripheral locations.[23] Only 15 turnkeys were provided from Spike Island to attend to the duties at both of the new depots. So while the military were keen to emphasise

21 NAI, CSORP/1850/G4853.
22 HMSO, *Prisons of Ireland Report 1850*.
23 NAI, CSORP/1850/G4853.

that their role was merely one of support, it is clear that their numbers made them an essential part of the running of Camden and Carlisle during the early years of operation.[24] By the end of 1851, two large rooms at Fort Carlisle provided shelter for 84 convicts, while 132 convicts were accommodated in five smaller rooms at Fort Camden.

Figure 6.4 Fort Camden from the east. (Image © Cork County Council)

While Camden and Carlisle could provide much needed work for increasing numbers of convicts, it was very quickly apparent that they could not be run as effective depots. Within 12 months of their establishment, the Inspector General of Prisons commented:

> It being expedient that the defences of Cork Harbour should be put in order, and there being no parliamentary vote [i.e. funding] for such service, the evils inseparable from the detention of convicts under such unfavourable conditions,

24 NAI, GPO/LB/14/654.

were not, in the opinion of the Government, to be compared with the advantages to the public from their free labour. But while I express my full concurrence in this opinion, it should be distinctly understood, that it is physically impossible to carry out in these Forts, to any extent, the improved system of prison morals. That the number located here, and required for the works, are far beyond the amount which could be suitably detained here, assuming even the existence of more favourable circumstances; and that the whole course of prison arrangement adopted is necessarily defective and unsatisfactory.[25]

In short, the works being undertaken at Camden and Carlisle required far more convicts than could have been reasonably accommodated in either fort. In the context of the widely held belief that prisoners could best be rehabilitated by accommodation in single cells, the overcrowding rendered any prospect of reforming prisoners redundant, but it was considered that the updating of Cork harbour's defences was more important than reforming convicts. However, the unsuitability of Forts Camden and Carlisle as convict depots had another serious consequence, as several prisoners were quick to demonstrate.

Two unsuccessful escape attempts were made from the outer forts in 1850. In each case the escapees were recaptured not long after they had absconded.[26] On 8 April 1851, convict John Kearns made his escape when two sentries turned their back on a Fort Camden work party. He was recaptured in Cork city that evening.[27] On 2 May 1851, William Johnson, convicted of theft at Hillsborough (Co. Down) in

25 HMSO, *Prisons of Ireland Report 1851.*
26 HMSO, *Prisons of Ireland Report 1850.*
27 NAI, GPO/LB/2/257.

1848, effected his escape from Fort Carlisle. He, too, was recaptured.[28] Towards the end of 1851 another such attempt was made at Fort Carlisle when a convict managed to jump a considerable height from one of the fort's ramparts and make his way to the road at Corkbeg, near Whitegate. He was quickly recaptured when his absence was discovered at roll call.[29] An isolated piece of correspondence from January 1852, in relation to this escape or another that occurred shortly afterwards, reveals that the military and the prison service were actively seeking to blame each other for the lack of security at the fort. The Inspector General of Prisons went so far as to suggest that 'the military authorities at the fort would accept the direction and control of the prison officers so that the Superintendent Turnkey might be allowed to report to them'.[30] The Lord Lieutenant did not issue any recommendation in that regard and it seems that some ambiguity was allowed to continue.

The most ingenious escape of all came when John James escaped from Fort Carlisle on 30 April 1852. The Inspector General of Prisons reported James's audacious escapade as follows:

> I have the honour to report for the information of the Lord Lieutenant, that on Saturday evening, a prisoner John James effected his escape from Carlisle Fort.
>
> It appears that he was wardsman employed in cleaning officers' quarters and in the absence of Head Turnkey

---

28 NAI, CSORP/1852/G2768 and GPO/LB/2/269.

29 *The Cork Examiner*, 29 December 1851. It is curious that the Inspector General reported four escapes from the outer forts in 1851, stating that two of the four escapees were recaptured. The alternative records (above) indicate that at least three escapees were recaptured. The discrepancy is likely to be accounted for in one of two ways: either the Inspector General was mistaken; or the final escape, as reported in *The Cork Examiner,* never occurred.

30 NAI, CSORP/1852/G99.

Graham entered his room, broke open his boxes, and having dressed himself in his uniform, walked through the fort un-challenged. He took with him a sum of money lying in Graham's box. Every effort has been made to affect his recapture but hitherto without success.[31]

The sum of money referred to was substantial. As Fort Carlisle was a considerable distance from Spike Island, Governor Grace was in the habit of sending significant sums to the fort to cover various accounts, including wages, during periods when high seas made access difficult. James may well have waited for his opportunity as such an amount of money had arrived at Carlisle the day before his escape. John James walked from the fort with more than £24, which equates with some €4,000 in 2016. Like all of the smartest escapees, his name vanished from prison records.[32]

On the other side of the harbour, Fort Camden was also the site of a daring escape in early 1853, when two prisoners simply walked out of the fort. Again, the prison service sought to place the blame at the door of the military, when Governor Grace reported as follows:

I regret having to report the escape of two prisoners from Fort Camden yesterday morning. I have been out there and it appears that immediately after unlocking, 7 O Clock, whilst Turnkey Colgan was inspecting his class and particularly the irons of one of them, those two passed out of the open door as if to wash. No.6 is the South end of the prison, at the angle of

31 NAI, CSORP/1852/G414.
32 NAI, GPO/LB/3/295. John James is another potential match for the notorious New Zealand outlaw, Isaac Robinson. James escaped from Fort Carlisle in the very same year that it was suspected that Robinson had escaped from Spike Island. Robinson's third escape, from custody in New Zealand, also resembled James's escape from Carlisle, in that he disguised himself as a warder and walked brazenly from the prison (NAI, CSORP/1867/12313).

which stands a water barrel and where the area wall is rather lower than elsewhere if not capped but as there is a sentry planted directly over the spot, they could not have got off if he had been on his post. I could not discover that any blame is imputable to the Turnkeys, business took its usual course. A few of the military officers told me it must have been from the sentry's neglect. He has been sent to Headquarters and will be tried for it. Turnkey Noonan saw him off his post. In 10 minutes they were missed and the alarm given. An officer & 20 men, with the spare Turnkeys were sent in pursuit. They tracked them some distance and searched the cabins on the way, but they continued to hide themselves in an adjacent wood or amongst the rocks I suppose last night.

I may say that every police station to Kinsale in one direction and to Cork in the other were immediately informed of it.[33]

Three days later, the men had completely vanished.[34] While the outer forts provided useful labour for Spike Island's ever-expanding convict population, their overcrowded accommodation and position on the mainland meant that they were seen as less than ideal from a reformatory or security perspective. Escapes such as these only served to prove the point.

On the island itself, the expansion continued. The opening of Mountjoy Gaol in Dublin on 27 March 1850 was a pivotal moment for the reorganisation of the Irish penal system and the use of Spike Island. Mountjoy was also deemed a convict prison, but unlike Spike Island it consisted of blocks of single cells and was therefore capable of housing convicts in isolation from each other. As noted above,

33 NAI, CSORP/1853/467.
34 Ibid.

this was considered an essential part of rehabilitation of convicts and had been a cornerstone of the British convict operation for several decades.[35]

In theory, by the late 1840s a male prisoner undergoing a sentence of transportation anywhere in Britain or Ireland was supposed to undergo three phases of punishment and rehabilitation. First, he completed a period of separate confinement in a given prison. Secondly, he worked as part of a prison-gang outside of the prison walls. Thirdly, he was removed to the colonies on a 'ticket of leave'. This ticket allowed him to obtain employment within a given area in the colonies, whilst under the supervision of the authorities there. In Ireland, it was intended that Mountjoy Gaol would provide the first phase by imprisoning convicts in separate cells for the first six months of their sentence, and that Spike Island would provide the second phase by offering labour for those who had already served time in separation. Convicts would then be transported and while they would eventually be freed in the colonies, their financial circumstances usually dictated that they could never return.[36] However, in order that Mountjoy could begin to function, and to relieve the general overcrowding of Irish prisons, it needed prisoners. The courts could only provide those prisoners as quickly as they were convicted, so filling the new gaol to capacity would require the transfer of a considerable number of convicts already within the system. Inspector of Government Prisons Henry Hitchins later described how this problem was addressed:

---

35 London's Millbank Prison consisted of almost 900 separate cells and had opened in 1816. Pentonville Penitentiary was superior in design to Millbank and opened in 1842, with accommodation for 520 prisoners. Mountjoy's design was heavily influenced by Pentonville.

36 Freed convicts were issued with Certificates of Freedom, of which there were three grades: Ticket of Leave, Conditional Pardon and Absolute Pardon. Only those with an Absolute Pardon could return home.

In the selection of convicts for removal to this depot, besides the ordinary medical grounds, the crowded state of the Irish prisons rendered it necessary that special reference should be had to qualifications for tickets of leave, and an early transfer to the colony under this system, without previous employment on public works at Spike Island. To obviate the evil of this departure from the usual probationary system, 350 prisoners were transferred from the other depots convicted of offences more or less resulting from the distressed state of the country, or under circumstances which, in some degree, mitigated the offence, and who had already undergone in most cases, protracted periods of imprisonment. The residue, chosen indiscriminately from the county gaols and prisons, were persons who had been convicted of the highest offences, and of character and habits on whom ordinary prison discipline appeared to have no effect. These last it was proposed, after twelve months separation, to remove to Spike Island for employment on public works.[37]

Thus, in 1850 Spike Island transferred 133 of what were perceived as its more inoffensive prisoners to Mountjoy, and in 1851 it received 76 of the most hardened and badly behaved convicts in the system. These 76 men were the first prisoners to land on Spike Island having already served a period of separate confinement in Mountjoy. Every effort was made to keep them entirely separate from the general population of the Spike Island depot. They were placed in three adjoining wards in Block B, sharing one yard between them. The schoolmaster taught these men independently of his other charges. They worked in separate gangs from the rest of the population and

---

37 HMSO, *Prisons of Ireland Report 1850.*

they even attended their own Catholic mass every Sunday.[38] This grand experiment, within which Mountjoy and Spike Island each provided separate stages of a convict's sentence, worked well on paper. It quickly became apparent that it could not work in reality.

In 1851, the new prison on the east side of the square was opened. Referred to as Block G, it initially detained 460 convicts (Fig. 6.5). Governor Grace then began to segregate the prisoners received from Mountjoy by housing them in that building. A Protestant church was constructed during 1852 on the upper floor of this new building (now known as Mitchel Hall; Fig. 6.6). The Roman Catholic chapel remained in its original location, in front of No.2 Bastion and between the stockades at the gables of Blocks A and B (Fig. 6.7).[39]

The authorities also began constructing new prisoner accommodation in No.4 Bastion. This was made of a newly available material: corrugated iron. This so-called Iron Prison was opened in 1852 and housed 90 prisoners.[40] It was designated Block D, as the old Block D in the former magazine/hospital and subsequent juvenile prison in No.6 Bastion had been re-appropriated by the military (Fig. 6.8). The Iron Prison was the most uncomfortable of Spike Island's prison blocks, reflecting the general inexperience with its new building materials. The corrugated iron made it extremely cold in the winter and much too hot in the summer. This problem was eventually remedied somewhat when the structure was lined with timber and felt.[41]

---

38 NAI, CSORP/1851/G3021.
39 HMSO, *Prisons of Ireland Report 1852*. The reference to a 'church' being completed for 'divine service' indicates that the church probably wasn't Roman Catholic. See also: NAI, CSORP/1847/G8814. The location of the first Roman Catholic chapel was recommended by Cottingham. The structure seems to have survived for many years and was marked as 'Work Shops' on the 1879 military map.
40 During its construction, it was envisaged that it would hold twice this number.
41 To examine the substantial alterations and expansions to Fort Westmoreland throughout 1850, 1851 and 1852, see: HMSO, *Annual Reports of the Inspector of Government Prisons*

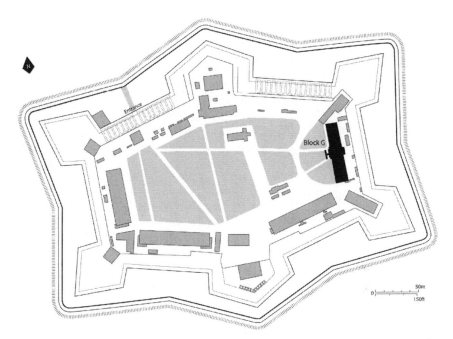

Figure 6.5 Location of Block G, which opened in 1851. By the 1870s, this building had been renamed C Prison. (Image © courtesy of Department of Archaeology, UCC)

By the end of 1851, Spike Island was home to 2,041 convicts. The outer forts at Camden and Carlisle detained a further 216 men, making a total of 2,257 under Grace's governorship. In 1852, the largest number located in the three forts at one time rose to 2,461. This made Spike Island the largest convict establishment, or prison of any kind, in the then United Kingdom. Indeed, for a few years in the mid-19th century, Cork harbour was probably home to the biggest prison in the British Empire, if not the world, in terms of numbers of prisoners. It certainly dwarfed infamous establishments like Kilmainham, Mountjoy, Dartmoor, Reading, Pentonville, Millbank, and even far away Hobart Town Prisoners' Barracks and Port Arthur.[42]

---

in Ireland for the Years ended 31ˢᵗ December 1850, 1851 and 1852.
42 HMSO, *Report on the Discipline and Management of the Convict Prisons And Disposal*

Figure 6.6 Block G today: the room surmounted by the clock tower housed the Anglican church. (Image © authors)

---

of Convicts 1851. See also: HMSO, *Reports of the Directors of Convict Prisons on the Discipline and Management of Pentonville, Parkhurst and Millbank Prisons And of Portland, Portsmouth and Dartmoor Prisons And the Hulks for the Year 1852.* See also: HMSO, *Seventeenth Report of the Inspectors Appointed under the Provisions of the Act 5 & 6 Will. IV. C. 38, to Visit the Different Prisons of Great Britain (I Home District, II Northern and Eastern District, III Southern and Western District).* See also: HMSO, *Thirteenth Report of the General Board of Directors of Prisons in Scotland to the Right Honourable Sir George Grey, Bart., One of Her Majesty's Principal Secretaries of State.* The largest prisons in Britain were Millbank and Dartmoor, each of which had a capacity of approximately 1,100 inmates. It is considered unlikely that any of the prisons in the then comparatively undeveloped continents of Africa, Asia or South America had prisons on Spike Island's scale. India's Madras Central Prison was extended to a capacity of 1,500 in 1855 (*The Indian Express,* 18 February 2009). The infamous French Penal Colony on Îles du Salut consisted of three islands, one of which was Devil's Island. The Colony began life in 1852 and eventually reached a population of 4,000, spread across the three islands. However, it had not approached that population in the 1850s, and no one island ever did. The convict depot in Bermuda never exceeded 1,500 prisoners, who were mostly detained in hulks *(Annual Reports on the Convict Establishments at Bermuda and Gibraltar).* New York's Sing Sing Prison was designed to accommodate 800 prisoners in single cells (John H. Lienhard, *Engines of Our Ingenuity: No. 1034 Sing Sing Prison* @ http://www.uh.edu/engines/epi1034. htm). Today, Rikers Island, New York, is said to be the world's largest prison, with a population of approximately 12,000. It began its life as a prison in 1932.

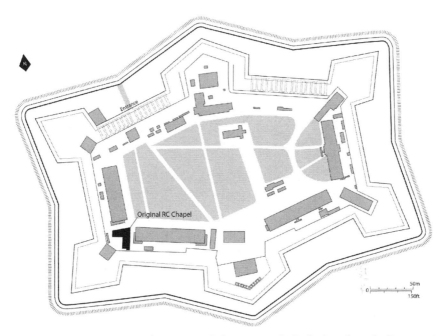

Figure 6.7 Approximate location of the original Catholic chapel. (Image © courtesy of Department of Archaeology, UCC)

On Christmas Eve 1851, disaster struck Spike Island when a fire ripped through Block F. 'Five houses in the range F, comprising six hospital wards, general store, and turnkeys' quarters, were destroyed, with clothing, bedding, furniture, and accounts.'[43] Soldiers from Haulbowline, and even sailors from HMS *Ajax*, then anchored in Cork harbour, were drafted in to fight the fire. Lieutenant Wentworth from Haulbowline was commended for organising the hasty extinction of the blaze and Captain Burnestru for his 'presence of mind in suggesting the demolition of the adjoining roof and personally carrying it out', thereby preventing the destruction of occupied wards in the hospital.[44]

---

43 HMSO, *Prisons of Ireland Report 1851*.
44 NAI, CSORP/1852/G191.

While the damaged Block F was being rebuilt, two casemates formerly within the military barracks were added to the prison. By this time the population had fallen temporarily, standing at 2,085 between the three forts, with 1,882 on Spike Island alone.[45] Block F was repaired at an estimated cost of £700 (almost €116,000 in 2016) and all of it was redesignated a hospital in 1852.[46]

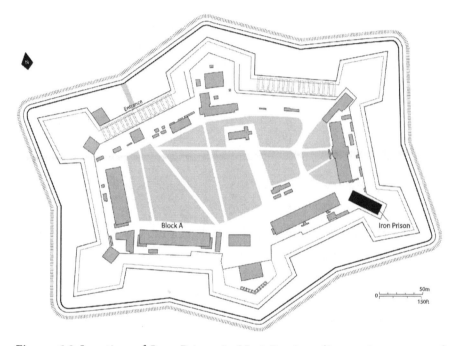

Figure 6.8 Location of Iron Prison in No.4 Bastion. (Image © courtesy of Department of Archaeology, UCC)

Spike Island had thus become one of the world's first super-prisons. Its size and scale were unprecedented. The prisoners and staff were part of an unforgiving and sometimes brutal regime. That regime involved years of continual hard labour, through the harsh contrasting weather of both winter and summer, on an exposed

45 HMSO, *Prisons of Ireland Report 1852*.
46 Ibid.

Atlantic sea-coast. Over time, the regime changed and evolved, and some of the men could gain limited privileges. On a pretty little island in one of the world's finest harbours, they toiled away the years watching their lives pass them by. One man who saw his best years overtake him on Spike Island was considered one of Ireland's most notorious murderers. He was William Burke Kirwan, and he arrived on the island in January 1853.

7. The Infamous William Burke Kirwan

William Burke Kirwan was a middle-class Dubliner with an air of haughtiness that offended some of those with whom he associated. He was a former medical student and a talented artist, making his living by creating anatomical sketches for various members of the medical profession. Moving in these affluent circles, Kirwan and his wife, Maria Louisa (Fig. 7.1), made their home in rented rooms at 11 Merrion Street, Dublin. However, Kirwan had a dark secret that would prove his undoing. Just a few miles away from his seemingly happy marital home, Kirwan kept a mistress, Teresa Kenny. With Kenny, Kirwan had fathered seven children; he had none with his wife. William Burke Kirwan had lived this double life for some 12 years. In September 1852, his deception was unveiled in a most dramatic way.

In June 1852, Kirwan and his wife took lodgings in the little seafront town of Howth, in north county Dublin. While staying there, the couple regularly journeyed to the nearby island of Ireland's Eye (Fig. 7.2). On the island, Kirwan painted landscapes while his wife indulged her passion for swimming. On the evening of 6 September, as the daylight faded from the skies above Howth, the boatmen who had deposited the Kirwans on the island returned to ferry them back to the town. They were met by Mr Kirwan, alone, who informed them that he had lost track of his wife. They immediately began a search of the island beneath the gathering gloom. Sometime later, they made a rather gruesome discovery. Mrs Kirwan's body was found lying on a rock in a little inlet known as the Long Hole. Some cuts and abrasions were visible, but nothing that immediately aroused suspicion.

Figure 7.1 William Burke Kirwan's sketch of his wife, Maria Louisa. (Image © courtesy of National Library of Ireland collection)

The body was brought back to Howth, where a coroner's inquest concluded that Maria Louisa Kirwan had suffered death by accidental drowning. Mrs Kirwan was buried in Glasnevin cemetery and it might have been assumed that there the matter would rest. However, the Dublin rumour mill kicked into overdrive. Stories circulated about Kirwan, his violent nature, his double life, his treatment of his wife, and of his threatening her life. Some of the rumours were without foundation. Some of them were not.

Figure 7.2 Watercolour by Kirwan of Ireland's Eye at sunset. (Image © courtesy of National Library of Ireland collection)

Maria Louisa's body was exhumed four weeks after its burial and, based on the autopsy then carried out and evidence gathered by the police at Howth, William Burke Kirwan was charged with the murder of his wife. His case was postponed in October, and he eventually stood trial on 8 December 1852. Kirwan was defended by a newly elected MP, and later champion of Irish Home Rule, Isaac Butt (Fig. 7.3).

Given Kirwan's high profile in Dublin society and the sensational nature of his domestic affairs, the case was one of the most notorious ever tried. It excited considerable interest from all sectors of society and his arraignment took on many of the characteristics of a circus. The excitement prevailing before the trial was described as follows:

Figure 7.3 Isaac Butt MP, Kirwan's defence lawyer and later champion of Home Rule. More than 20 years after Kirwan's trial, Butt was to defend the Fenian, Robert Kelly (see p.305). (Image © National Library of Ireland)

Long before the arrival of the judges the avenues leading to the court were thronged with a vast number of gentry seeking admission. However, as a result of the excellent arrangements made by the Sheriff, ample accommodation was secured by the bar and the public press area. The galleries and the seats in the body of the court were densely crowded with an assembly which included a number of ladies ... Intense anxiety prevailed among the crowd to catch a view of the prisoner whose demeanour was firm and collected. He was a good-looking man in his thirties with dark hair and eyes, dressed with evident care in a close-fitting paletot of fine black cloth. He also wore a black satin stock and black kidskin gloves. He was obviously a person who devoted considerable attention to his clothes and general appearance.[1]

---

1 Sheridan, M. 2012. *Murder at Ireland's Eye.* Dublin: Poolbeg Press, pp.43–4. Sheridan's text is the most authoritative text on the Ireland's Eye murder yet produced. Kirwan was a medical student in 1837. (See: *Freeman's Journal*, 27 May 1837.)

The trial revolved around the suspicious position and condition of Mrs Kirwan's body when it was found, as well as the dubious results of a post-mortem carried out after the exhumation. The prosecution claimed that the body was found lying on a sheet and exhibited injuries consistent with having had a wet sheet inserted in the mouth for the purposes of suffocation. They also pointed to several cuts and abrasions on the body and the blood seeping from several orifices. They produced witnesses who had been on the mainland and who testified that they had heard cries coming from Ireland's Eye just prior to dusk. Finally, but perhaps most damning, was testimony relating to Kirwan's double life and testimony of his arguments with his wife whilst lodging in Howth.

For their part, the defence claimed that Mrs Kirwan was not found lying on a sheet and that the sheet referred to was placed around her body after it was found. They had a witness who seemed to corroborate this story, but the prosecution had one who flatly denied it. They claimed that the cries heard from Howth were probably the result of another party on the island calling for a boat. Their contention was that Mrs Kirwan had drowned as a result of an epileptic fit caused by entering the water with a full stomach, and that her injuries were entirely consistent with those happenings. The defence claimed that the superficial cuts found on her person were caused by crabs, which were known to attack the bodies of drowning victims, and that blood flowing from the orifices of drowning victims was a normal occurrence in similar circumstances.

Both sides produced expert medical witnesses to testify to the validity of their theories. After three days of testimony, and a very short deliberation, the jury decided that they believed the prosecution. They returned a verdict of guilty, and Kirwan was sentenced to death.

His execution was scheduled for 18 January 1853, but on New Year's Eve the Lord Lieutenant commuted the death sentence to penal servitude for life. (Later that year, the Penal Servitude Act replaced most sentences of transportation with those of penal servitude at home. An exception was made for those with life sentences, who could still be transported.)

Kirwan was transferred from Kilmainham Gaol to Spike Island on 10 January 1853.[2] Although he was surely relieved that his life had been spared, he had 26 years to question the cost of his reprieve. Spike Island's celebrity murderer caused an administrative headache for all of the penal authorities. A Cork-based newspaper reported his arrival in Cork as follows:

> The last mark of distinction that has been conferred on the wretched Kirwan is well calculated to create feelings of disgust and honest indignation and must, in a great measure, tend to justify the assumption that the theory of one law for the rich and another for the poor has been in this instance fully realised...
>
> On the arrival of the train in Cork which conveyed Kirwan, for the purpose of his being transmitted to Spike Island, he was distinguished from his fellow-convicts not only by remaining unmanacled, but by appearing in the garb of a gentleman, and being suffered to associate on terms of equality with those from whose social position his crimes had forever removed him.
>
> ...we wish to protest in the most emphatic manner against the adoption of a course of conduct, which is calculated, as in this instance, to engender in the minds of the vulgar

2 NAI, CON/LB/3/January 1853. Kirwan never served time in Mountjoy and his months in Kilmainham appear to have answered for the separation portion of his sentence.

a respect for crime, and to carry home to those of others the firm conviction that the dignity of the law has not been maintained, and that impartiality has been outraged.[3]

It was true that Kirwan had left Kilmainham Gaol wearing an overcoat and top hat, but he was wearing his prison clothes beneath them. He had also fallen into a fit of despair after his conviction and was considered quite ill before and after his journey to Cork.[4] On being ordered to explain the circumstances of Kirwan's transport, the constable in charge of same, reported:

> I considered from his health and inferior appearance I thought it not only unnecessary but inhuman to handcuff a man in his feeble state. As I and the Sub-Constable had to assist him in getting on the car as he was quite unable to move or walk without assistance. With regard to his associating with any person while in my custody is totally false and unfounded as he was placed in a corner of the carriage guarded by myself and the Sub-Constable and was thereby prevented from either discoursing or conversing with any person. After arriving in Cork I immediately conveyed him by covered car to the steamer and placed him in a small apartment in the boat apart from other passengers where he had not the slightest communication with any person.[5]

At the time of his arrival on Spike Island, Kirwan was still a very ill man. It is possible that the enormity of his sentence had begun

---

3 NAI, CSORP/1853/406. Newspaper cutting within prison records.
4 *The Cork Examiner*, 15 December 1852 and *Freeman's Journal*, 11 January 1853. See also: NAI, CON/LB/3/January 1853.
5 NAI, CSORP/1853/407.

to dawn on him and may have been the root cause of some of his outward symptoms. Four months had seen him change from fashionable gentleman artist to convicted murderer and notorious convict. However, if he thought that the prison system would have any sympathy for his plight, he was very much mistaken. His first stop on the island was the hospital, but the Dublin authorities immediately intervened to ensure that he would not be allowed to avoid the rigours of prison labour for too long. On 12 January, they wrote to Governor Grace as follows:

> Sir,
>
> I have to call your special attention to the case of Convict Kirwan, now in your custody and to direct that he be treated in all respects, as any other ordinary felon. That he be employed at the usual works on the island, and that under no pretence whatever is any visitor to have access to him, without a written order from the under-Secretary or this Department.
>
> You will also exercise special care, that he be not allowed to respond by letter or otherwise, with any person outside the prison or receive any communication from without. You will strictly charge the officer in whose ward he is placed to attend to these instructions, the slightest deviation from which will result in instant dismissal. He is to be retained at Spike Island and every care taken to prevent his escape.
>
> If any longer in hospital, the medical attendant should be called on to certify as to his illness. I have to request your report on this subject where you will be pleased to state, the name of his officer, of ward, and the labor [sic] he is employed in.[6]

---

6 NAI, CSORP/1853/474.

It is worth noting that in interfering to ensure that Kirwan did not receive any preferential treatment, the authorities may have been ensuring that he ended up receiving harsher punishment than many of the island's other prisoners. How many sick convicts were to have their illness certified? How many prisoners were specifically singled out as potential escapees? How many warders were threatened with dismissal should they depart from the rules in relation to one particular prisoner?

All of this ensured that Kirwan's time on Spike Island did not pass pleasantly. On 14 January, Governor Grace responded to his superiors by outlining his specific plans for Spike's most notorious prisoner:

> I have to acknowledge the receipt of your letter of the 12th in relation to the Convict Kirwan. You may depend that your instructions shall be carefully observed. He came out of hospital last evening and I was with him at 8 O'C to set him to work, but as he told me he was yet ill, I waited till 10 O C when I brought the doctor to him, he has got medicine and is excused from work for this day. I have removed him from the Iron Prison to B near the Guard room and he belongs to Turnkey Duggan's class. This class has very hard irksome labor [sic] pumping water, except that I do not think it prudent to send him outside the fort for the present, there is too much curiosity about him, and I have no doubt he would prefer it to being kept inside.
>
> His request for change of diet and exemption from labor [sic] I have of course refused and you have nothing to apprehend respecting visitors or any communication.[7]

---

7 Ibid.

So Kirwan was deliberately moved into Block B, near the staff accommodation, and was also tasked with 'irksome' labour by a governor who knew the interest of his superiors in this specific prisoner. While other prisoners might be allowed to remain in hospital until fit for work, or be allowed outside the confines of Fort Westmoreland whilst engaged in labour, Governor Grace intended to ensure that Kirwan saw little but walls and sky. The former artist probably passed his days manning one, or both, of the forcing pumps mounted on internal wells near No.2 Bastion and No.3 Bastion.[8]

Kirwan spent the next 14 months in Cork harbour.[9] Although his immediate transport to Bermuda or Gibraltar was considered desirable, a lack of space in those places during those months meant that the possibility of Irish ships making the voyage was remote.[10] Some may have considered Spike Island an appropriate detention place for a man who had been convicted of a foul crime on a very similar island. Indeed, the calling of the seabirds and the churning of the tides may have been a torturous reminder of the events that had changed Kirwan's life, and ended his wife's. While the infamous convicted murderer languished on Spike Island, some of his well-connected supporters began to cast very serious doubt on his guilt. Foremost among them was the Dublin solicitor John Knight Boswell (1806–1865), who produced quite a convincing argument for the prisoner's innocence.

---

8 NAI, CSORP/1847/G8814. The wells near No.2 Bastion and No.3 Bastion were the only internal wells recorded prior to 1853. If Kirwan was indeed employed in pumping water within the fort, he would have done so at either of these locations.
9 NAI, Mountjoy Prison Convict Classification 1857-1866, 1/11/23. It is important to note that the so-called 'Mountjoy' classification records refer to all convicts who entered the convict system, most of whom served the majority of their sentences on Spike Island.
10 NAI, GPO/LB/3/189.

Boswell began by casting doubt on the motivations of Kirwan's neighbour in reporting her suspicions of murder to the police. It seems that this report was partly responsible for the instigation of the investigation, and Boswell now asserted that it was motivated by a long-standing dispute between neighbours. He also argued that Kirwan's double life was no motive for murder as both of his partners had known of each other's existence for 12 years, and it was claimed that several witnesses could testify to that knowledge. The question as to whether the body lay on the sheet was again discussed, and Boswell pointed to the evidence given by one of the boatmen at the Coroner's inquest, in which he had stated that the sheet was brought down from the rocks in order to cover the body. It was argued that Kirwan would have found it very difficult to commit and cover up a murder between the time the cries were heard from Howth, and the time he met the boatmen at the shore. It was also alleged that people in Howth became more convinced that a murder had taken place when the local Roman Catholic priest inferred it. It was also argued that several people had sworn that they had witnessed Mrs Kirwan suffering epileptic fits and it was again asserted that this was the cause of her drowning. Perhaps Boswell's most shocking allegation was his insistence that there was another man on Ireland's Eye at the time of the murder and that he could testify to Kirwan's innocence, but did not want to be implicated himself. Boswell also appended a sworn declaration from Teresa Kenny, to the effect that each of Kirwan's lovers was aware of the other's existence. Boswell's argument was startlingly logical and appeared to unveil a serious miscarriage of justice.

Kirwan was never afforded the luxury of a retrial. There was no court of criminal appeal that might overturn his conviction. There may have been grounds for reasonable doubt regarding his guilt, but that did not prove him innocent. While the notion that Kirwan was innocent gathered some traction in the public arena, there were just as many grounds to doubt his innocence as there were to doubt his guilt. One hundred and sixty years later, Michael Sheridan's 2012 book, *Murder at Ireland's Eye*, may have revealed the reason why the authorities were never inclined to believe in Kirwan's innocence. That reason came in the form of a medical paper published just a few weeks after Kirwan arrived on Spike Island. The paper was the work of Professor Thomas Geoghegan of the Royal College of Surgeons in Dublin. Professor Geoghegan helped the prosecution construct much of its medical case, but for reasons unknown was not called as a witness in the trial. Geoghegan deconstructed Kirwan's epilepsy defence by stating, with reference to the work of many other eminent scholars, that Maria Louisa Kirwan's injuries were not consistent with those of a person who had drowned during a fit. Instead, he felt that her injuries were entirely consistent with death, not by drowning, but by strangulation. In addition he asked a number of very pertinent questions:

1. If, as the defence claimed, Mrs Kirwan's epileptic fit was caused by her having eaten immediately prior to entering the water, why was there no trace of food in her stomach upon exhumation?
2. Why had Kirwan never mentioned his wife's history of epileptic fits in the immediate aftermath of her death?
3. The prosecution had claimed that Mrs Kirwan fell and drowned in shallow water as a result of an epileptic fit. In Geoghegan's experience those who were seized by an epileptic fit did not turn over after falling. How, therefore, were there wounds on both sides of Mrs Kirwan's body?
4. One may say that her body was damaged as the tide carried it out, however how could the tide carry a body from a shallow rock pool

to a more elevated rock, as tidal evidence dictated it would have had to?[11]

While the prosecution's failure to call Geoghegan as a witness might indicate a lack of confidence in his evidence, his report certainly seems to eliminate any reasonable doubt about Kirwan's guilt. That may well have been the reason why nobody in authority paid the slightest heed to any protestations of Kirwan's innocence. In the opinion of Professor Geoghegan and the authorities in Dublin, William Burke Kirwan was guilty of his wife's murder.

While Kirwan languished on Spike Island and his friends argued his innocence, his mistress, Teresa Kenny, was faring rather badly. She had become embroiled in a legal dispute regarding the ownership of Kirwan's property. That dispute in itself had helped resurrect a long forgotten story from Kirwan's past, and it was a story that did not serve him well.

During his late teens, the young Kirwan had become friendly with an elderly artist by the name of Richard Downes Boyer. Some sources asserted that Kirwan had claimed to be Boyer's nephew, others merely that he studied under him. Whatever the truth of it, it appears that by January 1837 their relationship had taken a new turn, when the feeble, and some claimed senile, Boyer parted from his younger wife. She claimed that Kirwan had entered her home with five or six other men sporting blackened faces, that they proceeded to tie her up while they ransacked the house and then made off with a bank savings book and her elderly husband. Kirwan had denied that he kidnapped Boyer, claiming that the latter had voluntarily left his violent wife and that although he had provided lodgings for his friend for a period, he

---

11 Sheridan, M., pp.276–304.

had lost contact with him and had no idea of his whereabouts. Mrs Downes Boyer pleaded before the court that they should 'let him give me my husband, that is all I want', but the court could do no such thing. Boyer's whereabouts were unknown and, 15 years before he was convicted of murdering his wife, there was no reason to suspect Kirwan of any wrongdoing. Of course, after Kirwan's conviction, that changed.

The police set about excavating the garden of one of Kirwan's old residences. Some reports claimed that human remains (those of a child) were found on the property. Other reports referred to Kirwan having used the bank book to withdraw money from Boyer's account. In the end, in spite of the continued and determined lobbying of Boyer's wife, no charges were brought against Kirwan in the case of the disappearance of the elderly artist. The primary reason may have been the intervention of Kirwan's supporter and friend, John Knight Boswell. This time, Boswell petitioned the magistrates, claiming that he could produce certificates issued by a doctor and a rector to prove that Boyer had died in November 1841 and was buried in Killeshandra, Co. Cavan. The matter appears to have rested there. The authorities may not have been able to convict Kirwan, but their suspicions that he may have been involved in another murder were surely enough to deafen their ears to his claims of innocence. Her failure to attain the justice she felt her husband was due appears to have been the primary motivation for Anne Downes Boyer's suicide on 7 July 1853.[12]

12 *Freeman's Journal*, 27 May 1837, *The Advocate*, 13 July 1853, *Freeman's Journal*, 12 January 1853, *Dublin Evening Post*, 5 February 1853, *Southern Report and Cork Commercial Courier*, 15 January 1853, *Dublin Mercantile Advertiser, and Weekly Price Current*, 4 February 1853, *Roscommon Journal, and Western Reporter*, 20 August 1853. See also: Gibson, C.B. 1863. *Life Among Convicts, Vol II*. London: Hurst and Blackett, pp.42–5.

Teresa Kenny now claimed ownership of property the elderly Boyer had sold to Kirwan. That property had been forfeited to the State upon Kirwan's conviction. Kenny produced a deed to assert that claim, but in the end the courts decided that she had no legal claim to the property. She had the added misfortune of engaging George Townley Balfour Darling to represent her interests. It was later alleged that Darling represented himself to Kenny as a solicitor, when he had no such qualification. He then proceeded to extract considerable sums of money from Kenny. When that matter came before the courts, it was decided that Kenny's status as a 'fallen woman' made her a less than creditable witness. However, Darling was convicted of having obtained money under false pretences from others involved in the Kirwan property saga. Having already amassed a number of convictions, on 12 April 1854 this career fraudster was sentenced to four years' penal servitude. Whether by accident or design, Kirwan departed Spike Island bound for Bermuda aboard the *Amazon* the day after Darling's conviction. When Darling arrived on Spike Island a few months later, he did not have to face the convicted murderer whose mistress he had allegedly cheated. He would be released by the time that Kirwan returned to a greatly changed island almost a decade later. [13]

---

13 *The Cork Examiner*, 28 November 1853 and 17 April 1854, *The Limerick and Clare Examiner*, 23 November 1853, *Freeman's Journal*, 8 April 1854, *The Dublin Evening Mail*, 6 February 1854, *The Advocate*, 15 July 1854, NAI, Mountjoy Convict Classification & Richmond Bridewell Registry (Balfour Darling), *The Dublin Evening Mail*, 6 February 1854.

8. Change and Reorganisation

Following the passage of the Penal Servitude Act 1853, the most common sentence of transportation, that of seven years, was abolished. Instead, offenders would be sentenced to 'penal servitude' at home in government prisons. While most of those sentenced to transportation never left Ireland and many sentences of transportation were already being carried out in Irish prisons anyway, this Act effectively made that process official and rendered it impossible to transport the overwhelming majority of Irish convicts. It was obvious that this would lead to serious overcrowding in Irish prisons. Indeed, Spike Island had become so overcrowded by this time that the possibility of once again mooring a prison hulk (or hulks) in the harbour was briefly considered.[1]

The Chief Secretary eventually appointed a Commission to make recommendations aimed at alleviating the overcrowding. In so doing, he was anxious that the Commission benefit from the experience of officials involved in the administration of the English convict service. As a result, the governor of Portsmouth Convict Prison, Captain Charles Raleigh Knight, was dispatched to Ireland. Knight was 40 years old and had considerable experience of administration within the penal system, having spent five years superintending military prisons in Canada and having served as governor of Portland Convict Prison before his transfer to Portsmouth. Captain Walter Crofton, a retired military officer then serving as county magistrate for Wiltshire, also made the crossing to Ireland. These Englishmen were joined on the Commission by J. Corry Connellan of the Inspectorate of Govern-

---

1 NAI, GPO/LB/4/92. The mooring of a hulk off Spike Island was reconsidered in 1853 when convicts returning from Bermuda threatened to overcrowd the prison again. This hulk was considered as a suitable location for the detention of the infirm (NAI, GPO/LB/3/26).

ment Prisons in Ireland, and Captain H.D. Harness, a member of the Board of Works in Dublin.[2]

The Commission reported back to the Chief Secretary on 16 March 1854. It made interim proposals regarding the removal of all invalids and juveniles from Spike Island and other prisons to separate accommodation. It also proposed the erection of another female convict prison and forwarded lists of specific prisoners for whom it recommended release on tickets of leave.[3] The Commission reported on a number of occasions throughout 1854. In order for its recommendations to be acted upon and for the convict system to be reorganised and that reorganisation to be placed on a legal footing, legislation was required. That legislation came in the form of the Convict Prisons (Ireland) Act, which was passed in August 1854. Under its provisions, a new system of governance was to apply to the Irish convict system.

On 29 November 1854, the Inspectorate of Government Prisons was abolished and replaced by the Directors of Convict Prisons for Ireland. This was the visible manifestation of a complete overhaul of the convict services in Ireland. Under the new regime, three directors were made responsible for all of Ireland's convict prisons. The first of those directors was 51-year-old John Lentaigne, who was a Commissioner of Loan Funds, a magistrate of counties Dublin and Monaghan, a sheriff in the latter county, a governor of the Richmond District Lunatic Asylum and a vice-chairman of the South Dublin Union. His fellow directors were Captains Charles Knight and Walter Crofton.[4] These three men were to have a profound effect on the

2 HMSO, *Copies of Correspondence Relative to the Management and Discipline of Convict Prisons, and the Extension of Prison Accommodation with Reports of Commissioners (Ordered by the House of Commons to be printed, 3 July 1854)*, p.15.
3 Ibid.
4 HMSO, 1854-55 (29), *Government prisons (Ireland). Copies of minutes constituting the Board of Commissioners, pursuant to provisions of 17 & 18 Vict. c. 76, for the management*

internal politics surrounding the relationships between senior officers in the Spike Island prison. Their first task, though, was the reorganisation of the Irish convict system.

Two of the three new directors had not seen the deprivations of the Irish famine at first-hand. And although Knight had significant experience of English convict prisons, he and his colleagues were surprised at the poor condition of Irish convicts. They reported as follows:

> The deplorable aspect and apparent destitution of the Irish convicts appeared to us to require immediate attention, and we have endeavoured, as far as possible, to remedy this state of things, which contrasts strongly with the condition of those in England...The condition of the Irish convicts...is the result of the want of a proper system which has hitherto existed in this country, together with a deficiency of suitable prison accommodation.[5]

Much of the motivation for the reorganisation of the convict system was the result of an awareness that the transportation of convicts could not continue indefinitely. The death knell of the entire convict transportation system had already sounded. Colonial authorities were raising the standard for acceptable convicts, and the Irish system could not produce convicts of that calibre. By 1853, the anti-transportation movement in Australia had succeeded in ending transportation

---

of the government convict prisons establishment in Ireland; and of order directing the dismissal or removal from office of the officers entrusted with the management of said convict prisons previous to the passing of said act; &c.
5 HMSO, First Annual Report of the Directors of Convict Prisons in Ireland, for the year ended 31st December, 1854; with appendix. Hereafter, these will be referred to as 'Directors' Report', with the relevant year stated thereafter.

to New South Wales and Van Diemen's Land.[6] The only Australian colony still accepting convicts from any source was Western Australia. The authorities in that territory had expressed strong reservations regarding the condition of Irish convicts after the *Robert Small* and the *Phoebe Dunbar* arrived there in August 1853, complaining that the men were in bad health, idle, insolent and irreverent. Furthermore, the Superintendent of Fremantle Gaol was able to demonstrate a tangible difference between Irish and English convicts:

> The English prisoners maintained an exemplary course of conduct the percentage of crime amongst them being singularly small. The Irish prisoners per 'Robert Small' and 'Phoebe Dunbar' exhibit a percentage of prison crime, during the period of their detention within the establishment, far in excess of the average proportion of the English fellows.[7]

The then Inspector of Government Prisons, Henry M. Hitchins, was somewhat dismissive of the charges relating to the health of Irish convicts. The Australian authorities had assumed that convicts aboard the *Robert Small* and *Phoebe Dunbar* were removed directly from prisons operating the separate system. Hitchins pointed out that these assumptions were entirely incorrect in the case of the *Robert Small,* as that vessel had removed convicts engaged in public works directly from Spike Island. While 174 of the *Phoebe Dunbar*'s 295 convicts were removed directly from separation cells in Mountjoy (Fig. 8.1), Hitchins concluded that there was no historical or contemporary evidence that suggested such a removal would impact on the physical

---

6 To mark a break with its past as a penal colony, the name of Van Diemen's Land was changed to Tasmania on 1 January 1856.
7 HMSO, *Directors' Report 1854.*

health of convicts. His view was supported by the Medical Superintendents of Spike Island and Mountjoy.[8] The matter may have rested there if those other concerns regarding the demeanour and behaviour of the Irish convicts hadn't surfaced soon afterwards. Those concerns were dealt with by Hitchins's successors, the Directors of Convict Prisons.

Figure 8.1 Aerial view of Mountjoy Gaol today. Mountjoy opened in 1850 and the radial building dates from that time. (Image © courtesy of Dennis Horgan)

The Directors tended to agree that 'it would be a grave injustice to inflict the Irish convicts in their <u>present state</u> on Western Australia'.[9] They were in the process of implementing a new regime and commented that:

> With regard to the physical condition of the Irish convicts who have arrived in Western Australia, we regret that the lamentable state of health of the criminal classes in this country (attributed in part to the results of the famine) is such, and phthisis and other scrofulous diseases so prevalent that we cannot anticipate any amelioration in this respect

8 NAI, CSORP/1854/17485 & 16905.
9 NAI, CSORP/1855/2321.

for some time to come, farther than what we may be able to produce through sanatory [sic] improvements, and alterations in the dietary and Prison Construction.

In conclusion we beg to state that although in the present transition state of Prison Discipline in this Country, we have thought it unadvisable to recommend the deportation of Irish convicts to a Colony for some time to come, yet their character generally gives us strong grounds to expect that when they have had similar Advantages of Education and proper treatment with the English Convicts, they need fear no comparison with them on the trial grounds of Western Australia.[10]

By the end of 1853, Spike Island held almost 59% of Ireland's male convict population, and 52% of its entire convict population.[11] The removal of all invalids and juveniles meant that this was about to change.

Under the new regime, all juvenile convicts were immediately removed to Philipstown (now Daingean, Co. Offaly; Fig. 8.2) and to Mountjoy. The new Directors were anxious that modern thinking on the reform of juvenile criminals should be implemented in Ireland and commented:

We highly appreciate such efforts, which in so many instances have been productive of the most favourable results; we observe that the secret, if we may so term it, of these successes has been through individualising cases ... We feel no doubt

---

10 Ibid.
11 HMSO, *Copies of Correspondence Relative to the Management and Discipline of Convict Prisons, and the Extension of Prison Accommodation with Reports of Commissioners (Ordered by the House of Commons to be printed, 3 July 1854)*, p.12.

whatever as to the favourable results of such treatment if pursued more in the Government Prisons than has ever yet been the case. When we consider that we have several boys at the tender ages of twelve and thirteen years sentenced to four years penal servitude for stealing potatoes & c., whose cases we have endeavoured to sift, the majority of whom have no parents, no home excepting the low lodging houses, whose owners have sent these children forth to commit the crimes for which they are now suffering, we feel that this same reformatory treatment carried out as described with the best results by different institutions, must exercise a large and important influence on any system adopted...[12]

Spike Island was not conducive to such a reformatory process. Neither, according to the Directors, was it conducive to the recuperation of the invalid convicts, who accounted for almost half its population.

The tendency to tubercular consumption, and the different forms of scrofula, at Spike Island, early engaged our attention. That island, situated near the mouth of Cork harbour, is exposed without shelter to cold winds, which frequently blow from the east and north-east. Its climate is variable, and totally unsuited to the class of maladies to which the convict, and more especially the Irish convict, is peculiarly liable; indeed we have ascertained that a residence on the island, is found to confirm the strumous tendency in constitutions pre-disposed to the disease, which quickly develops itself in its worst form, and assumes a fatal character.[13]

---

12 HMSO, *Directors' Report 1854.*
13 Ibid.

St. Conleth's School, Daingean, Offaly.

Figure 8.2 Early 20th-century aerial view of Philipstown Gaol. Originally the King's County Gaol, the prison became a convict depot in 1852. This closed in 1862 and the site later became a children's reformatory school. It is now a storage facility for the National Museum of Ireland. (Image © courtesy of Offaly Historical and Archaeological Society)

In short, Spike Island had been the destination for all prisoners suffering from two distinct manifestations of tuberculosis, phthisis (pulmonary tuberculosis) and scrofula (tubercular infection of the lymph nodes of the neck), but the cold winds present on the island, along with its variable climate, were thought to aggravate those conditions. From the end of 1854, all new cases of phthisis and scrofula were to be sent to the hospital in the Philipstown depot. There, the Directors of Convict Prisons intended making up to 500 spaces available for invalid convicts, and converting that prison for the exclusive use of juveniles and invalids. The removal of cases of phthisis and scrofula from the island would certainly improve the death rate. In 1854, Spike Island's overall mortality rate was almost 12%.[14] Of those 228 deaths, more than 77% were attributed by the Medical Officer to either phthisis or scrofula.

---

14 This was down from a peak of just under 12.5% in 1853.

In early December 1854, 245 invalid convicts were transferred from other depots to Philipstown; most of them came from Spike Island. In exchange, the King's County depot sent 280 of its healthy convicts to the Cork harbour island.[15] By March 1855, the immediate removal of 25 invalids from Spike Island to Philipstown was seen as 'the only way of saving their lives'. Their recovery on Spike Island was deemed 'impossible'.[16] By the end of 1855, Spike Island's convict population had been reduced to 1,433. This represented a 35% reduction in its population during the course of 1854 and 1855.[17] With 67 invalids moved to Philipstown, in 1855 the mortality rate fell to just over 5%. The removal of much of its infirm class allowed great improvements to the hospital accommodation on Spike Island. In August 1855, the south end of Block G was opened as a hospital, facilitating the closure of the older hospital accommodation in Block F.[18]

With many of the invalids and juveniles thus removed, the prison's contraction was further cemented by an administrative quirk of the convict system. The Penal Servitude Act 1853 had replaced a sentence of seven years' transportation with that of four years' penal servitude. In April 1854, the Commission of Convict Inquiry, recognising the overcrowding of Irish prisons, had recommended that those who had already served four years of their seven-year transportation sentence should be released. By the end of 1855, 920 such prisoners had been released on free pardons, 683 of them from Spike Island.[19] Even with so many prisoners already released, the Directors were anxious to continue trying to relieve numerical congestion in

15 HMSO, *Directors' Report 1854.*
16 NAI, GPO/LB/4/120.
17 HMSO, *Directors' Report 1855.*
18 Ibid.
19 Ibid.

Irish government prisons (previously known as convict depots). Thus, during 1855 they began implementing a scheme already in operation in England, whereby convicts of 'exemplary character' who had already served the greater part of a transportation sentence could be considered for release on a 'Ticket of Licence'. The scheme was also extended to convicts undergoing penal servitude sentences.

This 19th-century precursor of the parole system was quite controversial at the time of its introduction. Critics claimed that such convicts were prone to reoffending and were unable to support themselves by honest means. The Directors of Convict Prisons in Ireland argued that as most colonies would no longer receive convicts, they had to be released at home. The Directors aimed to address criticisms of the licensing system by providing accommodation outside of the main prisons where convicts could be gainfully employed, and their characters assessed, while living under a more relaxed disciplinary code prior to their release. The largest of these innovative establishments was to be at Lusk, Co. Dublin, while in Cork, and still under the governance of Spike Island, Fort Camden was also to become one of these 'Intermediate Prisons':

> ...we are endeavouring, as a preliminary step or stage to so important an undertaking, to collect prisoners eligible for discharge ... in certain establishments belonging to our service, and specially devoted to that purpose – at Smithfield, in Dublin, where those acquainted with trades, and the infirm of the selected class, can be profitably occupied, and at Fort Camden, near the mouth of Cork Harbour, where the able-bodied of the same class can be employed on the fortifications. These establishments will act as filterers between the prisons and the community; but to enable them to be *really* such, the

system pursued in them must be of such a character as to test the reformation of the prisoner, and throw him more on himself; hard work and coarse fare must be the rule and in the evenings carefully selected lecturers may inculcate lessons of practical utility.[20]

During the course of 1856, Fort Carlisle was converted into another intermediate prison. Portable iron huts modelled on those that housed soldiers in Beggars Bush Barracks in Dublin were constructed at each of the mainland forts. It was thought that these more mobile huts would allow convict labour to be directed to locations outside of the prisons.[21] From 1 January 1858, Carlisle's function was changed from intermediate prison to a feeder prison for Fort Camden. The best behaved of Spike Island's prisoners who were within eight months of eligibility for intermediate prison were transferred from Spike Island's Iron Prison to Fort Carlisle. As soon as they reached eligibility for intermediate prison, they were then transferred across the harbour to Fort Camden 'to receive their licence or otherwise be disposed of'.[22] As the intermediate prisons couldn't contain all of those who were eligible for them, convicts from less privileged backgrounds were to receive priority when allocating available places. This tended to exclude agrarian offenders, and the exclusion of this class was pursued as a formal policy in 1863.[23]

---

20 Ibid. Convicts located in the intermediate prisons also received tobacco allowances, which were much sought after at the time (NAI, GPO/LB/17/41 & 76).

21 NAI, GPO/LB/15/483 & 573 & 1298.

22 HMSO, *Directors' Reports, 1855-58.* See also: NAI, GPO/LB/16/1750, 2187, 2232 & 2302. Convicts were later permitted to transfer from Spike Island to Fort Carlisle once they were within 18 months of eligibility for intermediate prison. In early 1858, some convicts located in Fort Carlisle expressed the desire to return to Spike Island (NAI, GPO/LB/17/232).

23 NAI, GPO/LB/17/480, GPO/LB/18/1552 & GPO/LB/20/336 & 346.

This newly established probationary system served a dual function. It certainly helped relieve overcrowded Irish prisons. However, it also facilitated the implementation of a new disciplinary process for the prison establishment. After the abolition of shorter transportation sentences, the authorities feared the breakdown of discipline. Local Inspector Atkins wrote to the Inspector General of Prisons in order to explain those fears:

> I wish to impress upon you the great importance of our having some additional powers of punishment beyond the mere locking up in a cell for a few hours with bread and water a refractory convict. Since they have discovered that transportation is to be abolished and no more tickets of leave there has been a manifest change in their tempers and inclination to work. <u>Frequent acts of insubordination and positive refusal to work</u> have taken place within a few days. In one instance a convict who was learning the trade of stonecutter, and had made considerable progress in the trade, after completing the cutting of a block for the public works deliberately took up a sledgehammer and broke the stone to pieces.[24]

Whether granted in Ireland or in the colonies, a 'ticket of leave' had been an important motivational tool for good behaviour among convicts. As soon as this carrot was removed, the prison authorities were left with far less effective sticks. However, the introduction of a ticket of licence reinstated a more positive approach to motivation and was cemented by the classification system that came with it.

Under the new system, each prisoner on Spike Island was placed in one of five classes: the probation, third, second, first and

---

24 NAI, CSORP/1853/6712.

exemplary classes. As before, the first stage (usually six months) of a sentence of penal servitude was served in separate cells in Mountjoy, or on some occasions in county or city gaols. Having served their period of separation, the convicts were sent to the various government prisons, of which Spike Island was the largest. Those who had left Mountjoy having been certified by the governor as being of 'bad' or 'very bad' character were placed in the probation class. They would remain in that class until the Directors promoted them to third class, on the recommendation of the governor. Others placed in the probation class included those who had not served the desired period of separation in Mountjoy for various reasons. This included those who had been deemed 'medically unfit to undergo the strictly separate system of confinement carried out at the Mountjoy Government Prison, but who nevertheless may be equal to labour on the Public Works, and fit to undergo a modified system of separation'.[25] This seemed to imply that the authorities were already aware of a group who were mentally unfit for the silence and frightening introspection of the separate system. Yet warders were instructed to limit the communication of the probation class insofar as was practicable. Such mentally challenged individuals would become a serious problem for the authorities on Spike Island. These prisoners would remain in the probation class until they had served the time equivalent of the separation they should have served in Mountjoy, after which they were promoted to third class.

Third class prisoners were eligible for promotion to second class after time periods that varied in accordance with their character reports on their release from the probation class. During this time period they had to maintain an 'exemplary' character. Likewise, second class prisoners could only be promoted to first class after they had

---

25 HMSO, *Directors' Report 1855*.

maintained exemplary conduct for a period of six months. Prisoners in the first class had to maintain exemplary conduct for 12 months before their promotion to the exemplary class.

The different classes were to be distinguished by differences in their prison uniforms and by a series of badges worn on the sleeve (Fig. 8.3). Probation and third class prisoners were dressed in the plain grey prison uniforms that were previously worn by all convicts. The second class had light blue collars and cuffs on those grey uniforms, while the first class wore red collars and cuffs. The exemplary class wore an entirely different uniform, which was described as 'a sort of brick or brimstone colour'.[26] For a period from 1850, some, or all, of Spike Island's convicts wore wooden shoes or clogs known by the French term *sabots*.[27] In addition, with the introduction of the new classification system in 1854 all prisoners were to wear register and conduct badges on their right and left sleeves, respectively. The register badge displayed the prisoner's number along with details of his sentence. The conduct badge recorded the class in which the prisoner was currently placed, how many good conduct marks he required before he could be promoted to a higher class, and how many such marks he had received in the previous month, and in months prior to that month. In order to ensure that the conduct badge was accurate, it was to be reissued to each prisoner every month.[28]

---

26 Gibson, Rev. C.B. 1863. *Irish Convict Reform: The intermediate prisons, a mistake.* Dublin: McGlashin and Gill, p.20. (National Library of Ireland (NLI), P 477.)

27 The *sabots* were 'peculiarly adapted for the labour on Spike' and were only introduced on trial in 1850. We do not know how long this trial lasted (NAI, CSORP/1850/G4033/326).

28 HMSO, *Directors' Report 1855*. It is important to note that this system was applied to those serving older Transportation sentences, as well as Penal Servitude prisoners.

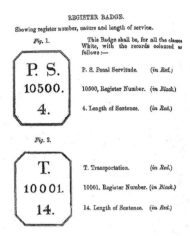

REGISTER BADGE.
Showing register number, nature and length of service.

Fig. 1.

P. S.
10500.
4.

This Badge shall be, for all the classes White, with the records coloured as follows :—

P. S. Penal Servitude.   (in Red.)

10500, Register Number. (in Black.)

4. Length of Sentence.   (in Red.)

Fig. 2.

T.
10001.
14.

T. Transportation.   (in Red.)

10001, Register Number. (in Black.)

14. Length of Sentence.   (in Red.)

Figure 8.3 Illustrations from the 1855 Annual Report of the Directors of Convict Prisons, giving details of the badges associated with the new system of prisoner classification introduced the previous year. (Image © HMSO, *Directors' Report 1855*, 154)

While the marks system provided an incentive to good behaviour among the convicts, perhaps the most powerful motivator was the system of gratuities that had been established in England for some years prior. From the time of their appointment, the new Directors were anxious to establish such a system in Ireland.[29] By 1855, exemplary convicts practicing skilled trades in the Smithfield prison were in receipt of gratuities for their labour. The governor of Spike Island soon found himself involved in a bureaucratic tangle regarding the payment of gratuities to English convicts who were placed in his care when the *Waterloo* transport was forced to put in to Cork harbour for repair whilst transporting exemplary convicts from Bermuda back to England.[30] In 1855 and 1857, the governor was in receipt of gratuity money for Irish convicts returning from Bermuda to the in-

29 NAI, GPO/LB/4/21.
30 NAI, CSORP/1854/13826.

termediate prisons.[31] From about this time the scheme was extended to those labouring in the Spike Island establishment. Convicts could earn reasonable sums and on their release could draw down these funds on a weekly basis. They could draw down a lump sum if they agreed to emigrate, and it is likely that much of this money was used to fund emigrant passages. Convicts returning from colonial prisons in Bermuda and Gibraltar to Irish intermediate prisons had the cost of their passage deducted from the gratuities they had earned.[32]

By the end of 1856, the Irish convict service had been completely overhauled. It was a much leaner and more efficient bureaucratic machine than what had existed prior to the 1854 Commission report. Its directors also claimed that they had seen much improvement with regard to permanent reformation of convicts.[33] A new broom had swept across the landscape of the convict system. But the dust was slow to settle. On Spike Island, a hostile and recalcitrant staff dug in to fight for their careers. Accusations were met with recriminations and counter-recriminations. Reputations were trashed, livelihoods lost and individuals dragged toward financial ruin. Spike Island was about to witness some very bad behaviour by some of its most senior staff.

---

31 NAI, CSORP/1857/1410.
32 HMSO, *Directors' Reports 1855, 1856 & 1857 (Accounts Spike Island)*. See also: NAI, CSORP/1855/2601.
33 HMSO, *Directors' Report 1855*.

9. Accusations and Machinations

By the end of 1853, Richard Grace had served more than six years as governor of the Spike Island convict depot. When his years of service in Cork County Gaol were considered, it was obvious that Grace was a man of great experience in the prison system. Even so, his ability to run a prison that had expanded as rapidly, and to such a size, as Spike Island was being called into question. When asked to explain why the Ordnance Department had made unfavourable comparisons between labour practices on Spike Island and in England's Portland Prison, Hitchins, the last Inspector of Government Prisons prior to the 1854 reforms, wrote a lengthy explanation of the differences between the two complexes and the health and skill-sets of their prisoners. To this explanation he added a separate letter, which could be attached to or detached from the explanation as the Chief Secretary desired. Its contents were of a very personal and private manner, and there might have been good reason to detach it from the 'official' explanation. In it, Hitchins explained what he felt was a major contributing factor to the inefficiency of Spike Island's prison:

> Whilst I have put forward that grounds on which the difference between the system at Portland and this prison can be explained other grounds exist which may in some degree also account for it. I allude to the unfitness of the Governor of Spike Island for the office he holds. I cannot speak in too high terms of Mr Grace's character and conduct, but he is from temperament and otherwise quite unequal to the arduous duties imposed on him. In fact when appointed to the office he holds, the number of prisoners in Spike Island did not exceed 600 and when it is considered that the prisoners detained

there are of the worst class convicted of the highest offences and that it is essential to enforce a high degree of discipline and to give to the employment a penal character, I cannot conceal from His Excellency that Mr Grace is quite deficient in that firmness and decision of character so essential for a satisfactory fulfilment of these important requirements.

If His Excellency should concur ... in requiring a stronger and more efficient management in this prison, and a greater development of its industrial resources as applicable to the completion of the public works on the island, the transfer of Mr Grace to one of the Dublin prisons will be an essential preliminary...[1]

Whether as an attempt to save his own face or motivated by a genuine concern for the management of Ireland's largest prison, Hitchins accused Grace of being too mild-mannered in his dealings with Spike Island's convicts. Luckily for Grace, his experience with juvenile and invalid convicts on Spike Island seemed to make him an ideal candidate for the governorship of the Philipstown convict depot while it was in the process of conversion for the reception of those classes. Some 10 months after Hitchins's letter, Grace departed Spike Island bound for Philipstown on 1 December 1853.

On Spike Island, the governor's torch was passed to William Stewart. Although described by the Directors of Convict Prisons as 'an able, active and judicious officer', Stewart had no previous experience of the convict service. His governorship did not last long. The beginning of the end came less than a year after his appointment when, on 27 September 1854, and for the first time since the fire of Christmas Eve 1851, the alarm bells rang out around Spike Island.

---

1 NAI, GPO/LB/3/15.

Prison staff made haste to the site of the alarm, which was the Timber Prison, then known as C Prison. It was soon discovered that the bell had been sounded too hastily as there was no sign of fire. The commotion had begun because a prisoner in one of the Timber Prison's two wards had attempted to slit his own throat. The prisoner was removed to the hospital. Then the recriminations began.

Over in Queenstown, Deputy Governor George Downes was availing of a few hours' leave from the depot. By his own admission he had just landed on the mainland when one of the boatmen told him of having heard an alarm from the island. For whatever reason, it seems that Downes was not inclined to rush back to Spike Island. Instead he sent a boat boy up the hill in Queenstown in order to observe the island and see whether there were any signs of fire there. When the boy reported back, he informed Downes that there was no evidence of smoke on Spike Island. Downes decided to go about his business on the mainland and return to the island at a later hour.

From the time of his return to Spike Island later that evening, Downes's behaviour was described by some witnesses as 'excited' and by others as 'drunk'. Nonetheless, he set about making enquiries regarding the ringing of the alarm bell. He asked to meet with Governor Stewart, who had left orders with the gatekeeper that he should be summoned as soon as Downes returned. The governor made his way to the gate as soon as Downes appeared. Downes soon ascertained that the bell had been rung by Warder Edmund Callon. On being questioned by Downes, Callon claimed that Governor Stewart had ordered him to ring the bell. Hearing Callon implicate the governor, Downes became extremely annoyed. For his part, Governor Stewart, who was later described by Downes as displaying the manner 'of a child who feels he has done wrong and is afraid to tell of it', stated that he had no recollection of giving any such order. Downes told Governor Stewart (his superior) that his staff had made a fool of him. Then, although the governor had initially ordered that investigations and any disciplinary action should be delayed until the morning, Downes ordered that Turnkey Callon be escorted to the guardroom. The governor made no objection to the order at that time, and so the unfortunate turnkey was taken to his place of punishment. The meeting in the gatehouse then broke up.[2] As the governor crossed the square, he was asked by Head Warder Thomas McCall whether Callon should be detained for the night. Governor Stewart went to the guardroom and promptly released Callon.[3]

At the subsequent inquiry, the governor admitted that the heated meeting in the gatehouse had annoyed him. After releasing Callon, he returned to his quarters and thought about his next move. At about 11.30pm, Stewart went back down to the Timber Prison, in order to ensure that all was well. There, he met McCall and they spoke of the events in the gatehouse some hours earlier. Later, both of them swore that during this meeting they had agreed that Downes had returned from Queenstown under the influence of alcohol.

The following morning, Governor Stewart went to Local Inspector Atkins in order to report the happenings of the previous night. Both of them later testified that Stewart informed Atkins that Downes was under the influence of alcohol on his return from Queenstown. Whatever he may or may not have said, and however accurate the memories of the two parties to that conversation, it seems that Atkins told Stewart that a verbal report was not sufficient.

---

2 The gatehouse was demolished by the Irish Prison Service during the remodelling of the fort undertaken in the aftermath of a riot in 1985.
3 NAI, CSORP/1860/14362.

He instructed the governor to make his report in writing. Stewart then penned the following:

Sir,

I beg to inform you that last night, about 8 O' clock, I heard a great disturbance and whistling in the square. On hastening down, I found the turnkeys running and crying from every quarter that the C Prison was on fire. On investigation I found that it was a false alarm – which had arisen from a prisoner in the above prison having attempted to cut his throat. On first hearing the cries of fire – I gave the Military Sergeant of the Guard notice to acquaint the commanding officer that his men might be required. I then opened the prison and saw the man lying on the floor – with blood on his throat – which was caused by a mere scratch. He was taken to the hospital where it was found necessary to put on a strait-waistcoat as he still threatened to destroy himself and has been long known to be a bad character. The prison bell being rung on the first alarm the turnkeys all hastened to the depot. I then placed a guard round the C Prison to prevent any of the prisoners taking advantage of the turmoil to escape several of them having already broken panes of glass and were increasing the confusion by calling fire.

I then gave directions to the head turnkey to close the C Prison and count the prisoners. The numbers being found correct and a strict examination having been made of all the building, the usual order and routine of the prison was soon established.

The Deputy Governor who had been absent for a few hours on leave, returned towards 10 O' clock, slightly excited which was revealed by the accounts of what had occurred during his absence.[4]

As ordered, Stewart presented this written report to Atkins. But Local Inspector Atkins was not satisfied with the contents. Governor Stewart's vague description of his deputy's 'slightly excited' condition was insufficient. He and Atkins spoke for a time and during the course of that conversation it was agreed that a second, and more descriptive, report should be produced. It seems that Atkins was anxious that a written record of the interaction should be established and so he returned the first report along with the following note:

> I have to request that in reference to the latter paragraph of your report of the 28th inst. that you will furnish me with a more detailed report as to the state of the Deputy Governor on the evening of the 27th inst.[5]

The second report delivered a serious blow to Downes's career prospects when it substituted the words 'slightly inebriated' for 'slightly excited'.

These reports formed much of the basis for an inquiry into Downes's behaviour some two-and-a-half months later. What transpired between Atkins and Stewart on the presentation of the first report was crucial to Downes's defence on the charge of drunkenness. He claimed that the first report did not mention his being under the influence of alcohol because he had not been so. He produced several witnesses who testified to his being sober when leaving Queenstown and on his passage to Spike Island. Stewart, Atkins and Head Warder

---

4 Ibid.
5 Ibid.

McCall all testified that Downes had been under the influence of alcohol on his return to the island. This prompted another question that needed to be answered: if Downes was not under the influence of alcohol on his return, why would Atkins insist that the governor report that he was?

According to Deputy Governor Downes, the answer might have had something to do with the origins of a mysterious anonymous letter 'in which the Local Inspector was charged with improprieties in the discharge of the duties of his office, such as being a participator in contracts & buying and selling prison property by & under false names for his own benefit, & screening misconduct in others, partiality etc etc.'[6] The specific charge of Atkins having sent 'in his own rotten straw to this prison at double the market price' was also levelled against the Local Inspector.[7] Downes claimed that Hitchins had notified him of Atkins's suspicion that the deputy governor was the author of the letter. Atkins had even threatened to resign his post unless Downes was dismissed. Downes vehemently denied that he had had anything to do with the mysterious letter. It should be noted, however, that Hitchins 'had been under the necessity of twice reprimanding Mr Downes, on one occasion he considered the circumstances gave rise to suspicions as to his honest intentions'.[8] This would seem to imply that Atkins was not the only person who believed that Downes was the author of the anonymous letter, and that the truth of anything he said, or wrote, might be called into question. Atkins's suspicions

---

6 NAI, CSORP/1855/10967.
7 NAI, CSORP/1860/14362. It should be noted that the quotations regarding the anonymous letter are taken from documents written by George Downes. Thus, they do not represent the authors' interpretation of the anonymous letter, but rather Downes's précis of its contents. Our research was unable to locate the letter and it is assumed that it is no longer extant.
8 NAI, CSORP/1860/14362.

about Downes's alleged letter writing was the source of substantial tension between the two men. The bitterness they felt for each other might have been enhanced by a row over Downes's erroneous over-payment for stores some months previously.[9] According to Deputy Governor Downes, this bitterness manifested itself in deliberate per-secution perpetrated by Local Inspector Atkins. At about this time, Downes's daughter became ill, and he later wrote:

> One of my daughters who had returned from Dublin after fin-ishing a costly education became very dangerously ill from cold caught by sleeping in a damp closet, I never having got suitable room for the accommodation of my family, about this time a room adjoining my quarters became vacant and I ap-plied to Mr Hitchins for it. He immediately granted it to me, upon hearing which, Capt. Atkins ordered one Turnkey each from several other rooms to occupy the room I was promised and he then reported to Mr Hitchins that the room in question could not be spared from the Public Service, and the result was my Daughter all but lost her life and only recovered after I had been driven to an expenditure little short of one hundred pounds, for lodging, Medical advice as well as Medicine and medical comforts to all of which my position in the Service fully entitled me Gratis.[10]

Whether or not Downes had written the anonymous letter, Atkins probably believed that he had and the whole affair certainly led to a less than cordial relationship between the two men. So when Governor Stewart reported the incidents of 27 September to him, it

---

9 NAI, GPO/LB/14/224.
10 NAI, CSORP/1860/14362.

surely occurred to Atkins that he now had an opportunity to settle an old score. The question remains as to whether or not he was entirely honest in doing so. The inquiry concluded that it had not 'been clearly proved that Mr Downes was <u>absolutely drunk</u> on the evening of 27th Sepr. 1854, [but] it is very evident from the testimony given on oath by the Governor and Head Warder of the Convict depot that he was <u>not in a state of sobriety</u> becoming an officer of his position in the prison.'[11]

Perhaps the most telling evidence against Downes was the illogical behaviour that he himself confessed to during the course of the inquiry. When he first heard reports of the alarm on the island, he was not excited enough to do his duty and return there at once. Instead, having directed a boy to check the validity of the reports by visually inspecting the island at some distance, he received a second-hand report that all was well and decided to remain in Queenstown. It is hard to reconcile this rather nonchalant reaction with the behaviour he exhibited when dressing-down his superior officer in front of two of their subordinates. It is clear that Downes only became excited several hours after he heard the alarm bell. Something seemed to have changed his temperament. It may have been something that was said, or it may have been the alcohol that he had consumed. Either way, Downes was guilty of overstepping the mark with his superior officer. During the course of subsequent correspondence, the deputy governor made it very clear that he did not consider Stewart's experience, or lack thereof, appropriate for the governorship of a convict prison. Indeed, it seems that Downes was under the impression that he himself was the real authority on the island. He later wrote:

---

11 Ibid.

I beg leave to state that in the presence of the Local Inspector, as was stated in evidence, I was told by the late Inspector of Government Prisons that owing to Mr Stewart's inexperience as well as his unbusiness like habits he would hold me responsible for the discipline and safekeeping of the establishment, thereby virtually investing me with the authority and responsibility of Gov. That for nearly five months after Mr Stewart's appointment I was obliged to govern the prison under very trying circumstances – which trust I executed according to the best of my ability, and I may add, in an efficient and proper manner, so much so as to elicit the commendation of Mr Hitchins. That afterwards and since charge was taken by Mr Stewart, he has never acted while I was present without my advice and direction.[12]

Downes was initially happy to have the matter inquired into. However, he may not have foreseen the events that were about to overtake him. The new Directorate of Convict Prisons for Ireland was in the process of installing itself and replacing Inspector of Government Prisons Hitchins at the helm.[13] As a result, it was the new Directors of Convict Prisons, and not Inspector Hitchins, who conducted the inquiry. With his old boss Hitchins departed from the scene, Downes faced the new administration alone. He was keen to persuade them that Hitchins had made him the effective governor of Spike Island, and consequently he questioned Governor Stewart as follows:

Are you aware that the Inspector General on the Occasion of his first visit here, after your appointment, stated that he would hold me almost, or all but entirely, responsible for the

---

12 Ibid.
13 NAI, GPO/LB/14/497.

discipline part of the prison, for a considerable time, as he would the Local Inspector for the other part owing to your inexperience and un-business-like habits?

To which Stewart responded:

> You told me so some time last week. Mr Hitchins told me that I was to be under the orders and directions of the Local Inspector and to be guided by him. Mr Hitchins may have said to me that you would help me with your experience.[14]

Thus, in his own mind at least, Downes may have felt that he had the moral authority to accuse his superior of foolishness opposite two warders. His ego and directness had driven him to address his superior in a manner that no subordinate should. In itself, this offence is somewhat understandable. What is less understandable, though, is his failure to acknowledge any wrongdoing on his part in the days, weeks and months that followed the incident.

While Hitchins may not have seen any grounds for an inquiry, the newly installed Directors certainly did. By the time the inquiry commenced, they had decided that another charge should be considered as well. That charge related to Downes having left the prison approximately one week before the events of 27 September 1854 and instructing the guard not to enter his name in the prison book, per the standing orders at the depot. We have already seen that the inquiry established that Downes was not drunk, but neither was he sober, on the night of 27 September. They did not record a definitive conclusion in relation to his departure from the prison a week prior. Nonetheless,

---

14 NAI, CSORP/1860/14362.

their ultimate conclusion was that Downes's:

> ...gross neglect of duty in not repairing at once to Spike Is-
> land on hearing of an alarm having sounded, together with his
> ... extraordinary conduct toward the Governor, and others, on
> his arrival at the prison, show the unfitness of this officer for
> his appointment.[15]

The Directors chose a rather unusual way of dismissing Downes. Instead of removing him from the office, they simply removed the office from the island. As they were then in the process of reorganising the convict service, they noted that 'the office of Deputy Governor may be dispensed with'. As both Downes and Stewart had been suspended from duty until the outcome of the inquiry was known, the Chief Secretary (presumably on the recommendation of the Directors of Convict Prisons) then wrote to Downes informing him that his office had been dispensed with and that his services were no longer required. The administration promised him a gratuity equal to one year's pay and probably hoped that this would be the end of the affair. George Downes, however, would not rest.

Even before the events that led to his downfall, in the latter half of 1853, Hitchins had promised Downes a raise in his salary. The increase was subsequently approved as part of the budgetary process. In December, Hitchens decided that the wage increase would not be required and should be struck off the estimates and he found a technicality that allowed him to do so. When, in October 1855, Downes decided to petition the Lord Lieutenant for the money which he felt he was due, the administration responded as follows:

---

15 Ibid.

In answer to your memorial claiming a sum of £25 as due to you for increased salary as Deputy Governor of Spike Island prison for the year 1853-54, I am directed by the Lord Lieutenant to inform you that His Excellency has no power to order the sum in question to be paid to you – it having been erroneously inserted in the estimate without the sanction of the Lord Commissioners of Her Majesty's Treasury having been first obtained for the increase of your salary and that sanction not having been subsequently given.[16]

In the briefing provided by the Government Prisons Office for the above reply, Downes's nemesis, Local Inspector Atkins, had informed the Lord Lieutenant's office that Hitchins had withdrawn the salary increase from a memo to the Treasury as he 'had reason to be displeased' with Downes. Atkins also pointed out that Downes later received a salary increase of £50, which he was paid for the year prior to his dismissal. Although Downes had claimed that he was unable to pay income tax demanded of him, Atkins noted that the tax was due for the year prior to his dismissal and not the year for which the £25 increase was withdrawn.[17] So whatever tax problems Downes had were entirely of his own making. The former deputy governor was arrested for income tax arrears on 10 March 1856.[18]

By now Downes had a very personal vendetta against the entire prison service and he continued to wage war on them periodically. On 30 June 1855, he petitioned the Lord Lieutenant regarding his claims to gratuity and superannuation. He produced a letter presented

16 NAI, CSORP/1855/9262.
17 NAI, CSORP/1855/561. The reason why Hitchins was displeased with Downes is unknown, but it is likely that it had something to do with the anonymous letter.
18 NAI, CSORP/1856/13099.

to him by the Chief Secretary at the time of the abolition of his office. The letter assured him that the Lord Lieutenant would recommend Downes for a gratuity amounting to 'one year's salary from the 1st Instant', but it also informed him that he was not entitled to any annuity as his service was not of sufficient duration. Although Downes claimed that he only received £50 gratuity on his £200 salary and that he was entitled to superannuation due to previous public service, his claims fell on deaf ears. What he had failed to mention was his dismissal from his post in the Rathdown Union, and its consequential irrelevance in the calculation of superannuation entitlements.[19] In April 1855, the Under-Secretary had communicated with the Lords of the Treasury ruling out any addition to the £50 gratuity already paid.[20] In 1860, Downes again tried to revive the matter of his gratuity with the Lord Lieutenant. He was simply informed that 'His Excellency can only refer mem. to answers already given'.[21] When he wasn't chasing his superannuation, Downes was making other accusations. In September 1855, he revived his hostility with Atkins when he wrote to the Directors informing them that the Local Inspector had stolen property from some of the convicts. The Directors asked him to substantiate his claims by naming the victims of the thefts.[22] There is no record of his having done so, and it seems that the matter was allowed to die.

Much of Downes's correspondence with the Dublin authorities was written from his house at Bellvue Terrace in Queenstown.

---

19 NAI, CSORP/1855/16469. Reference to Downes's dismissal from the Rathdown Union was made in the report of the Spike Island Inquiry (NAI, CSORP/1860/14362 & GPO/LB/4/53 1/2).

20 NAI, CSORP/1860/15783. The communications between the Under-Secretary and the Treasury were referred to during the course of Downes's correspondence with the (new) Lord Lieutenant's Office in 1860. Unfortunately, the contents of those communications are not annexed to the correspondence.

21 NAI, CSORP/1860/15783. Mem. is an abbreviation of memorialist, or petitioner.

22 NAI, GPO/LB/14/1841 & 1862.

His front windows commanded a stunning view of Cork harbour and Spike Island (Fig. 9.1). It was hardly a view that assisted him in forgetting the past. Neither did the death of his daughter, Sofia, on 28 September 1858.[23] If she was the girl who had suffered illness on Spike Island some years earlier, his loathing of the Prison Office was probably added to by her passing. Although he tried to obtain alternative employment, the Prison Office's refusal to provide him with testimonials did not help his cause.[24] By late 1860, Downes was operating as an insurance agent in Queenstown. He also continued an auctioneering business that he had run while serving on Spike Island. In 1868, the former deputy governor of the largest prison in the then United Kingdom served 24 days in prison for debts he had accrued. He was declared bankrupt later that year.[25]

A simple alarm bell on 27 September 1854 began a process that ultimately destroyed the career of the deputy governor of Spike Island. Few of the participants emerged from the affair in an attractive light. The Directors of Convict Prisons did not believe the accusations made against Local Inspector Robert Atkins. He remained at his post and died in an armchair at his home, just short of four years later, on 26 August 1858.[26] He was replaced as Local Inspector by another soldier, Captain John Barlow.[27] It may be the case that Governor William Stewart was used as a pawn in an ugly argument between Atkins and Downes. His reluctance to report Downes for drinking and his failure to assert his authority when Downes publicly chastised him may have been construed as weakness. The Directors concluded that his experi-

---

23 *The Belfast News-Letter*, 1 October 1859.
24 NAI, CSORP/1860/14362 and GPO/LB/14/1728 & 1804.
25 *Dublin Evening Mail*, 1 May 1854 and 10 February 1868; *The Cork Examiner*, 12 December 1860; NAI, Cork County Gaol Index of Prisoners 1861-73, 1/8/20.
26 NAI, CSORP/1858/17111. See also: *The Cork Examiner*, 27 August 1858.
27 *The Belfast News-Letter*, 14 September 1858.

ence was insufficient for the Spike Island job and he was transferred to the governorship of the female convict establishment in Cork city.[28] However, his reputation was already in tatters and he was removed from that post after only a few months.[29]

Figure 9.1 View of Spike Island from Bellvue Terrace in Cobh, where former Deputy Governor Downes lived in 1855. (Image © courtesy of S.H. Bean)

The new governor of Spike Island was Francis Hogreve, the former deputy governor at Philipstown. Hogreve was a much more

28 NAI, CSORP/1855/785-787.
29 NAI, GPO/LB/15/11.

experienced officer. Indeed, his experience was sorely missed in Philipstown where the ageing Governor Richard Grace now struggled to run that establishment. Soon the Philipstown depot was in a state of considerable disorder. Crofton sought Grace's removal from Philipstown and in September 1855 the elderly governor vacated that post, having suffered a violent assault at the hands of a group of convicts prior to his departure.[30] Hogreve was transferred back to Philipstown, where he became its new governor.

On Spike Island, Hogreve was replaced by a Scot, Peter Hay. Governor Hay had served as a police superintendent in Gloucester, but had no previous experience of the prison system.[31] For that, he had to rely on his chief warder, Cornelius Sporle, who was a man of considerable experience, having worked as chief warder in the convict prison at Portsmouth.[32] In that capacity he had served under Charles Raleigh Knight. Sporle's relationship with Knight seemed particularly irritating to the former deputy governor, Downes. Knight had presided over the inquiry into Downes's behaviour and Downes later claimed that Knight 'having a protégé of his own ready appointed to supersede me conducted himself ... with ... partiality towards my slandering accusers'.[33] Hand in hand with these accusations of partiality and nepotism was Downes's insistence that his office was not abolished but merely given a different title in order to facilitate Sporle's appointment.[34] However, even if Knight had deliberately removed Downes in order to install an old friend from England, he did so while paying that old friend less than half of Downes's salary.[35]

The new chief warder spent some time in Philipstown, assist-

---

30 HMSO, *Directors' Report 1855*. See also: NAI, GPO/LB/4/149 & GPO/LB/14/1810.
31 *Freeman's Journal*, 10 September 1855.
32 NAI, CSORP/1855/3685. See also: *The Belfast News-Letter*, 2 October 1856.
33 NAI, CSORP/1860/14362.
34 Ibid.
35 NAI, CSORP/1855/3527.

Too Beautiful For Thieves And Pickpockets

ing in restoring order there in the wake of Grace's hastened departure. In April 1855 he made his way south to take up his new post on Spike Island.[36] Sporle was described by the Directors as 'a most excellent and deserving officer'.[37] One of Spike Island's prisoners had an alternative view:

> Mr Sporles [sic] showed spite to me for making a report to
> him about the a faires of the prison but in doying so Mr Spor-
> les called me a ... scoundrel which he had no cal to me at all
> for I never was punished for 5 and 4 months. It was very hard
> your lordship to be treated so for worst characters in the pris-
> on got more justice than I have. I was called to go to Bermuda
> 2 and kept back each time. Dr Corr put me to work in a quarry
> ... I had no right to do for I am lame twelve years by a fall.[38]

Sporle may have had a vindictive streak, or the un-named prisoner may have been making a vexatious complaint. The arrival of Sporle was really symptomatic of an efficiency drive within the prison service generally, and on Spike Island in particular. The Directors of Convict Prisons in Ireland were aware of the poor behaviour of some prison staff in the decade prior to their arrival. They were determined not to tolerate such behaviour in the future and to establish a more professional convict service. In 1854, in their first report on the condition of the convict depots (which from this time onwards were known as Convict or Government Prisons), the Directors commented:

> We have found it necessary to call for special reports on the
> character and capabilities of the different officers of the pris-

---

36 NAI, CSORP/1855/3685.
37 HMSO, *Directors' Report 1855*.
38 NAI, CSORP/1858/13712.

ons, with a view to remove those who are not qualified for so important a position; and regret to add that we have been compelled to recommend the dismissal of several warders for drunkenness, a crime that cannot be tolerated for an instant in a prison where a good moral example should operate as one of the principal elements of reformation.[39]

They went on to describe particular deficiencies among the Spike Island staff:

> One of the principal defects has been the inefficiency and unfitness of many of the officers for the performance of the duties required, which in a "Public Works Prison" are of a very arduous and responsible nature, and demand (in order to be satisfactorily carried out) men possessing a high moral standard combined with an amount of energy and physical strength found only in persons in the prime of life.
>
> Heretofore, officers who had been guilty of drunkenness or who had otherwise misconducted themselves at other prisons, were frequently punished by being sent to do duty at Spike Island, a practice calculated to degrade the character of the officers generally, to lower them in the estimation of the convicts, and to lessen their authority and control. Many of the warders were men much advanced in years, and infirm, therefore totally incapable of efficiently performing any duties requiring either much exertion of body or energy of mind.[40]

Spike Island's ageing and unprofessional staff was to be culled and replaced with younger and more efficient men. This had to be a

---

39 HMSO, *Directors' Report 1854.*
40 Ibid.

gradual process, as the Directors couldn't dismiss large numbers of staff immediately. One of the problems they faced was that the salaries of Irish prison staff were lower than those of their English counterparts. Consequently, the Irish prison service tended to attract 'persons who can get nothing else'.[41] Disciplinary actions for infractions were also less effective. Whereas English warders were often dismissed for breaches of discipline, Irish warders were more frequently given second and third chances if their character was otherwise unblemished. The authorities knew that if they dismissed a capable and competent officer for one act of indiscipline (drunkenness being particularly frowned upon), he might well be replaced by a far less capable man who had been unable to secure any alternative employment. The Directors insisted that any effective reorganisation of staff, where unsuitable warders were to be replaced by capable and sober men, had to be accompanied by a rise in wages that 'put the salaries in Ireland more in accordance with the English scale'.[42] Thus, while the older and less competent staff members were gradually replaced, the staffing costs of the Spike Island prison establishment rose. For the 12-month period beginning 1 April 1854, the wages of the Spike Island staff cost the exchequer £6,717. Three years later, that figure had risen to £7,579.[43]

Staff members who were considered too old or otherwise unsuited to continue in service were simply informed of this and asked to retire on pension. One of Spike Island's most senior staff members was asked to depart after the governor had bluntly written to the Directors in Dublin:

---

41 HMSO, *Copies of Correspondence Relative to the Management and Discipline of Convict Prisons, and the Extension of Prison Accommodation with Reports of Commissioners (Ordered by the House of Commons to be printed, 3 July 1854)*, p.21.
42 Ibid.
43 HMSO, *Directors' Reports 1854, 1857*.

Gentlemen,

I respectfully beg to bring under your notice that, in my opinion Principal Warder Leonard is getting too old to be an efficient prison officer. He is willing but not sufficiently active for the duties of Principal Warder in Spike Island.[44]

The Directors acted on the governor's advice and Principal Warder Leonard was dismissed from his post in early April 1858. Curiously, Michael Leonard himself had written to the Directors on precisely the same day as the above correspondence. He too had referred to his declining state of health and his wish to retire from the service, if appropriately superannuated.[45] It seems that Governor Hay, Local Inspector Atkins and Warder Leonard had all agreed that the latter should retire due to his failing health. Leonard later claimed that Atkins and Hay had intimated that he would be well-remunerated through his pension, given his three decades of service in the police and various other prisons. However, Leonard later objected when the pension arrangements did not meet with the expectations that Atkins and Hay had helped him form. He then sought to withdraw his offer of retirement, but was forced to depart by Atkins. He sought additional superannuation, but was only partially successful. Eventually his appeals on his own behalf and on that of his dependent family were dismissed by the Lord Lieutenant's office, which insisted that 'His Excellency has no means of complying with this application'.[46]

---

44 NAI, CSORP/1858/12391.
45 Ibid.
46 Ibid.

10. The Murder of Warder William Reddy

While the Directors of Convict Prisons in Ireland enforced their new regime, the prisoners continued their arduous toil, permanently altering the landscape of Cork harbour. Work on the fortifications at Forts Camden and Carlisle and at Spike Island continued. By 1855 the convicts were beginning the process of laying thousands of tonnes of soil outside Fort Westmoreland to complete the artificial sloping embankment, or glacis (Fig. 10.1). Like much of Fort Westmoreland, the glacis had been left incomplete after the Napoleonic threat abated. Now, however, with sufficient unfree labour on hand, the job would be completed. Eventually the formation of glacis on all sides would remove all humps, hollows and variations in gradient, so that the island's surface would slope upwards towards the fort at a uniform ascent from the lower ground around the shore, thereby denying any attacking army the cover afforded by undulating terrain or by the outer walls of the fort.[1]

This work involved groups of convicts moving earth around the island in hand trucks. It was an operation to which the new Local Inspector objected as 'the prisoners being broken up into small parties, renders it difficult to ensure a proper amount of supervision over working parties; the amount of labour lost must also be very considerable'.[2] Each side of the faceted glacis was lined with a retaining wall of stone, cut from the island's quarry. As well as working on the glacis, within the fort the convicts had repaired and refitted several of the older buildings. They had installed and relined the Iron Prison (Block D) and erected the Timber Prison (Block C). They had removed much

---

1 *The Cork Examiner*, 17 October 1855. See also: PRO, MPH 1/191.
2 HMSO, *Directors' Report, 1859.*

of the remaining rock from the north side of the Parade Ground and at the easternmost end of this space had built Block G from stones cut and quarried on the island.[3]

Figure 10.1 Spike Island from the north, note the artificial slope of the glacis. (Image © courtesy of National Monuments Service)

These projects were supplemented by the addition of a few more major employment schemes for convict labour. The first was the extension of the sewage system on Spike Island. The island's large prison population had caused a potentially dangerous problem whereby vast quantities of human waste were being deposited just off its coast by two substandard sewers. The problem was exacerbated at low tide, when foul-smelling waste was left exposed by the retreating water. The solution was the extension of the sewers, and the labour required was readily available on the island. The sewers were extended to low-water mark and tanks placed at the exit point of each. In that

---

3 HMSO, *Directors' Report 1852.*

way, the waste was retained as manure, while the waste water was discharged into the harbour.[4] Such projects were not without dangers, however. For example, Convict M. Mulqueeny had been on Spike Island only seven months when an embankment caved in on him while he was working on the sewage system in 1859. The unfortunate 22-year-old suffered a compound fracture of the left thigh bone (i.e. a fracture with an open wound). Infection set in and he died in hospital three days later.[5]

Throughout the latter half of 1853, the prison's senior staff sought sanction to employ convict labour in dredging the sand bar that lay between Spike Island and Queenstown, in order to create a navigable channel for boats. Such a channel had previously existed, but it had silted up and as a result direct passage from Queenstown to Spike Island was no longer possible. Instead, boatmen had to row around Haulbowline Island and approach Spike Island from the west. Whether coming from Queenstown or Spike Island, this journey involved travelling west, then east and therefore rowing against the tide for a considerable part of the journey. Although it was first considered inadvisable to employ convicts aboard the dredges, Local Inspector Atkins had revised that opinion by November 1853.[6] The scheme was eventually approved by the Harbour Board in December, with work scheduled to begin the following year.[7]

In 1855, Spike Island's convicts also began labouring on nearby Haulbowline Island. They were initially engaged in the construc-

---

4 NAI, CSORP/1853/4192.
5 NAI, CSORP/1859/6687 (document no longer extant, but described on the correspondence register/index). See also: HMSO, *Directors' Report 1859.*
6 *The Cork Examiner*, 25 November 1853 and NAI, CSORP/1853/6411, GPO/LB/3/168 & 309.
7 *The Cork Examiner*, 2 December 1853.

tion of a sea wall and the clearing of a channel.[8] Soon, small parties of convicts made regular trips to the naval base on Haulbowline. There, they worked at loading and unloading ships and repairing naval buildings. Weather could inhibit their passage to the nearby island and thus their work there was sporadic. Nevertheless, Haulbowline Island would soon become a major source of employment for convicts as huge construction projects were already being considered there. In 1856, Spike Island's convicts began making regular trips to Queenstown in order to labour on the military hospital located there.

Convicts were becoming more visible and playing a more prominent role in Cork harbour and its surroundings. Reports indicated that most of the men were well-disciplined and few attempted to escape from these less secure locations, which suggests that there was some screening process involved in determining who could work outside the fort. Perpetrators of violent assaults are unlikely to have been considered for these work gangs and a number of such assaults are recorded in the archives. In June 1856, John Malony struck Michael Kelly with an iron bar which he drew from his sleeve while the two prisoners attended mass in Spike Island's chapel. In court it was suggested that Malony was seeking retribution for Kelly's complaining his misbehaviour to a warder some days earlier. Another report suggested that Kelly had actually prevented Malony from throwing a warder over a cliff on the east of the island. Either way, Malony's vicious assault resulted in his conviction for attempted murder.[9] He was sentenced to death, but the sentence was later commuted to life imprisonment and he was moved to Mountjoy

---

8 HMSO, *Directors' Report 1855.*
9 *The Cork Examiner*, 20 March 1857. See also: Rev. C.B. Gibson, *Life Among Convicts Vol. I*. London: Hurst and Blackett, p.198.

Gaol in Dublin to serve out his sentence.[10] Though close to death after the assault, Kelly recovered from the blow although he remained deaf for a considerable period after the event. Not all victims of prison violence on Spike Island were as lucky as Kelly.

On 22 November 1848, 14-year-old Edmond Power, originally from Ballykerogue in County Waterford, was convicted of vagrancy, which had been a criminal offence since the 16th century. His sentence was quite typical of the time, but was ludicrous by its nature. Power was sentenced to two months' imprisonment unless he could raise a bail of two £5 sureties. That is to say, the justice system wanted a homeless, and quite probably orphaned, child to raise a total of £10 during the height of the Great Famine, or face two months' imprisonment. Of course, Power could not raise any such sureties and so served two months in prison. Gaol probably provided Power with regular meals, something that he probably found difficult to procure on his release. It is of little surprise, then, that a second conviction came a little over one year later when he was found guilty of the theft of milk on 30 March 1849. Again, he was sentenced to two months' imprisonment, but this time he was to be whipped at the end of the first month, and again the day before his release. While whipping had been largely discontinued on convict ships and in Government Prisons like Spike Island, it was still considered an appropriate sentence for a 15-year-old boy in a county gaol.

On release from his second period of imprisonment, Power continued to live as a vagrant and was sentenced to one month's hard labour in January 1851. Shortly after his release, he was admitted to the Dungarvan workhouse. Inmates of the workhouse could not come and go as they pleased, so when Power absconded from there he was

---

10 NAI, *Cork County Gaol General Register 1853-1860*, 1/8/6.

sentenced to one month's hard labour in August 1851. Power's behaviour was now in decline. Where others sought the refuge of the
workhouse, he was happier alone in the world, making his way by
nefarious means. His fifth conviction came in October 1851 when
he was sentenced to 10 years' transportation for the theft of a cow.[11]
In October 1852, 18-year-old Edmond Power disembarked on Spike
Island's pier. Little did he know that four years later, he would leave
the island as a murderer.

Like Edmond Power, Patrick Norris was also from County
Waterford. He was convicted of arson on 16 July 1851. Although
this was 16-year-old Norris's first offence, it was precisely the kind
of 'Whiteboy' activity that incensed the ruling class in Ireland while
also provoking hostile reactions from the English press. The Crown
had little option but to convict and a severe sentence of 10 years'
transportation was imposed. While Norris awaited his transfer from
Waterford Gaol it is possible that he crossed paths with Edmond Power,
who was serving a sentence in the same gaol at that time. The two boys
were of similar age, and may have struck up a friendship.[12] Norris was
sent to Philipstown, before being transported to Bermuda aboard the
William in January 1855.[13] Before his departure for Bermuda, he was
probably sent to Spike Island among the small group dispatched from
Philipstown in 1854. As Edmond Power was already on Spike Island,

---

11 NAI, Waterford Prison General Register 1851-1853 1/39/3 & 4.
12 Ibid.
13 NAI, Dublin Prison Classification General Register 1854-1865, 1/9/65. See also: NAI,
TR11, p.157; *The Cork Examiner*, 15 January 1855. The convict ship *William* was in Cork
harbour in January 1855. According to the Directors of Convict Prisons Report for that
year, she was the only vessel that shipped convicts to Bermuda in 1855. The Transportation
Register cited above records that Norris was sent to Bermuda aboard this vessel. Yet documents relating to the Reddy murder trial record that 'Bermuda man' Norris was 'at Spike
Island since December 55'. Thus the most logical assumption is that Norris shipped out
aboard the *William*, spent only a few months in Bermuda, and returned in December 1855.

the two may have renewed an old acquaintanceship. Although they were held in Waterford Gaol at the same time, it is unknown precisely when these two young men first met. However, it is certain that they met after Norris returned from Bermuda in December 1855. Norris was described as revelling in breaches of prison discipline, which resulted from:

> ...a superabundance of animal spirits. He had all the *qui-vive* vivacity of a rough haired terrior, was as mischievous as a monkey, and as full of tricks as a kitten ... A favourite amusement of his was to steal out of bed at night, and tie a string to the great toe of a fellow prisoner, which he pulled until the other roared with agony.[14]

On Spike Island in 1856, Power and Norris made the acquaintance of John McCullagh, another youthful offender who had received a seven-year transportation sentence for the theft of a handkerchief. That offence resulted in the 17-year-old Dubliner's eighth conviction.[15] Another Dubliner, John Doyle, was also on Spike Island at the time, having served two years of a 15-year sentence for burglary.[16]

Power, Norris, McCullagh and Doyle had all served their period of separate confinement in Mountjoy, with its purpose-built single cells. One of the prison officers they came to know in that institution was William Reddy. Warder Reddy had since been transferred to Spike Island, where he once again found himself in the company of these four convicts. Several other convicts under sentence on the island in 1856 later claimed to have known Warder Reddy in the Dublin prison,

---

14 Gibson, *Vol. I*, p.198.
15 NAI, Mountjoy Prison Convict Classification 1857-1861, 1/11/22.
16 Ibid.

and alleged that he had mistreated them. Thus, when Reddy and Edmond Power had an altercation in September 1856, Power found quite a few sympathetic ears for his complaints against the warder. While we cannot say if Power and Reddy had clashed previously, we know that their first recorded altercation seemed to be of a minor and trivial nature. Even so, this squabble ultimately led to the death of Warder Reddy. Convict Mick Finn later recalled the argument:

> About a week prior to the attack on Warder Reddy I had heard him and Power have some words. Power's bed was empty and I heard Warder Reddy ask whose bed it was. Norris replied that "it was his bed" (altho' it was not). Reddy asked him to sit over on his own bed; he asked him to do so twice – when Norris replied "that he was near enough to it" Reddy then took the number of the bed and walked away, but in some time returned with Mr Nowlan one of the officers of the prison. Power then asked him why he took the number of his bed and Mr Nowlan told him to behave himself and he replied "you may go to the Devil." As he left convict Edmond Power got up and went to the lower part of the ward and brought up a trestle and placed it under his bed and seeing by his countenance that he was not inclined for good I went to advise him, when he told me that I had enough to do to mind my own affairs – but he afterwards prompted Smyth and Roche to remove the trestle. Upon the night Warder Reddy was killed, convicts Naughton and McCullough [sic] were violent and seemed anxious to quarrel with Warder Reddy. I often advised Convict Power to shun this company and that of convict Patrick Norris.[17]

---

17 NAI, CSORP/1856/19618.

Curiously, another account of this event described how Power and Norris had been 'larking and tossing each other on a bed' before Reddy took the number of the bed.[18] It seems that Finn witnessed the aftermath of their 'larking'. Finn was some eight years older than Power and was serving four years' penal servitude for theft, but had one previous conviction for assault.[19] He was hardly of unblemished character, yet his assertion that Power was led astray by others is worth considering. Finn had no discernible reason to stand up for Power, and not for his co-accused. His motivation was most likely sympathy for Power or antipathy towards the other prisoners charged with Reddy's death.

Convict Terence Doran witnessed the same argument and its ominous aftermath. He, too, seemed to hint at Power's subservience to Norris:

> About six or eight days before Warder William Reddy was murdered at Spike Island prison, I saw convicts Edmond Power, Patrick Norris, John McCullough [sic] and a convict named Burke sitting on two beds in No 6 Ward – and I heard Patrick Norris say "I will settle with this long policeman if I get any one to come along with me." Edmond Power replied "I will go by Heaven along with you." I told them to mind what they were saying. On this very evening Mr Reddy had taken the No. of Edmond Power's bed. When the No. of a convicts bed is taken by a warder it is usually for the purpose of having him punished for some breach of discipline, altho' they sometimes get off.[20]

---

18 Gibson, *Vol. I*, p.193.
19 NAI, Mountjoy Prison Convict Classification 1857-1861, 1/11/22.
20 NAI, CSORP/1856/19618.

Doran went on to claim that he had reported the threat on Reddy's life to Warder Mackey some days after the above incident. It seems as if Reddy was warned of the threat, but as a 'brave but blindly determined man ... he defied "the d-d scoundrels, the b-y rogues".'[21] If Doran was telling the truth, it seems that the days following the incident did nothing to quieten the emotions of the men involved. For their insolence to an officer, Norris and Power were each removed to the solitary cells in No.3 Bastion. There, they spent 72 hours on bread and water. Power was degraded from second to third class and lost 42 'good marks'. Norris was denied the award of any good marks for a month. On the convicts' removal to the solitary cells, Power and Reddy were involved in an ugly altercation. Power later alleged that he had been 'cut on the head with a sword, and knocked down by the warders'. The warders claimed that any injuries they had inflicted on Power were sustained as a result of his resistance to their discipline.[22] It seems that this was the latest of an unknown number of times that Power was placed in isolation.[23] The young man may have reached breaking-point.

While Power and Norris sat alone in the solitary cells for three days, they may well have continued to contemplate revenge against Reddy. If they did, they were not the only convicts making such plans. Indeed, it seems that revenge was being contemplated by some of the convicts with whom they shared Ward 6 and that their plot may have extended to warders other than William Reddy. Convict William McDonnell later testified:

---

21 Gibson, *Vol. I*, p.194.
22 *The Cork Examiner*, 18 March 1857.
23 NAI, CSORP/1856/19618. See statement of Michael Finn who, when speaking of Power, referred to when 'he was last put in the cells'.

About three days before Warder Reddy was killed at Spike Island prison, I went into the stone cutters shed there situated to look for some tools and I there saw, John Doyle, John Mc-Cullagh, John Donahue, Patrick Murphy, John Naughton and a man named Thos. Byrne. I heard McCullagh ask the others how they would go about taking the Long Policeman down. I knew they meant the warder that was killed for that was the name he went by. On the night after I heard this conversation, Warder Reddy that was killed was on guard and I told him not to into that prison and I told him what I had heard and I know that he Reddy told a warder named Hill that I had told him so. I heard McCullagh ask the others who would act. Some of the others, I can't say which of them said – "If we could meet the three of them in their different wards we would go and take them down." McCullough [sic] said "that they could not be worse off than they were and that they would draw lots for who would do it. McCullough [sic] said that he was sorry that Mr Dunne was on day duty that he could not get the same as the rest. As I was passing the shed – McCullough [sic] said "There is a stag." The fellow prevented me from sticking an officer in the C Prison.[24]

Unless McDonnell was confessing to his having plotted an attack on an officer in Block C, we must assume that the quotation marks are incorrectly placed (as is common in this transcript) and that it was McCullagh who had planned a previous attack. McDonnell's assertions were contested by Doyle and McCullagh, who cast doubt on his ability to stop and listen to this entire conversation during a working day, as well as on his understanding of an oath.[25]

---

24 NAI, CSORP/1856/19618. 'Stag' was a mid-19th-century term for informer.
25 Ibid.

Whatever the number of convicts involved in the plot and who-ever its masterminds were, it was carried into effect on the evening of 26 September 1856, by which time Edmond Power and Patrick Norris were back in their respective dormitory-style wards. Early that eve-ning, Warder William Reddy was seen disciplining a Kerry convict named John Naughton in Ward 6 of Block A (Fig. 10.2). Naughton shared that ward with John Power. At some time between 6.00 and 7.00pm, Power and Norris were seen in conversation under the arched entrance to Ward 6. Shortly afterwards each man returned to his bed. Norris slept next-door in Ward 5. Soon after this, Warder Reddy en-tered Ward 6. In it he found a number of prisoners lying in their beds before lights out. Convict Patrick Murphy was trying to read, but the light was not sufficient and Murphy suggested that the lamp be trimmed. John Neill had already asked Wardsman (an overseer ap-pointed from among the convicts) Timothy Sullivan to trim the lamp. Sullivan had refused to do so as it was too early. Neill now repeated his request to Reddy, who immediately asked for the wardsman. Sul-livan repeated his objection, but Reddy overruled him and stated that the convicts should have some light. He then had Sullivan hand him the lamp and began adjusting the wick with his pencil. As he did so, Edmond Power walked up behind Reddy and struck him on the head with a blunt object. Reddy moaned and fell to the ground. Power then immediately retired to his bed and hid his weapon beneath it. Some seconds later Norris entered from Ward 5 and struck the prone Reddy with a similar object. He attempted to hide his weapon under Patrick Murphy's bed. Murphy was understandably reluctant to receive the murder weapon and he insisted that Norris remove it, along with him-self.

Figure 10.2 The façade of Block A. Ward 6, where Warder Reddy was killed, is probably the middle of the 11 bays on the ground floor. (Image © courtesy of S.H. Bean)

Warder William Chapman was in Ward 3 when he heard the commotion coming from the centre of the building. He rushed immediately to Ward 6, where he found a group of prisoners crowding the outer archway. He pushed his way through them and saw Warder Reddy lying on the ground unconscious. Rushing to his colleague's side, he noticed that one side of Reddy's head was 'quite soft', indicating a badly fractured skull. Chapman also noted a whistle and its cord twined around the dying man's fingers. He unravelled the whistle and blew into it, raising the alarm. Reddy was still alive and groaned as Chapman cradled his head.[26]

Governor Hay saw the external guards running into Block A. He immediately followed them to the scene. Chapman was still cradling Reddy's head when the governor arrived. All of the prisoners were lying on their beds. Hay ordered that a guard be placed on the prisoners and that they immediately turn in the perpetrators of the

26 *The Cork Examiner*, 18 March 1857.

assault. His calls were met with icy silence. By now, William Reddy had died. The governor ordered that his body be removed and called the two convict wardsmen, Finn and Sullivan, to the chief warder's office for interrogation. He also ordered Chief Warder Sporle to make an immediate search of the ward for the murder weapon.[27]

In the chief warder's office, Sullivan and Finn began to talk. There is no indication as to why they experienced this change of heart. It might have been the result of coercion or persuasion on the governor's part; it might have been their desire to see justice done in the aftermath of a murder; or it may have been that they felt free to talk when away from the stares of 30 or so fellow convicts. Either way, in the absence of their fellow prisoners, Sullivan and Finn quickly pointed the finger at Power and Norris. Both of them reported that they had seen Power strike Reddy; they saw Norris aim a blow at the fallen warder, but could not say whether the blow had landed.

Meanwhile, Ward 6 had become the scene of an intensive search for the murder weapon. A small iron bar was found under John Power's bed. Chief Warder Sporle ordered that Power should be immediately escorted to the solitary cells. Power asked that Sporle accompany him to solitary, to ensure that he was not ill-treated. Nonetheless a witness later claimed that Power 'was taken rough enough'.[28] Indeed, it may have been 'rough enough' to almost provoke a prison riot. Warder Laurence O'Connell later recalled the aftermath of Power's removal:

> On the night of the 26th inst. at about 7 ½ O Clock Pm, I was placed by order of the Chief Warder on guard in Ward No 6

27 NAI, CSORP/1856/19618.
28 *The Cork Examiner*, 18 March 1857. It is worth noting that the smuggling of iron bars into the prison from the works was the subject of an enquiry by prison authorities (NAI, GPO/LB/15/1321).

A Lower immediately after the removal of the convict Power to the cells. After entering I was struck by the disorderly and agitated manner of the prisoners walking about the ward in open defiance of our frequently repeated orders to the contrary throwing out threats of a serious and mutinous import.[29]

Warder Thomas Greenham was one of those charged with escorting Power to the solitary cells. However, on hearing the commotion breaking out in Ward 6, he quickly went to the aid of his colleagues:

I escorted the convict Power about halfway to the cells. I turned back to the ward I came from under the impression that my services would be more required there. On my return the door of the said ward happened to be open and I went in accordingly and observed several of the prisoners walking about in a very disorderly manner. More particularly I remarked the prisoners

> 6026 John McCullagh
> 8024 Thomas Byrne
> 6987 Patrick Murphy
> 8831 Terrence Doran
> 7724 John Bourke
> 8979 John Naughton

On McCullagh being ordered by PW Gunning to go to his bed he said he would not. Herd Convict 8831 Terrence Doran say that the blood was boiling in his veins to have his fellow prisoners treated in such a manner. Saying there ought to be a law to protect them. McCullagh answered this remark of

---

29 NAI, CSORP/1856/19618.

Doran's by saying you may expect a great deal of law at the court held in hell. Also I herd McCullagh say it was his own fault. He would take a fellows number for nothing (alluding as I firmly believe to the murdered man). I herd an unknown voice say we will all suffer for this in the morning, when Burke replied we will not, if we do others will suffer too. I herd several of the prisoners mention Warder Reddy's name to the effect that he was in the habit of ill-treating them in Dublin. Some of the expressions were such as Reddy is the boy, I knew him in Dublin. I do not know particularly which of them said it.[30]

When the warders threatened to place Burke in the cells, he rushed to the door and told them that he wanted to go. The situation reached its boiling point when the prisoners from Ward 7 attempted to join in the disturbances and came to the archway between the wards. However, once the warders succeeded in dispersing those men by ordering them back to their beds, peace was restored in all of Block A. The moments before the men from Ward 7 backed down and returned to their beds were surely tense. Chief Warder Sporle later conceded that 'I did expect every moment they would have resisted us, if they could have got the others to join them'. Sporle also suspected that McCullagh was the ringleader of the group.[31]

The following morning Norris was also sent to the solitary cells. In an exhaustive search for his weapon 'in the sewers and all around the prison', nothing was found.[32] The iron bar beneath Power's bed was discovered to be a nipping bar (an iron tool used in laying tracks). Such a bar was found to be missing from the works on

30 Ibid.
31 Ibid.
32 Ibid. Atkins to Whitty, 06/10/1856.

No.1 Bastion, the morning after the attack. The Presbyterian chaplain, the Rev. Charles Bernard Gibson, claimed to have met Power that morning. He stated that, 'Nothing could equal Power's surprise and consternation when he heard that the warder was dead. It was too natural to be feigned. So much so, that I seriously doubted whether it was his *intention* to kill the warder.'[33] There seems to be an element of truth in the Reverend Gibson's story because that afternoon Governor Hay went to Edmond Power's solitary cell. He asked the prisoner if he had anything to say about the events of the previous evening. Hay later claimed that a remorseful Power then confessed to Reddy's murder. However, the prison's Medical Superintendent, Dr Jeremiah H. Kelly, could not recall whether or not he had urged Power to confess on the grounds that others had already informed on him. Thus, Power's confession was deemed inadmissible during the subsequent trial. Dr Kelly also swore to having seen minor injuries on Power's person on the night of the murder.[34]

Power and Norris were transferred to the County Gaol on Western Road (now part of the UCC campus) in Cork on 1 October 1856. As investigations continued on Spike Island, the authorities there became convinced that the two men in Cork were part of a wider conspiracy. They suspected that several prisoners had planned to assault, or kill, three different warders, and that the leader of the conspiracy was John McCullagh. Indeed, the investigating magistrate commented that he believed 'convict John McCullagh to have been the man who incited the others to the preparation of this barbarous act'.[35] The 'others' referred to were Norris, Power, Doyle, Naughton

---

33 Gibson, *Vol. I*, pp.194-5.
34 NAI, CSORP/1856/19618. Hay to Directors, 28/09/1856; and *The Cork Examiner*, 18 March 1857.
35 NAI, CSORP/1856/19618; Magistrate's Report, Castlemartyr, 13/11/1856.

and Byrne. It was recommended that the Attorney General prosecute all six men on charges varying from murder, to accessory to murder, to conspiracy to murder.

The murder had caused quite an amount of public comment, and one old enemy of Spike Island's authorities couldn't help but weigh in. Still smarting from his dismissal in 1854, George Downes dispatched a letter to the administration in Dublin alleging that the authorities on Spike were a part of the conspiracy to murder Reddy. According to the former deputy governor, a warder had informed him that Sporle and two other senior warders had been aware of the plot to kill Reddy. The warders and the Directors strenuously denied the allegations, reminding the Chief Secretary of Downes's bitterness at his dismissal and alleging that his unnamed informer was a warder who had been dismissed from Spike Island for drunkenness.[36] The authorities had had their fill of Downes and there is no indication that they entertained his allegations any further. In the end, only Norris, Power, Doyle and McCullagh faced trial and that began on St Patrick's Day, 1857.

Doyle and McCullagh asked the court to face trial separately. The court agreed that they should do so, and their case was held over. Nobody had ever reported having seen Doyle or McCullagh strike Reddy, making the case against them harder to prove. They were removed to Mountjoy while they awaited their trial.[37] Eventually, almost one year later, the prosecution entered a *nolle prosequi* against Doyle and McCullagh.[38] This meant that the Crown was unwilling to prosecute at that time, probably because it was felt that a conviction could not be secured. However, should the Crown become more con-

---

36 NAI, GPO/LB/5/83.
37 NAI, GPO/LB/5/310.
38 *The Cork Examiner*, 17 March 1858.

fident of a prosecution in the future, it could then seek to try the case. Luckily for Doyle and McCullagh, no further evidence came to light and it was never proven that they had had anything to do with the murder of William Reddy. Nonetheless, the prison authorities delayed their stay in custody for as long as they could, carefully noting every incident of misbehaviour and using it to slow their transit through the penal system. McCullagh served his full seven-year sentence, being released just one day shy of the seventh anniversary of his conviction on 30 August 1859. In October 1864, Doyle was officially denied parole on account of his not being 'sufficiently cleared from the charge of implication in the case of <u>fatal assault</u> on the late Warder Reddy'. He was eventually released in October 1865.[39]

Power and Norris were both convicted of murder. The prosecution outlined the facts of the case as detailed above using several convict witnesses, including Sullivan, Finn, Doran, Murphy and the irrepressible John Burke. Doran stated that Burke was present when McCullagh, Power and Norris discussed an assault on Reddy. Burke's cross-examination was a humorous demonstration of the defence's argument that the witnesses were seeking to extricate themselves from their responsibility in a conspiracy to murder and were therefore unreliable:

> John Burke ... swore that Norris gave the deceased a blow on the right cheek, and two other blows on the body.
>
> Mr Exham – Honest Mr Burke, how long were you in custody for this yourself? – No man could bring a charge against me for it. Were you not put into a cell? – I was but not for that. What were you put in for? – For some angry words

39 NAI, GPO/LB/6/1135. See also: NAI, Mountjoy Prison Convict Classification 1857-1861 1/11/22; and Cork County Gaol General Register 1853-1860, 1/8/6.

I spoke to some of the officers, when I heard the unfortunate prisoner, and beside I did not know at that time that the man was killed. What prisoner was that? – The prisoner Power. Did you give your information to Mr Knaresborough? – I did as far as God and my conscience allowed me (laughter). What made you go to Spike? – The doctor sent me there for the good of my health (laughter). What were you sent to prison for? – For what a good many others beside me are – theft. There are thousands of men do it as well as me. What were you convicted for? – For burglary. You did not try to get into a gentleman's house? – I did (laughter). What did you do that for? – Robbery of course (laughter). What did you take out of it? – I won't tell you. Oh, you may. You have already been convicted, Jack, and they can't convict you again for it. What was it you took? – Clothes. How long were you sentenced? – Six years.[40]

While Burke's testimony provided considerable hilarity for those present in the court, there is an implication that he may have been involved in a wider conspiracy to murder. The case against him remained unproven. The same could not be said of the charges against Power and Norris. The jury considered the evidence for only 15 minutes and gave little credence to the defence's attempts to undermine the credibility of the witnesses. After a guilty verdict was returned there was only one sentence that the judge could impose:

> The prisoners who had ben [sic] put back while the jury were consulting, were then put forward again, and in reply to the Clerk of the Crown, as to whether they had anything to say

---

40 *The Cork Examiner*, 18 March 1857.

why sentence of death should not be passed on them, said they had nothing to say.

His Lordship - Edward Power and Patrick Norris you have been together indicted for the murder of the late William Reddy. A jury of your countrymen have found you guilty of this crime and I doubt if, upon the evidence, they could have arrived at any other conclusion than that to which they have come ... You were convicts both of you in the prison of Spike Island. The deceased man, William Reddy, was an officer or warder in that establishment. In the course of his duty he found it necessary to make a report of misconduct on your part, and both of you, by order of the governor, were subjected to punishment. That punishment you attributed, no doubt, to the report of Reddy. You took offence against him, you meditated revenge against him, and you openly threatened that you would take revenge on him. About a week after this transaction you had an opportunity, and you seized that opportunity ... How can I characterise this diabolical act. It was not done in the heat of blood or sudden passion, but upon deliberate premeditation on your parts. The malignant feeling was working in your minds, and you sought this opportunity to wreak your vengeance upon Reddy. There is but one sentence that I am able to pronounce by law upon you. It is not in my power to mitigate that sentence. It may be in the power of His Excellency the Lord Lieutenant to do so, but I must warn you against cherishing any false hopes on that subject, for I feel persuaded that under the peculiar circumstances of your case, any hopes on that subject must be disappointed, if you entertain them. I think there is no pardon for you at this side of the grave...I trust that the short period that may remain before you shall be compelled to bid farewell forever to this present world, will be occupied happily for yourselves your souls and your mortal interests. Your thoughts, your hopes, your expectations, wean them all from this world, for it is closing upon you, and the darkness of the grave is about to come on you. Look only to that place where you can have pardon and peace of mind. It remains only now that I should pronounce upon you the awful sentence of the law, and it is this (his lordship put on the black cap), that you, Edward Power and Patrick Norris, be taken from the place where you now stand to the place from which you came, the gaol, and that from thence you be taken, on a day to be named, to the place of execution, the gallows, and that you there be hung by the neck until you are dead, and that your bodies be buried within the precincts of the prison in which you are confined, and may the Lord God Almighty have mercy upon your souls.

The Prisoner Norris – A long day, my Lord.

Both prisoners were then removed, Power seemingly somewhat affected, but Norris, notwithstanding the request he had made, appearing to be little moved by the sense of the awful position in which he stood.[41]

Fortunately for Power and Norris, the Judge's assessment of their future was not entirely accurate. There was one more twist in the story. Throughout the days that followed the trial, the newspapers and their correspondents began to ask whether the men might be shown the mercy that the jury had recommended. It was argued that they had not intended to kill Reddy when they assaulted him, and thus they did not deserve the gravest sentence of the law. One account errone-ously stated that Power was a well-behaved convict who had been on the verge of release and emigration to America with his mother and

---

41 Ibid.

brother.[42] Reverend Gibson was one of those who lobbied on behalf of the men. The campaign seemed to gain some traction in Dublin Castle, and on 27 April 1857 the Lord Lieutenant eventually commuted their sentence to transportation for life.[43] Power and Norris left Cork County Gaol on 11 May that year. Although their sentence specified transportation, and not penal servitude, the convict stations in Bermuda and Gibraltar were already winding down. Neither Power nor Norris ever left Ireland. Instead they were sent to Mountjoy, where they began another period of separate confinement.[44] Some years later, Reverend Gibson encountered William Reddy's notorious murderers in Mountjoy:

I raised the iron cover of the "spy hole," and looked in at a prisoner, at Mountjoy, who had murdered a night warder at Spike. The murderer was seated on the floor, picking like a bird, at a piece of bread. When I saw the change which a few months of solitary imprisonment had produced, and marked his blank pale face, without a ray of hope, I reproached myself with having done him and his companion in crime an injury, by saving them from the gallows. "There they lie buried," I soliloquized, "inside the walls of the jail. The latter part of the Judges sentence has been carried out at all events."

I have seen Power and his accomplice Norris since writing the above. It is over six years since they committed the murder. During this period they passed from Mountjoy to Philipstown, and when Philipstown prison was closed, back again to Mountjoy, but not to the separate cellular discipline. They still sleep – as do all the prisoners – in separate cells,

42 *The Cork Examiner*, 20, 25 & 30 March 1857. See also: *Dublin Evening Post* in *The Cork Examiner*, 6 April 1857.
43 NAI, Cork County Gaol General Register 1853-1860, 1/8/6.
44 Ibid.

but they work through the day in the associate departments of the prison.

The expression of Power's face is greatly changed. It has lost the heavy and stolid appearance of the ox. He looks less muscular and more intelligent. He has less of the brute and more of the man. He is now what is styled a "wardsman," a high position among prisoners. He knew me at once and showed me his books. He has learned to read and write and seems to take an interest in the improvement of his mind. I did not, on this occasion, regret that I had aided in saving his life.

Norris, his companion in murder, seems to have been very little changed in any way. He is very muscular with a tremendous head. He is possessed of great mental and animal activity, and as hard to tame as a hyena. I met him in a passage of Mountjoy Prison, going before the Director, Captain Whitty, for some breach of prison discipline. His face lighted up and his eyes flashed fire as he recognised me. "There is gratitude in that look at any rate," was my remark.[45]

Patrick Norris was eventually discharged from the Dublin prison on 2 March 1881. Having spent the previous 30 years in prison, he emigrated to Liverpool. Edmond Power was released around the same time, and he too boarded an emigrant ship. Indeed, the release of both men was conditional on their leaving Ireland. William Reddy's widow was granted a pension of £15 per annum for the loss of her husband.[46]

---

45 Gibson, *Vol. I,* pp.94-6.
46 NAI, Dublin Prison Classification General Register 1854-1865, 1/9/65. NAI, GPO/LB/15/1759 and GPB/LB/110/396, 429, 435 & 522.

11. Close Confinement and the Punishment Block

William Reddy's murder highlighted a deficiency in the Spike Island prison, one that had been highlighted several times previously, most recently in the governor's report for 1855. That deficiency was the lack of separate cells and the consequential association of prisoners in large wards, often under the cover of darkness. In 1857, the authorities noted that violence between prisoners on the island was increasing and at least one other warder became fearful for his life. It was in this climate that the process of subdividing Spike Island's large prison wards into single cells began. This was achieved by the use of wire mesh and corrugated iron supported by timber panels. The first wards to be subdivided in this way were those in Block A. The wire-mesh cells were lined against the side walls of each ward. They were 8ft deep and 5ft wide (2.4m x 1.5m). Each cell had a hammock hung lengthways along the cell wall in addition to a small seat and table and a shelf for religious books and eating utensils. The entire division could be removed and the wards restored quite easily.[1]

The transformation of the wards was just one of a series of radical alterations that took place as a result of the reduction in the numbers of inmates. Some of the prison buildings were renamed at this time. The original naming of prison blocks (A to G) was based on the sequence in which buildings in the fort became convict accommodation. The resulting scheme made no sense on the ground, with adjacent buildings having non-sequential labels. The new labelling system (which, confusingly, also used the same letters) sought

---

1 NAI, GPO/LB/16/1783, 1846 & 1914. See also: GPO/LB/15/1674 & 1895, GPO/LB/16/1994 & GPO/LB/18/2118 & 2134 and *Freeman's Journal*, 2 September 1861. It is also worth noting that from 1859 warders were not supposed to be left in sole charge of prisoners whom they had caused to be disciplined (NAI, GPO/LB/18/16).

to remedy this and replace the eccentric scheme with a more logical sequence running anti-clockwise from Block A. In this way, the new labelling of buildings mirrored the anti-clockwise logical sequence of bastion numbering. In this new scheme, Block A became A Prison and its wards, which had been dormitory-style, were now subdivided into single cells. The neighbouring Georgian building, Block B, which had been built as officers' quarters, reverted to this use when it was relieved of its convicts and given over for the exclusive use of the prison staff. In 1859, the prison hospital was moved from Block G at the easternmost side of the fort and back to its earlier location in Block F, which was renamed B Prison. Block G was then given over as accommodation for most of the married warders and their families. Until that time, those warders had to cross between Spike Island and Queenstown every day, regardless of the weather.[2] Despite its use as warder rather than convict accommodation, Block G was redesignated C Prison, as by then the old Blocks C, E and D had closed.[3] So by 1860, Spike Island's convict population was housed in three buildings: Block A (now A Prison), Block F (now B Prison), and the Iron Prison (now known as D Prison). In addition, the construction of the island's most modern and forbidding prison building was already underway: the Punishment Block.[4]

---

2 NAI, GPO/LB/5/1041. The warders paid one shilling per week for this accommodation (HMSO, *Directors' Report 1859*, 30). With most of the warders and their families now living on the island, a substantial community was established. The warders were expected to send their children to the school provided, and a considerable controversy emerged in 1865 when it appears that some of them had failed to do so (NAI, GPO/LB/21/492). By 1870 warders failing to send their children to school were to be ejected from their accommodation on the island (NAI, GPO/LB/23/1274).

3 HMSO, *Directors' Report 1859*, p.32.

4 The Punishment Block was called the Solitary Cells by the military when they eventually regained possession of the fort in 1883. In the annual reports of the civilian prison, the building was usually referred to as the Cells. As noted in Chapter 4, due to an erroneous connection with the detention of John Mitchel, in the 20th century this new block would become known as 'the Mitchel Gaol'.

Immediately after the murder of Warder William Reddy, 'in September 1856 it was considered necessary for the discipline of Spike Island Prison that 30 punishment cells should be erected'.[5] The construction of this new, modern block kept Spike Island's convict labour force heavily occupied in the years that followed. These were not ordinary punishment cells, however. As the convict prison was still a temporary tenant on a military base, the cells had to be built to the specifications of the military. This meant that they were bomb-proof and suitable for the detention of military offenders after the departure of the convicts. This process was time-consuming and laborious and ended up costing three times what an ordinary cell block might have cost.

While construction of the new block continued, Spike Island's inability with regard to 'carrying out any lengthened course of separate confinement' was addressed by having its most recalcitrant characters transferred to Mountjoy's penal class.[6] Eventually, after four-and-a-half years of construction, the new block was opened and was occupied by the end of 1860 (Fig. 11.1). Spike Island then established its own penal class for its most disobedient prisoners, and they were the first inmates of the new Punishment Block. The penal class presented a frightening aspect to all who encountered them, and the Rev. Gibson left the following account of his interactions with one of their number:

> He went on in this way from bad to worse, until he was placed
> in the penal gang, heavily chained from wrist to ancle [sic],
> dressed in black frieze, with a horrible masked cap contain-

---

5 NAI, CSORP/1861/362.
6 NAI, GPO/LB/16/2050 & 2108. Thirty-two such offenders were transferred to Mountjoy in 1857.

ing two holes for the eyes. It often thrilled my nerves to hear the clanking of his chains as he came into church guarded by a warder ... I entreated him one day to change his line of conduct and get out of that horrible penal gang, that looked as like a company of damned spirits as could well be.[7]

Figure 11.1 The façade of the Punishment Block, completed in 1860, before its recent restoration. (Image © authors)

The Punishment Block became the most feared of Spike's residences. Yet behind the black hoods lay some of the island's most colourful characters. One of them was William Johnston.

When he escaped from Cork County Gaol while awaiting trial in January 1859, Johnston had been compared to the notorious English prison-breaker Jack Sheppard.[8] This was Johnston's second prison break, as he had escaped from Kilmainham Gaol the previous October whilst imprisoned there under the alias of Denis Johnston. The freedom he enjoyed after his escape from Cork lasted only a mat-

---

7 Gibson, *Vol. I*, pp.5–6.
8 Sheppard escaped from English prisons four times in the early 18th century. His escapes were audacious and ingenious and made him a folk hero of the time.

ter of days and he was returned to the County Gaol by 18 January 1859. This time Johnston had a warder specifically assigned to guard him and was given the use of two separate cells. He worked in one by day and slept in the other by night, thereby removing any necessity to leave those two rooms or to associate with other prisoners. As a further precaution, he slept naked in his night cell while his clothes remained in the day cell.

On 31 January 1859, it was proposed that Johnston should be deprived of one of the cells. While the prisoner was supposed to be sleeping, a warder went to his day cell in order to prepare it for its new function. He noticed Johnston's clothes were positioned suspiciously, as if he were preparing for departure. On moving to the night cell to check on Johnston, the warder discovered that the prisoner was in the process of digging a hole in the wall with an iron bar he had smuggled into the cell. His work had evidently been underway for some time, as the breach was almost big enough for him to fit through. The thwarted Johnston was then secured in irons until his eventual conviction for theft and his transfer into the convict system and Mountjoy Gaol on 14 March 1859.

By then it had been discovered that William or Denis Johnston had also been known as Denis O'Brien, but that his real name was Denis Hourigan. During his eight months in Mountjoy, Hourigan made two more attempts to escape. By the time he arrived on Spike Island for the hard labour portion of his sentence, warders were warned that 'great caution should be used with respect to him – he is most plausible in his conversation and will endeavour to throw the officers off guard'. After two successful escapes and three failed attempts, Hourigan still wasn't giving up.

On the morning of 18 October 1860, Hourigan, along with

another convict called James Dywer, were absent from their cells in Spike Island's A Prison. It was apparent that they had removed the bars from their cell windows and climbed through using ropes they had fashioned from sheets. Then, carrying their sheet ropes with them, they had scaled the walls of the fort, crossed the ramparts and descended into the moat. It was assumed that the makeshift ropes were again deployed in climbing their way out of the moat. The alarm was raised and notice immediately dispatched to police stations all around the harbour. Soon, one of Spike Island's ladders was found floating in the harbour along with two convict caps. As this discovery was made a considerable distance from Spike Island, it was assumed that the convicts had attempted to paddle the ladder to the mainland, but that they had been capsized and drowned by the rough seas that prevailed on the night in question. However, just as the search was winding down, the convicts were located. They had never left the island. It seems that the rough seas had deterred them, and the caps and ladder were merely an attempt to deceive. They had hoped that they could remain concealed on Spike Island until calmer seas might aid their departure on the following night.

Hourigan was returned to the fort where he was most likely stripped naked, confined in an unfurnished cell in the Punishment Block and placed in the penal class. Throughout 1863 and 1864, he was returned to those cells on several occasions when prohibited articles like pen-knives and pieces of tin were found in his cell. He eventually left Spike Island on 13 March 1866 and was returned to Cork County Gaol to serve two years' hard labour for his previous escape. The authorities showed him some mercy, however, and he was released in December. He returned to his native Limerick, where he was soon imprisoned again for the theft of a coat and boots. His reputation as a prison-breaker was now well-established so he was stripped of his clothing each night before he slept. Somehow, on the evening of 23 February 1869, he managed to keep hold of his trousers. Early the following morning he was absent from his cell. He had again removed the bars from his window and dropped to the yard beneath, before somehow scaling the 30ft (9.1m) wall to freedom. Denis Hourigan alias William Johnston alias Denis Johnston alias Denis O'Brien had made his third and final successful escape from an Irish prison. If he ever entered such an institution again, he did so under yet another alias.[9]

After Hourigan's initial attempt to escape Spike Island, he may well have come in contact with another infamous escape artist from an entirely different part of the world. That escapee landed on Spike Island in March 1862, after the *Flower of the Forest* entered Cork harbour. This ship had arrived from Callao, the port of Lima in Peru, with a cargo of guano. Aside from this rather common cargo of Peruvian bird manure, the *Flower of the Forest* carried a very unusual convict. Going by the name of Daniel Stephens, alias Sutherland, was an escaped prisoner who had almost circumnavigated the globe in his efforts to remain a free man.

Stephens was a military convict, having been convicted of the assault of a petty officer aboard HMS *Impregnable* as she lay in Plym-

---

9 See: HMSO, *Directors' Report 1860*; *The Cork Examiner*, 10 January 1859 & 19 October 1860; *Cork Daily Reporter*, 19 October 1860; *Tipperary Free Press and Clonmel General Advertiser*, 10 January & 11 February 1859; *The Dublin Evening Mail*, 16 February 1859; *Saunders' News-Letter and Daily Advertiser*, 12 January 1859; *Wexford Independent*, 24 October 1860. See also: NAI, Richmond Prison General Register 1859-60, 1/13/13, Mountjoy Prison Convict Classification 1857-66, 1/11/23, Dublin Prison Classification General Register 1854-65, 1/9/65, Limerick Prison General Register, 1869-77, 1/24/10. Given that their prison records indicate at least 1.5in. (3.8cm) difference in heights and that their first known convictions were in Belfast and Limerick respectively, it is highly unlikely that this is the same person as the William Johnston who escaped from Fort Carlisle in 1851.

outh on 5 May 1859. He was initially sentenced to be hanged from the yardarm of his ship, but this grotesque sentence was later commuted to 10 years' penal servitude. He served the initial part of his sentence in Portland prison before departing England for Western Australia aboard the *Palmerston* on 10 November 1860. He then served approximately one month at the Swan River penal colony before his naval experience landed him a job on the pilot boat at King George Sound, a few hundred kilometres southeast of Swan River.

On 6 October 1861, Stephens was involved in piloting the *Malakoff* to sea. While engaged in this process, he cleverly hid himself away aboard the outbound ship, causing those who were with him to believe that he had fallen overboard and to abandon any hope of rescuing him. The hidden convict was discovered mid-voyage by the crew of the *Malakoff* and on their arrival at Callao they promptly delivered him to the British Consulate. Stephens could not deny that he was a stowaway, but he emphatically and repeatedly denied his convict status. So impressive were his denials that the English authorities had to consult their own convict records and request that the Irish prison service do the same. Neither authority could track the elusive Stephens among their records, but they never confessed as much to him. Meanwhile, Stephens was placed aboard the outbound *Flower of the Forest* and her captain was ordered to hand him up to the authorities at their first British-held port of call. For the *Flower of the Forest*, that port happened to be Cork.

On 10 March 1862, Stephens was officially handed over to the governor on Spike Island. He still denied his convict status and Governor Hay had him lodged in separate confinement in the Punishment Block. The familiar surroundings of a convict prison may have had an impact on Stephens's mind. He may have begun to assume that he had been returned to prison and that any further denials of his convict status were pointless. Whatever his reasons, just a few hours after he had arrived on the island, Stephens asked to speak to Governor Hay. When Hay arrived at Stephens's cell, the convict, 'in order to avoid giving any further trouble', admitted that his real name was Langley Southerdon and that he was a military convict. Hay wrote to the Directors in order to confirm that Stephens was indeed an English convict.[10] Stephens left Spike Island on 11 April, when he was handed over to the local constabulary.[11] Twenty-two-year-old Southerdon was returned to England and from there to the Swan River penal colony on board the *Lord Dalhousie*, which left Portland in September 1863 and docked in Fremantle the following December.[12]

Spike Island's new Punishment Block oversaw a disciplinary regime that terrified many of those who encountered it. Convicts needed to be of sound and strong mind to cope with incarceration there. Many of those who entered the cells allowed the isolation to penetrate their minds, resulting in rage, or even madness. The Reverend Gibson left accounts of prisoners in the Punishment Block who exhibited signs of both, but he also told the tale of a calmer prisoner, one who seemed to enjoy the isolation of solitary confinement:

> There he seemed perfectly content. He always met me with a smile, was "quite well" and wanted "nothing."
>
> "Now M___" I said addressing him when he came out, "I know you deliberately committed yourself in order to get into the cells. Why did you do it?"

10 NAI, CSORP/1862/11832.
11 NAI, Mountjoy Prison Convict Classification 1857-1866, 1/11/23.
12 PRO, TS18/507.

He smiled as he replied "I left a book behind me the last time I was there – a book of difficult calculations – and there were some of them I had not mastered, and so I went back to them again."

"Where did you put the book," I inquired, knowing that such a book would not be allowed to a prisoner undergoing cellular punishment; and also knowing that the cell contained no furniture during the day but a small round boss, or footstool, on which the prisoner sits.

"I had it in the heart of the boss."

..."But how did you work out your calculations without pen and ink, or slate and pencil?"

"I did them on the whitewash of the wall with a pin."[13]

Unfortunately, not all of the island's more distressed convicts were able to occupy their troubled minds as this man did. The effects that the Punishment Block could have on such men became graphically apparent on 15 September 1862, when convict Thomas Morris hanged himself by a sheet from the window of Cell 18 (Fig. 11.2). Morris was so determined to take his own life that he had succeeded in putting his feet through the chains of his handcuffs, in order that they could not reach the floor as he was suspended from the bars. Morris had been convicted of burglary and larceny in Loughrea, Co. Galway, on 1 July 1861 and was sentenced to five years' penal servitude. On his arrival at Mountjoy, however, it was soon discovered that Thomas Morris was in fact Thomas Ellis, who had been released from one of the intermediate prisons in February 1860.

---

13 Gibson, *Vol. II*, pp.6–7.

Figure 11.2 The headstone of Thomas Morris. This stone was moved from its original location in the 20th century and now stands against the east wall of the enclosed convicts' burial ground on the west side of Spike Island. (Image © courtesy of F. Cole)

An inquiry into the convict's death found that the prison ward-ers had not been negligent in their duty of care and that Morris had taken his own life as a result of his temporary insanity. It was known that the prisoner was facing rape charges on the expiration of his sec-ond penal sentence and perhaps the contemplation of a third stay on Spike Island was too much for him. Morris had exhibited violent ten-dencies on a few previous occasions and had been in the punishment cells after he threw a stone at one of the warders. Another warder referred to Morris exhibiting a stare that one wouldn't usually asso-ciate with a sane person. But it was Rev. Gibson who left the clearest indication that Morris's mental illness should have been apparent to all. When first taken into custody, Morris stated that he was a member of the Church of Ireland. On 15 October 1861, while still at Mountjoy, he converted to Roman Catholicism. This was a common strategy used by prisoners in an attempt to improve the conditions of their confinement, but in Morris's case the circumstances may suggest that he was searching for some elusive spiritual peace or guidance. This is suggested by the fact that Morris again changed his religious affilia-tions just three months later. This time he was indoctrinated into the Presbyterian faith.[14] By the time he arrived on Spike Island in 1862, the Presbyterian chaplain was aware of the special care this prisoner might require and gave the following testimony to the inquest:

> The deceased came here in May last from Mountjoy Pris-on. The Presbyterian Chaplain of Mountjoy Prison wrote to me stating that he believed his mind was a little affected. On account of this report, I gave him the greatest attention. He stated to me that there were attempts at Mountjoy Prison to

14 NAI, CSORP/1862/18259 & GPO/LB/6/639.

poison him. If he had a mental delusion it was on this subject. He made similar statements to me of attempts of the same kind having been made here; that he had got arsenic in his food; but that it was of no use as an ounce of it would not kill him. I was under the impression that he was feigning but there was something very peculiar in his eyes and from the catastrophe that has now taken place, I am under the impression that he was insane.[15]

Reverend Gibson later wrote that some days before he succeeded in killing himself, Morris had attempted suicide by jumping off the ramparts of the fort while tied to a stone. Indeed, according to Gibson, this was the reason that Morris was placed in the Punishment Block.[16] Morris's suicide seemed to have a profound effect on Gibson, and perhaps on some of the island's other inhabitants too. One of his fellow convicts immortalised the unfortunate 26-year-old in a poignant poem:

Sacred to the Memory of Thomas Morris

He now lies numbered with the dead,
The deed was not his own;
His friends and parents, brothers dear,
Are forced to sigh and moan.

Oh! Satan, thou most cruel fiend,
Of enemies the worst;
You tempted our first mother Eve,
By which frail man was cursed.

15 NAI, CSORP/1862/18259.
16 Gibson, *Vol. I*, pp.70–71.

And now this poor dejected lad
Was with your poison killed;
When suicidal thoughts at night,
Both heart and soul had filled.

You first suggested life was nought,
While he in handcuffs lay;
You raised the arm, the deed you wrought,
He died before 'twas day.

'Twas in the silence of his cell,
When pain his feelings stung,
That Morris, with his handcuffs on,
Himself he slowly hung.

He rose, and wrought his foes' design,
Good people when you read,
True Christians ponder well on this,
Let hearts of stone here bleed.

Richard Hastin No 11,203 [17]

Richard Hastin was a 27-year-old former soldier from Leeds. He was two years into a four-year sentence at the time of Morris's death.[18]

Thomas Morris's suicide may have acted as the oil that greased the cogs of dissension already turning in Reverend Gibson's mind. He had noticed some fundamental flaws in the Irish convict system and did not feel that it served the convicts, or the public, as well as it

---

17 Ibid., p.73.
18 NAI, Mountjoy Prison Convict Classification 1857-1866, 1/11/23 and Bridewell Richmond Prison General Register Male 1856-1865, 1/13/10.

should. With these ideas weighing on his mind, Gibson departed from his clerical duties and decided to take a hand in the management of the convict system. He was not the first of the chaplains to do so. The clerics of Spike Island had been in conflict with the civil authorities for some time.

12. Clerics, Convicts and Teachers

In keeping with the stated aim of caring for both the bodies and the souls of convicts and transportees, chaplains were an integral part of the Victorian prison and transportation systems. The convict depot at Spike Island served the entire island of Ireland and at the time of its inception in October 1847, both Anglican and Roman Catholic clergy were attached to it. There was also a small cohort of Presbyterian convicts and ministering to these men was the subject of considerable debate in the early years of the prison.[1]

Spike Island's first Roman Catholic chaplains were priests from nearby Passage West, Fr John Holland and his curate, Fr Thomas Walsh.[2] The necessity of their travelling to and from the island by boat eventually made their ministry impossible, and by November 1847 the numbers of Catholic prisoners had increased enough that the Bishop of Cork wrote to the authorities seeking the appointment of a permanent chaplain to reside on the island.[3] The bishop's request

---

1 NAI, CSORP/1847/G8973; NAI, CSORP/1851/G2615 and CSORP/1847/G12306. See also: NAI, GPO/LB/2/262 and GPO/LB/3/221.

2 PRO, AO19/44/14 and NAI, CSORP/1847/G12306. We know that Spike Island's Roman Catholic chaplains were initially from 'the neighbouring parish to which the island is attached' (NAI, CSORP/1849/G12306). An undated letter by the schoolteacher Edward Walsh, probably written in October or November 1847, mentions a Fr Walsh travelling to the island every Sunday to say mass (see Ó Ríordáin, J.J. 2005. *A Tragic Troubadour: life and collected works of folklorist, poet & translator Edward Walsh (1805-1850)*, p.167). Fr Thomas Walsh was curate of Passage West in 1848–9 (See: Bolster, E. 1989. *A History of the Diocese of Cork: from the Penal Era to the Famine*. Cork: Tower Books). Thus it would seem that the priests from Passage West were the island's first RC chaplains. Fr John Holland was a native of Kilbrittain and ordained at St Patrick's College, Maynooth, in 1826. He was appointed parish priest of Passage West in June 1847 and died in 1858 (Bolster, 1989).

3 NAI, CSORP/1847/G12306. It should be noted that the prison authorities had initially (in 1847) asked the Bishop of Cloyne to attach a chaplain to the prison and it was he who pointed out that it was part of the diocese of Cork (NAI, CSORP/1847/G9193 & G9455). The appointment of a chaplain to the island may not have received the support of Fr Holland, who later claimed that the island was part of his parish and pressed his claim by landing on the island to say a station mass (NAI, GPO/LB/3/343).

was granted and in 1848 Fr Denis O'Donoghue was appointed Spike Island's first resident chaplain. Similarly, Cove's Rev. Henry Woodroffe MA was described as 'Chaplain to the Church of England Convicts' and provided spiritual guidance to Spike Island's Anglican prisoners, though he continued to journey to and from the island by boat.[4] This difference is explained by the distribution of convicts across the different religious traditions. Of the 600 men admitted to the prison between 31 March 1849 and 7 March 1850, 580 (96.66%) were reported to be Catholic, 19 (3.16%) were listed as Protestant, while one convict's religion was not declared.[5]

These statistics masked the small numbers of Presbyterian convicts. In late 1852, the authorities began to transfer Spike Island's few Presbyterian convicts to Philipstown, shortly after the latter depot opened. It was intended that Philipstown would then provide the public works portion of the sentence of all Presbyterian convicts. Despite this policy, a handful still remained on Spike Island. These Presbyterian convicts voluntarily attended the services of the Anglican minister. It appears that they could refuse to do so and that such a refusal would normally result in a transfer to Philipstown. Nonetheless these men were the subject of an ongoing debate between the Presbyterian community and the government. The Presbyterian community (including the Synod of Ulster) wanted a chaplain appointed to Spike Island, but while the government was happy for a minister to tend to his flock on a voluntary basis, it refused to create a salaried position. The conversion of Philipstown to a juvenile and invalid depot meant that the plan

---

4 HMSO, *Prisons of Ireland Report 1848.* See also: NAI, CSORP/1847/G12465. The only Denis O'Donoghue listed as a priest in the Cork diocese at this time was from Bandon and ordained at the Irish College in Paris in 1839, though he is listed as curate of Courceys parish from 1842 to 1849 (Bolster, 1989).
5 NLI, MS 3016.

to use it for the imprisonment of the Presbyterian convicts was abandoned. Now, these men were imprisoned on Spike Island in sufficient numbers to make the refusal of a chaplain an impossibilty. Spike Island's first Presbyterian chaplain was Rev. James B. Huston, who was transferred from Philipstown along with his flock in 1855. Huston did not last long in the job and following his resignation in January 1856, he was replaced by Charles Bernard Gibson on 21 February 1856.[6]

In the early years of the prison's establishment, Protestant services were held in one of the rooms on the upper floor of Block B, while Catholics held mass in a temporary wooden building that doubled as a schoolroom and stood between the stockades of Blocks A and B.[7] These latter premises were described by Fr O'Donoghue's successor as 'a timber shed' that was 'unfit and indecorous, besides being too small, badly ventilated and adjoining to a dust-pit and water closets'.[8] At the time this description was written, a new permanent church was being completed on the upper floor of the new range at the eastern side of the Parade Ground, but as this was too small for the large numbers of Catholics, it was used instead for Protestant services.

Apart from the times set aside for religious services and instruction, there was no segregation of prisoners based on denominational affiliation in the early years of the prison. Although the Roman Catholic bishop had requested such segregation, Governor Grace explicitly stated that he thought this would be a bad idea.[9] It is interesting that despite the overwhelming preponderance of Catholic inmates, the

---

6 NAI, CSORP/1851/G2615, CSORP/1855/2031, GPO/LB/2/262, GPO/LB/3/18, 221 & 563; HMSO, *Directors' Report 1856*.
7 HMSO, *Prisons of Ireland Report 1847*; HMSO, *Prisons of Ireland Report 1848*; NAI, CSORP/1847/G8814.
8 HMSO, *Prisons of Ireland Report 1852*.
9 HMSO, *Prisons of Ireland Report 1850*. See also: NAI, CSORP/1847/G12306.

annual reports of the prison authorities always printed the report of the Anglican chaplain first, followed by that of his Catholic colleague, which after 1856 was always in turn followed by their Presbyterian associate. This reflects the position of the Established Church as an organ of the state and this privileging of the Church of Ireland continued after the parliamentary vote for its disestablishment in 1869.

The chaplain for each denomination reported each year on the 'moral state' of their charges and in his first report, Rev. Woodroffe made it clear that when he began his role on Spike Island, he feared the worst. He had no experience of being a prison chaplain and was worried that the convicts would 'treat the services of religion with inattention, if not disrespect'.[10] He was pleasantly surprised to be proven wrong and found that not only was his congregation attentive and respectful but that the convicts were willing to acknowledge their guilt and expressed their gratitude to him for his efforts. In his report for the year ending 31 December 1848, Rev. Woodroffe asked for and was granted funding for a small library for the convicts and his mention of the Catholic chaplain in this request suggests a level of co-operation between them. This library was kept in a corner of the schoolroom, though a later chaplain complained that the texts were 'too hard and dry', too 'heavy and spiritless' to be appreciated by the prisoners.[11]

Fr O'Donoghue also reported that he found himself welcomed by the prisoners and that a year later, and 'with very few exceptions', they continued to avail of his ministry on Sundays and church holidays.[12] O'Donoghue mentioned that he had been very assiduous in instructing the juvenile prisoners. When Fr O'Donoghue wrote his only

10 HMSO, *Prisons of Ireland Report 1848*.
11 Fr Timothy O'Sullivan, Assistant RC chaplain, HMSO, *Directors' Report 1856*.
12 HMSO, *Prisons of Ireland Report 1848*.

annual report, in early 1849, work was underway converting what had been the convict hospital in the old two-bay ammunition store in No.6 Bastion into Block D, with accommodation for 100 juveniles (i.e. under 16 years of age). Fr O'Donoghue also reported himself to be pleased with the progress made by the convicts in the school and his stating that he had 'every reason to be pleased with ... the attention of the master to his duties' suggests that he saw himself having a supervisory role there.

By the time the following annual report was submitted in early 1850, the numbers of convicts detained on Spike Island had almost doubled and Fr O'Donoghue had been replaced as Catholic chaplain by Fr Timothy F. Lyons and his assistant, Fr Timothy O'Sullivan.[13] While Rev. Woodroffe submitted a very brief 'steady as she goes'-type report in February 1850, Fr Lyons noted that his daily visits to the hospital occupied much of his time and that of his assistant, an ominous sign of the overall deterioration in prisoner health.[14] The mortality rate among the convicts rose sharply between 1850 (52 deaths) and 1851 (122 deaths). Both the Anglican and Catholic chaplains later reported spending more time visiting the sick, while in his report for the year 1851 Fr Lyons reported that he or his assistant officiated at the burial services of 115 Catholics.[15] The dead from these years were interred in a cemetery on the east side of the island that was later

---

13 Timothy Lyons was born in the Cathedral parish of Cork (north inner-city) and his early clerical education was in Killarney Diocesan College. He attended Killarney to improve his Irish language skills as this was considered essential for priests in the Cork diocese. He studied at the Irish College in Paris before being ordained at Le Mans in 1839. He had served in Passage West prior to his appointment on Spike Island. Timothy O'Sullivan was originally ordained for the Kerry diocese, but had transferred to Cork by 1847 when he was a curate in Bantry (Bolster, 1989).
14 HMSO, *Prisons of Ireland Report 1849*.
15 HMSO, *Prisons of Ireland Report 1851*.

buried under the glacis when this was completed in the early 1860s.[16]

As the prisoner numbers grew, Rev. Woodroffe suggested that a full-time Protestant chaplain be appointed and both he and the governor noted that it was difficult to minister to the island's Protestant prisoners while also looking after parishioners in Queenstown.[17] Woodroffe felt that the strain of doing so and of the boat trips back and forth had damaged his health. As a result, in his report submitted on 1 January 1853, he made it clear that he was about to retire from his chaplaincy role.[18] His place was taken by the Rev. Joseph G. Bouchier, who had filled in for Woodroffe during an illness in 1852 and who was to remain as Anglican chaplain until discharged on medical grounds in 1880.[19] The Rev. Bouchier took up his post as the prisoner mortality rate peaked: 190 deaths in 1852; 286 in 1853; 228 in 1854.[20] Bouchier made no mention of the high death rate in his first report, which he submitted in February 1855. By then, William Stewart had taken over the governorship of the prison and Bouchier had convinced him to segregate the Protestant prisoners from the Catholics. The Protestant church on the upper floor of Block G had been completed and 'neatly carpeted, [and] cushioned'.[21] The Catholic congregation seems to

---

16 Gibson, *Vol. I*, p.144.

17 Ibid., p.31. In the Church of Ireland, Spike Island is part of the parish of Clonmel and the diocese of Cloyne.

18 Woodroffe was transferred first to the parish of Ballynoe then to Aghern, both in Cloyne, before moving to Lisee in Ross in 1869. He was appointed Archdeacon of Ross in 1883 and died on 1 November 1889, aged 77 (Cole, J.H. 1903, *Church and Parish Records of the United Diocese of Cork, Cloyne, and Ross*. Cork: Guy and Co. p.280).

19 HMSO, *GPB Report 1881* – hereafter all such Reports will be referred to as *'GPB Report'* and the relevant year(s) will be quoted. Curiously, there is no biography provided for Rev. Bouchier in Cole (1903), where Rev. J.G. Bourchier (sic) is mentioned only in a table showing the distribution of churchmen in 1863 where he was listed as 'Chaplain for Spike and Haulbowline Island'. Rev. Bouchier's retirement occurred after 'the failure of this gentleman's health mentally'. See: NAI, GPB/LB/110/428.

20 1853 figure given by Fr Lyons, HMSO, *Directors' Report 1855*.

21 HMSO, *Directors' Report 1854*.

have remained in its original chapel at this time and in the report Fr Lyons submitted in early 1855, he mentioned how his duty to visit the sick was a very onerous one due to the 'great amount of sickness and deaths in the year 1854' (conveniently for the government, no report was issued for 1853, the year of the highest mortality, due to the reorganisation of the convict service).[22] In early 1855, Fr Lyons also alluded to 'various defects in the system' that he felt were 'seriously detrimental to the moral and physical welfare of the prisoners'.[23] Lyons praised the work of Captain Knight, whose commission was then examining the issue of overcrowding in the Irish system, and that of Governor Stewart, but he implied that the problems still persisted. While it might appear at first glance that the chaplain was referring to the mortality rate among the convicts, his reference to the physical welfare of the prisoners might also be connected with an ongoing feud between the priest and the Medical Superintendent, Dr Corr.

Maurice Corr MD, FRCSI, who at the time of his appointment had an address at Willow Place, Booterstown, Co. Dublin, had been hired as Medical Superintendent in April 1852 after the death in the previous year of his predecessor, Dr Robert A. Calvert.[24] Dr Corr and Fr Lyons appear to have clashed very soon after the doctor took up his post as just four months later, in August 1852, the Inspector General of Prisons wrote to the chaplain asking him not to interfere with the running of the hospital. This followed a report from the Local Inspector, Captain Atkins, that did not paint Fr Lyons in a very positive light.[25] The problems between the two men continued and on 18

22 HMSO, *Directors' Report 1854*.
23 Ibid.
24 In his *Jail Journal*, Mitchel described Dr Calvert as 'a young man from the county Monaghan' (p.13). During Dr Calvert's long final illness, a Dr Bradford acted as his substitute (HMSO, *Prisons of Ireland Report, 1851*, p.24).
25 NAI, CSORP/1860/14776.

February 1853, Dr Corr complained to Governor Grace that:

> … the RC Chaplain Mr Lyons has interfered with Hospital arrangements in direct contradiction to the letter from the Inspector General dated 18 August 1852 wherein the duties of the Chaplains were specifically laid down and requested that steps might be adopted to prevent the recurrence of such interference.[26]

Both the Medical Superintendent and each of the chaplains appear to have kept daily journals in the governor's office, where Governor Grace initialled each day's report. Grace reminded Fr Lyons that if the chaplain was aware of any impropriety on the doctor's part, he should note this in his own daily report. A few days after Dr Corr's complaint of 18 February 1853, Governor Grace sent a letter to Fr Lyons giving some details of the grievance: 'I have learned that a few nights ago when in the Hospital you found a patient lying in filthy sheets and that you censured the Hospital Sergeant very harshly for it which he reported to Dr Corr.'[27] The doctor's assistant, Mr Sharpe, denied that the patient had been in this condition for very long and stated that the sheets were immediately changed once he had been alerted to the situation.[28] The governor reminded Fr Lyons of a note the chaplain had received from the Inspector General in which the priest had been told that his duty was entirely confined to the spiritual concerns of the prisoners.

Matters deteriorated even further the following year when Fr Lyons made more complaints about Dr Corr. In the first of these,

---

26 Ibid.
27 Ibid.
28 In 1847, a Mary Sharpe had been included on the payroll as a nurse (PRO, AO19/44/14).

Lyons made charges of culpable neglect against the doctor, alleging that Corr had been absent from the island for the weekend of 9–12 September 1853 and that a prisoner called John Irwin had died as a result.[29] Things got worse for the administration when on 28 October 1853, the *Sunday Times* newspaper published an article that was critical of the management of the Spike Island prison in general terms, but reserved particular censure for the Medical Superintendent. Perhaps spurred on by the negative media attention, an inquiry was ordered by the executive in Dublin and this was held on the island between 23 January and 2 February 1854, just a matter of weeks before Fr Lyons wrote the above-mentioned report about 'various defects in the system'. The inquiry was held by the former Inspector General of Prisons Henry Hitchins, and a Captain Hugh Pollock. These men exonerated Dr Corr on the charge of culpable neglect, noting that he had a locum, Dr McArthur, on the island for the weekend in question, but it seems that Fr Lyons was not going to let the matter rest. Captain Pollock reported back to Dublin that during the inquiry, Fr Lyons had intercepted Hitchins at Passage West as the latter was travelling to Spike Island. The chaplain asked to speak to the former Inspector of Prisons off the record and told him that Dr Corr 'was a person of intemperate habits'.[30] This accusation was to result in another inquiry, one that was to damage the reputation of the doctor while also suggesting that Fr Lyons may have been pursuing an agenda based on self-interest.

Pollock and Hitchins agreed that the manner in which Fr Lyons made this new complaint against Dr Corr was inappropriate, but they felt duty-bound to investigate it as they stated that if it were true, it

---

29 Irwin had been convicted in July 1851 of housebreaking and robbery. He was 25 years old at the time of his conviction in Queen's County, where he was sentenced to transportation for 10 years (NAI, TR11, p.133).
30 NAI, CSORP/1860/14776.

would mean that the medic was unsuited to his job. They began a new inquiry on Friday, 3 February 1854 and asked the chaplain to prove his allegation. Fr Lyons said that he would have to bring a witness, Turnkey Reidy, from Mallow. This turned out to be a lie as Captain Pollock later established that Reidy had been in Queenstown since the previous Sunday, lodged there at Fr Lyons's expense. Captain Pollock was also able to produce a note from Lyons to Reidy dated 1 February 1854 in which the priest asked the former prison guard if he 'Could … say anything of the neglect of the Doctor to the prisoners or of his cursing or violent conduct'.[31] When Pollock investigated further, he found what he felt was the reason for the Catholic chaplain's hostility towards Dr Corr: Fr Lyons had a brother who was a medical doctor and the priest wanted to remove Corr so that his sibling could be appointed in his place. Pollock reported to Dublin that Lyons had written to a number of MPs and other people of influence canvassing for his brother's appointment as Medical Superintendent to the prison. Captain Pollock also noted that on 8 October 1853, Fr Lyons had sent the governor a list of queries about Corr's medical duties. Pollock noted that this list bore a strong resemblance to the points made in the *Sunday Times* article later that month and he concluded that Lyons was the instigator of the article. Pollock concluded that no one had ever seen Corr drunk or, with one possible exception, 'the worse for drink'. This one exception was mentioned by Local Inspector Atkins, who reported that there was an occasion when the two men were crossing to Queenstown together when Captain Atkins suspected that Dr Corr was under the influence of liquor. Atkins sought to temper this statement by also noting that the effects were so slight that he would, at the time, have allowed the doctor to bleed him! Pollock concluded his

---

31 Ibid.

report saying that while Corr was 'a person of abstemious habits', he did not consider Fr Lyons 'to be a safe or proper person in any position in such an establishment as Spike Island'.[32] Hitchins appended a note to Pollock's report agreeing that Lyons was not suited to the job and that he should be replaced.

In a response from the Lord Lieutenant's office to the Hitchins and Pollock report, Dr Corr was exonerated of the charges Fr Lyons had brought against him but was reprimanded for the one instance when Local Inspector Atkins thought him to be under the influence of alcohol. This reprimand tarnished his reputation.[33] The Atkins incident was resurrected nearly two years after Fr Lyons's accusations when Governor Hay reported that Dr Corr had been under the influence of alcohol on 6 December 1855. Later that month, Captain Knight, by then one of the three Directors of the convict service, was asked to investigate the claims and took evidence from Corr, Hay, Atkins and others. Dr Corr outlined that he had experienced medical problems since February 1854, the month of the Hitchins and Pollock inquiry. Specifically, he stated that he suffered from sudden attacks of difficulty in breathing and from dry retching. The doctor gave details of medicating himself with 'ether, black drops and two drams of Hoffman's'.[34] He also called a number of expert witnesses to support his case, including a professor of Forensic Medicine from his *alma mater*, the Royal College of Surgeons in Dublin.

An appendix to Knight's report on the accusation gave details of all of the leave that Corr had taken since joining the prison staff on 1 April 1852: a total of 23 days in over three-and-a-half years. No mention was made of the fact that over 750 convicts had died on Dr

---

32 Ibid.
33 Ibid.
34 Ibid.

Corr's watch nor does there appear to have been any sympathy for the enormous burden that the high rates of mortality and morbidity must have placed on him and his one assistant. It is clear from the details of his leave that Corr was overworked and the symptoms he reported are consistent with someone suffering from stress. The medications he was taking may indeed have produced the symptoms reported by Governor Hay and earlier by Captain Atkins, and it is possible that Corr's self-medication may mean that Fr Lyons's earlier actions were driven by genuine concerns. Black Drop was a 19th-century medicine made from vinegar, spices and opium. Hoffman's anodyne was a painkiller made by diluting ether in alcohol. Both ether and opium are addictive and the effects of ether intoxication and of opium overdosage can mimic those of alcohol intoxication.

At the end of January 1856, the Lord Lieutenant's office informed the governor that Dr Corr's explanation of the events had been accepted, but suggested that he be transferred to a smaller prison where he would not be exposed to the elements as he was while working at Spike Island and the harbour forts. A week later, Corr was informed that he was to be transferred to the prison at Philipstown. Corr appealed the transfer to the Lord Lieutenant, saying that he had worked on Spike Island for four years and had spent most of that time separated from his family and moving around the harbour in all weathers in open boats. He also mentioned that while he was paid £250 per annum at Spike Island, his pay at Philipstown would be £150.[35] His appeal came to naught and he moved to Philipstown in March 1856. Perhaps in light of the cut in his salary, a little over a year later the government sanctioned payment of £7.10.2½ to defray Corr's and his family's moving expenses. Dr Corr was the victim of

---

35 Ibid.

a violent assault at the hands of a number of Philipstown convicts the following year.[36]

Despite having been found to have lied in his attempt to have Corr dismissed and his own brother appointed Medical Superintendent in his place, Fr Lyons fared better than the doctor. The recommendation made by Hitchins and Pollock that Lyons be dismissed was ignored by the administration in Dublin. In a letter of apology sent after the inquiry, the priest provided a clue as to why. In this letter to Hitchins and Pollock, dated 7 February 1854, Lyons included a copy of an earlier letter to Hitchins in which he noted that the prison authorities and the Catholic Bishop of Cork, Dr Delany, were anxious that the priest and the doctor should develop a way of working together.[37] William Delany (1804–1886) was Bishop of Cork from 1847 until 1886, and Fr Lyons would not have remained in his post without the continued support of his superior (Fig. 12.1).[38] In these early decades after Catholic Emancipation when the Catholic Church in Ireland was increasingly asserting its new-found authority, Lyons may have survived in his post precisely because the authorities wanted him removed.

It is worth noting that Hitchins had originally regarded Lyons as an experienced man of 'liberal and enlightened views' and that the priest's concerns about Corr's medical department may have been genuine. Lyons seemed to have a protective concern for those under his care and on at least one occasion he was admonished for not bringing suspicions of 'indecent practices' to the attention of the

---

36 NAI, GPO/LB/5158.

37 Ibid. As the Catholic Church was organised after Catholic Emancipation, there was a dispute between the diocese of Cork and Cloyne over the jurisdiction of the harbour islands. This was not resolved until after the convict depot had closed (Bolster, 1989).

38 Bishop Delany appears to have visited the island once a year during the 1850s to confirm prisoners.

governor.[39] On another occasion he questioned the governor's power to punish convicts.[40] It is also worth noting that the Corr affair did not prevent Fr Lyons from expressing concerns about the medical department again in the 1860s.[41]

Figure 12.1 Monument in the grounds of the North Cathedral in Cork city to William Delany (1804–1886), Bishop of Cork 1847–1886. (Image © authors)

39 NAI, GPO/LB/17/475. The 'indecent practices' referred to were alleged to have been committed by two convicts 'together in one of the privies of the prison'. Lyons claimed that he tended not to report such matters 'to keep the knowledge of such disgustful guilt from the Prisoners'. While his description of what appears to be homosexual activity as 'disgustful' reveals an intolerance that was typical of the era, his reluctance to report it may reveal a forgiveness that was not.
40 NAI, GPB/MB/2/20270.
41 NAI, CSORP/GPO/LB/2/180.

Figure 12.2 The headstone of Fr Timothy Lyons in St Joseph's cemetery, Cork. (Image © authors)

Although, for unknown reasons, he resigned his post and subsequently changed his mind in 1862, Fr Lyons was to continue working in the prison until the time of its closure in 1883, when his total salary was £327. At this time, the salary of the longest-serving first class warder was £85. Fr Lyons was awarded a pension of £218 per annum in respect of his 33 years of service on the island. To put this in some perspective, three of the first class warders who had each served for 32 years at the prison were awarded annual pensions of £56 each.[42] Fr Lyons retired to a house in Sunday's Well in Cork city and died there in March 1886 (Fig. 12.2).[43]

Father Lyons had an assistant Catholic chaplain throughout his time in the prison. Six assistants served under Lyons in his 34 years as chaplain.[44] Two of these priests had already served as prison chaplains to Cork City and County Gaols.[45] Due to the large numbers

---

42 PRO, T1/15663. See also: NAI, GPO/LB/6/586 & 683.

43 Bolster, 1989. See also: Cork City and County Archives, St Joseph's Cemetery Register, 2 January 1877–18 August 1892.

44 Timothy O'Sullivan, 1849–1857; Daniel Finn, 1857–1862; Cornelius Twomy (sic), 1862/3–1865; John A. Barry, 1865–1871/2; John Murphy, 1872–1876; John O'Connor, 1876–1883.

45 Fr Cornelius Twomy (ordained at the Irish College in Paris before 1853, died 1865) had served at Cork City Gaol for seven years prior to his appointment at Spike Island in 1862/3 (*Directors' Report 1862*), while Fr John Barry (ordained at St Patrick's College, Maynooth,

in their congregations in the 1850s, the Catholic chaplains held three masses each Sunday and holy day and also appear to have distributed communion at other times. In the first few years of the prison, religious instruction classes were held daily (from 10am to 2pm in winter, from 10am to 3pm in summer) with groups of up to 70 prisoners at a time (this provides an indication of the size of the original chapel, which doubled as a schoolroom), but these classes were gradually reduced and moved to the evenings by 1854 so that they would not disrupt the exploitation of convict labour.[46] A significant part of the religious instruction involved preparing large numbers of men (794 in 1852, 798 in 1854) for Confirmation, which suggests that the conferring of this sacrament was not yet common practice, at least among the poor. As the longest-serving member of the prison's staff, Fr Lyons was in a position to notice secular changes in the character of the institution and its inmates. After nearly a decade in his post, on New Year's Day 1858 he commented how during 'the first six years of my ministry here the prisoners were, for the most part, victims of the famine years, men who passed their lives honestly, until driven to the commission of crime by the extreme poverty of themselves and their families. But not so with prisoners convicted during the last three or four years, who are generally ... practised criminals from the cities and towns ...'[47]

Given that the overwhelming majority of convicts identified as Catholic, the Anglican and Presbyterian chaplains ministered to smaller numbers. Rev. Bouchier reported a considerable increase in

---

1857, died 1895) had served as chaplain to both Cork City and County Gaols for two years prior to his transfer to Spike Island in the summer of 1865 (HMSO, *Directors' Report 1865*; Bolster, 1989).

46 HMSO, *Prisons of Ireland Report 1851*.

47 HMSO, *Directors' Report 1857*.

the numbers of his congregation in 1863 when he ministered to 120 convicts, while Rev. Gibson reported that the average number of Presbyterian convicts was between 20 and 43 during his first year, 1856. Gibson appears to have visited the island on Sundays, Tuesdays and Fridays.[48] The Catholic chaplains were ministering to many multiples of these numbers and, ironically, it was only after the concerted effort made after 1854 to reduce the overall numbers of convicts in the prison that a new space was made available for Catholic services in the form of one of the two large rooms that made up the Timber Prison (Block C). This served as the Catholic chapel until 1877, when a new church was built in the Parade Ground opposite the Punishment Block.[49]

The prison authorities employed the chaplains to the full and insisted that they act as censors on top of their ministry roles. With literacy rates rising throughout the period, all letters written and received by convicts had to be seen by one of the chaplains. Reverend Gibson made liberal use of the prisoners' letters in his annual returns to the Directors of Convict Prisons. Gibson also quoted some of the letters in part and in full in his memoir, *Life Among Convicts*, published in 1863. In this work and in a pamphlet from the same year entitled *The Intermediate Prisons: A Mistake*, Gibson devoted considerable discussion to the merits or otherwise of the Irish convict system and the reforms introduced by Crofton in the 1850s. The latter had used the decline in the number of convicts in Ireland to suggest that reforms such as the intermediate prisons and conditional liberty had reduced overall criminality. Gibson argued instead that the numbers reflected

---

48 HMSO, *Directors' Report 1856*; *Directors' Report 1863*.
49 HMSO, *Directors' Report 1877*. The new church was demolished sometime between the 1930s and the 1960s.

the ending of famine conditions and the post-release emigration of many convicts. This contradiction of Crofton's view does not seem to have been appreciated by the Directors and instead of publishing Gibson's report for 1862, the Directors replaced it with the following note: 'The Presbyterian Chaplain's Report being composed almost wholly of observations on subjects not required by the Regulations to be included therein, and he having declined to remove all such observations, when called on to do so, his Report is omitted.'[50]

Gibson had already angered the administration in 1859 when he distributed booklets to his Presbyterian flock containing a passage that disparaged Roman Catholicism.[51] As Crofton's reforms and his innovative intermediate prisons were receiving international attention, Gibson was openly critiquing them from within the system.[52] Gibson's critique prompted others to question Crofton's achievements and the latter felt obliged to publish a defence of his methods of prison reform.[53] Bitter debates between Crofton and his critics continued for a number of years, but by then the man whose pamphlet seems to have initiated the row had already departed Spike Island. Gibson was

---

50 HMSO, *Directors' Report 1862*.
51 NAI, GPO/LB/181131. It seems that Fr Lyons brought the distribution of this booklet to the notice of the prison authorities.
52 British Library, Add MS 60844–60849; Von Holtzendorff, Baron Franz. 1860. *The Irish Convict System: More Especially Intermediate Prisons* (NLI Ir 365 h 2); Carpenter, Mary. 1857. *Reformatory Discipline as Developed by the Rt Honourable Sir Walter Crofton* (British Library X208/1839); Shipley, Orby. 1857. *The Purgatory of Prisoners: or an intermediate stage between the prison and the public; being some account of the practical working of the new system of penal reformation, introduced by the Board of Directors of Convict Prisons in Ireland* (British Library 6055.df.29); Krause, T. 2003. *The influence of Sir Walter Crofton's 'Irish system' on prison reform in Germany*. Dublin: British Legal History Conference: Adventures of the Law. In the 1870s the Spike Island prison was also studied by parties from India, Sweden, Norway and Spain (NAI, GPO/LB/24/221 & 375 and CSORP/1879/1079).
53 Burt, John Thomas. 1863. *Irish Facts and Wakefield Figures in Relation to Convict Discipline in Ireland; investigated by J.T. Burt*. London; Crofton, Walter. 1863. *A Few Observations on a Pamphlet Recently published by J. Burt on the Irish Convict System*. London.

dismissed from the service on 1 August 1863. He was given just one week's notice and his dismissal left him without any pension rights. Gibson appealed his termination to the Chief Secretary in Dublin and to the Home Office in London. The decision of the Irish authorities to dispense with the Reverend's services was not overturned. Gibson argued that he was entitled to disagree with aspects of the system and that public statements by the Lord Lieutenant had encouraged him to do so. The Directors of Convict Prisons argued that while he was entitled to raise concerns about the system in which he worked, he was obliged to bring those concerns to his superiors through the appropriate channels and not to publish them.[54]

Gibson moved to London and settled in Hammersmith. He obtained employment as a teacher but lost his job when the school closed. Without any form of income, he was forced to apply to the Royal Literary Society for a grant. He was a prolific writer and had published several articles and books. The society obliged and he was later placed on the civil list and granted a pension of £100 per annum for his literary achievements. He also returned to work as a teacher, but ended his working life as the chaplain to the Shoreditch workhouse and infirmary. After a two-year illness, Charles Bernard Gibson died in West Hackney, London, on 17 August 1885.[55] His *Life Among Convicts* remains a valuable primary and unofficial source of information on Ireland's 19th-century convict system. On Spike Island, Gibson was replaced by the Rev. William J. Kertland, who was Presbyterian chaplain until the closure of the prison in 1883.[56]

---

54 NAI, CSORP/1864/8307.
55 British Library, Loan RLF 1/1727.
56 Rev. Kertland's salary by 1883 was £185 per annum. After his 19 years of service he retired on a pension of £95 per annum (PRO T1/15663).

In their 1862 annual report, the Directors of Convict Prisons had also included the relevant regulation that stipulated that the chaplains should confine their reports to the religious and moral conditions of the prisoners in their congregation and the apparent effects of prison discipline. All of the chaplains seem to have taken note of Gibson's misfortune and their annual reports were shorter and more formulaic for the remaining 20 years of the prison's existence. A form of self-censorship appears to have operated during those last two decades as, when compared to the years before 1862, there was a reluctance to air publicly any defects or failures in the system. This impression is given added strength by what was omitted from the published reports. For example, in 1877 an American newspaper published the following account:

> During church service at Spike Island Convict Department on Sunday, Feb. 19th, an attack was made on the governor, Mr. Peter Hay, by one of the convicts, who was in chains. The convict managed to secrete two stones of about one pound weight each, and during the service, he threw one of them at the head of the governor, inflicting a severe wound. He was about throwing the second stone when he was stopped by a warder, and removed to a cell.[57]

If this report was true, no mention was made of this assault in the annual report for 1877.

By the time of Rev. Gibson's replacement in 1863, the transportation of convicts had ceased. Van Diemen's Land was closed to

---

57 *Irish American Weekly*, Saturday, 17 March 1877. We were unable to locate any official record of this attack. As considerable portions of the correspondence generated by the Spike Island Convict Depot are no longer extant, our failure to find such a record does not constitute proof that such an attack did not occur.

convict transportation in 1853, and from then until 1860 most transportation from Spike Island was to Bermuda or Western Australia. All of the chaplains reported that they paid particular attention to those about to be transported. The Bermuda convict depot, established in 1823, was being wound down in the later 1850s and a large contingent of convicts was returned to Ireland in early 1854, while 360 more were returned to Spike Island in December 1855 and in January 1856. Fr Lyons noted in his report for 1856 that the returned convicts appeared to be 'strangers to all the practices of religion, and the observance of discipline'.[58] The experience of incarceration on the convict hulks at the construction site of the Bermuda Naval Dockyard may explain some of what Lyons observed among these men.

One of the January 1854 returnees was Thomas Cronin from Co. Limerick.[59] Cronin was 23 years old at the time of his trial on 8 March 1847, when he was convicted alongside his brother, James, who was 21 years old. The younger of the two, James Cronin, who was 5ft 6in. tall (1.7m), had discharged a gun at a James Hogan during a failed burglary and was sentenced to be transported for life for shooting with intent to kill.[60] Thomas was sentenced to 15 years' transportation at the same trial.[61] A few months after their conviction, the Cronin brothers were transported, probably from Kingstown, to Bermuda on board the newly outfitted convict ship, *Medway*. This recently decommissioned battleship was refitted in 1847 not just to serve as a transport vessel for the 450 convicts it carried but also as a prison hulk. On the *Medway*'s arrival in Bermuda in January 1848, the masts were removed and extra accommodation was built on the

58 HMSO, *Directors' Report 1856*.
59 NAI, TR6, p.130.
60 NAI, TR6, p.129; AOT CON33-1-106, 25280.
61 NAI, TR6, p.130.

top deck. Newly arrived convicts were required to work out of doors for two years on probation. After this time, they could apply to work in some of the skilled trades indoors.[62]

The Cronin brothers caused a fatal riot onboard the *Medway* in 1849. They had been fighting with a fellow prisoner and Thomas Cronin refused to co-operate when instructions were given to put them in irons. When the guards attempted to enforce their orders, James Cronin grabbed one of the irons, broke loose and threatened the warders. He made his way on deck and then onto the breakwater where the hulk was moored before being subdued by the guards with the help of fellow prisoners.[63] In order to punish both of the brothers, the overseer ordered that James should be flogged publicly and that Thomas should administer the whipping. The older brother refused and was sentenced to a period of solitary confinement, but not before being brought to watch another prisoner administering the punishment. As was standard procedure, all of the other prisoners held on the *Medway* were mustered on deck to witness the flogging, under the supervision of armed guards. Just as the whipping was about to begin, James looked up at his fellow prisoners and Thomas broke from the crowd, provoking a riot. The guards opened fire, killing four and wounding another 10. Once order was restored, the punishment went ahead and James received his 24 lashes.[64]

The Cronin brothers were separated in 1851 when James made an escape attempt and was sent to England.[65] In London, he was put on board the convict transport ship *Aboukir*, which sailed for Norfolk

---

62 Hollis Hallett, C.F.E. 1999. *Forty Years of Convict Labour: Bermuda 1823-1863*. Bermuda: Juniper Hill Press, p.73.
63 PRO, CO37/128, pp.175–8.
64 PRO, CO37/142, p.273.
65 Hollis Hallet, pp.32–3; AOT CON33-1-106, 25280.

Island and Van Diemen's Land on Christmas Eve 1851, arriving in Hobart on 20 March 1852.[66] He was in and out of trouble in the former penal colony throughout the 1850s, but did not appear in police records in later decades. A note in his record indicates that he died of pulmonary apoplexy (haemorrhage in the lungs) at the Hospital for the Insane, Cascade, Hobart, on 16 July 1885 (Fig. 12.3).

Figure 12.3 James Cronin (1826–1885), pictured later in life. (Image © Tasmanian Museum and Art Gallery Collection)

Prior to 1853, most convicts who served time in Bermuda were later transported to Van Diemen's Land as the local population in Bermuda would not permit any permanent convict presence (Fig. 12.4). For many, this provided an incentive for good behaviour as convicts who had done their hard labour in Bermuda with a good record would be released on arrival in Hobart on a Ticket of Leave. The refusal from 1853 by the free colonists of Van Diemen's Land to accept any more convicts led to the demise of the entire transportation system and left the Bermuda authorities with no option other than returning prisoners to Ireland and Britain. This caused distress to some convicts who had hoped to start new lives in the colonies. Gold had been found in Victoria in 1851 and Australia was increasingly seen as a land of opportunity.

So instead of joining his brother in Van Diemen's Land, Thomas Cronin left Bermuda on board the *James* in December 1853 and disembarked at Spike Island on 12 January 1854.[67] He arrived at

---

66 PRO, HO11/17/323.
67 Hollis Hallett, p.118; NAI, TR9, p.14.

Figure 12.4 The Naval Dockyard at Bermuda, constructed 1823–1863 using convict labour. British and Irish convicts lived on prison hulks that were moored where the modern marina is located. (Image © authors)

the convict depot at the time of its greatest overcrowding and at the peak period of mortality, when over 12% of prisoners (286 men) had died in the previous year. Thomas was one of the fortunate ones as he was released from the depot on an unknown date and disappeared from the records.[68] Like some of their fellow Catholic prisoners in Bermuda, the Cronin brothers may have feared for their souls there because anti-Catholic sentiment in the local population had delayed the appointment of Catholic chaplains until the late 1840s and they would have heard of all convicts, regardless of religious background, being forced to attend Anglican services. This, along with the fact that the Church of England minister officiated at convict funerals, must have added to the burden of incarceration for prisoners who were committed Catholics.

When Fr Lyons noted in his 1856 report that the returnees were 'strangers to all the practices of religion', he would have been

---

68 NAI, TR6, p.130.

aware that there had been considerable resistance in Bermuda by the local population (descendants of 17th-century Protestant settlers) to the presence of Catholic clergy on the island.[69] However, it was the head schoolmaster at Spike Island and not any of the chaplains who reported to the Directors of Convict Prisons on the religious pressure experienced by some of the Bermuda returnees. Writing two years after Fr Lyons's observations, Head Schoolmaster Michael Harold reported that the convicts had attended school in Bermuda but learned nothing as 'the schoolmaster was a proselyte, and that they feared to learn anything from him'.[70] Harold was one of a small band of men who ran the convict schools that all prisoners had to attend. Along with discipline, forced labour and moral/religious training, education was regarded as playing a key redemptive role in the Victorian prison system. In his instructions regarding the initial establishment of the prison at Spike Island in 1847, Captain Clement Johnson, the Inspector General of Prisons, placed a lot of emphasis on the importance of instruction as part of the prison regime. There was one schoolmaster employed when the prison opened in October 1847 and in that first month he was joined by an assistant in the person of a former turnkey.[71] The teachers' annual reports were published from the end of 1849. By then, the island had already lost its first and best-known schoolmaster, the folklorist and poet, Edward Walsh.

Born in 1805 and brought up in Kiskeam in northwest Cork, Walsh began his career as a hedge-school master or private teacher in various locations around Munster. The new National School sys-

---

69 Wahl, J.A. 2003. *Planting the Banner of Christ on the Isle of Devils: the history of the Roman Catholic Church in Bermuda.* Waterloo, ON: St Jerome's University.
70 HMSO, *Directors' Report 1858.*
71 PRO AO19/44/14: the assistant teacher was John Hickey, who was initially paid as a second class turnkey.

tem was in its infancy and the older system of privately run schools was still extant, where teachers like Walsh depended entirely on direct payments from the students. Walsh moved to Dublin in 1843, where he was associated with Daniel O'Connell's Repeal movement and other nationalist groups.[72] He was appointed schoolmaster at Spike Island when it opened in October 1847, a move that his friend, the nationalist politician Charles Gavan Duffy, later wrote was due to 'the straitened circumstances of his family'.[73] Over 40 of Walsh's letters survive, at least in part, including four that were written on Spike Island. Two of the letters were written in November 1847 while the other two are undated. All four letters were addressed to Walsh's wife, Brighid Sullivan, who had remained in Dublin with their three youngest children for health reasons, while their six-year-old son, Adam, accompanied the teacher to Spike Island. The letters provide an insight into life in the prison during the first months of its operation. In one of the undated letters, probably from October or November 1847, Walsh described a stormy afternoon:

> The island is very high, and the winds seize upon it fearfully. I went at three o'clock to look out over the harbour from the ramparts, and was forced to lie down in the blast. However, we have a snug room, with solid stone walls, and a bomb-proof roof over our heads, and are very snug. ... I think we'd be very happy here till the children would be grown, did they permit you to reside with me. I'd have great leisure; the school business won't be more than four hours a-day.[74]

---

72 Ó Ríordáin, J.J. 2005. *A Tragic Troubadour: life and collected works of poet and translator Edward Walsh (1805-1850)*. Duhallow, Co. Cork: Duhallow Development Integrated Resource.
73 *The Nation*, 7 September 1850.
74 Ó Ríordáin, pp.167–8.

The description of their accommodation suggests that Walsh and his son were living on the ground floor of Block B, which had yet to be pressed into service as convict accommodation, and that the sub-divisions of two of the ground-floor rooms had yet to be removed. The reference to his short working day is matched in the other undated letter where he mentioned that there were 300 convicts in his care, which is close to the number that had been transferred from the Dublin depots by 31 December 1847.[75] Of his 300 charges he wrote:

> Most of the convicts are persons of the south and west, who were driven by hunger to acts of plunder and violence. I wept today in one of the wards, when some of the people of Skull [sic] and Skibbereen told me the harrowing tale of their sufferings from famine, and the deaths – the fearful deaths – of their wives and little ones.[76]

In the same letter, Walsh provided some details of his diet when he mentioned that he and Adam were:

> ...sitting down to our supper of boiled bread and milk. We have both to spare, as the storm did not permit the milkman to land in the morning, and we now have a double portion. Adam says, 'Mamma will be in great glee when she comes here, to find such lots of boiled bread and milk.' I am annoyed from little turns I am forced to do about myself and Adam. Fancy me cooking ham and cabbage, and cleaning up the crockery?[77]

---

75 HMSO, *Prisons of Ireland Report 1847*.
76 Ó Ríordáin, p.168.
77 Ibid.

Food and accommodation were also mentioned in the letter dated Wednesday, 10 November 1847, when Walsh told his wife that he had ordered beef and groceries in Cork. He went on to exhort his wife to stay in Dublin until her doctor said she was fit to travel and continued:

> When he says that you should get a change of air, you must come down to Cove at least, which is a beautiful place, or to some neighbouring village. I don't think there is a decent room in this whole island. But if you were permitted here, you could have nice apartments, coals and candles, and two pounds of bread each day, 'gratis'; and then the salary would leave us enough for minor wants.[78]

Walsh's early optimism about his working hours cannot have lasted long as the number of prisoners on the island had doubled by the end of March 1848 and continued to rise at an exponential rate over the next few years. We get another glimpse of Walsh and his life on the island in May 1848 from the island's most famous prisoner, John Mitchel. The Young Irelander had arrived on Spike Island on 28 May and in his *Jail Journal* recorded how two days later, the turnkey guarding him had quietly asked him to step through a door in the high wall surrounding the yard he was in, accessing another enclosure, where:

> ...immediately a tall, gentleman-like person in black, but rather over-worn clothes, came up to me and grasped both of my hands, with every demonstration of reverence. I knew his face, but could not at first remember who he was. He was Ed-

---

78 Ó Ríordáin, p.169.

ward Walsh, author of *Mo Chraoibhín Chnó*, and other sweet songs, and of some very musical translations from old Irish ballads. Tears stood in his eyes as he told me he had contrived to get an opportunity of seeing and shaking hands with me before I should leave Ireland. I asked him what he was doing at Spike Island, and he told me that he had accepted the office of teacher to a school they kept here for small convicts – a very wretched office, indeed, and to a shy, sensitive creature like Walsh it must be daily torture. He stooped down and kissed my hands. 'Ah!' he said, 'you are now the man in Ireland most to be envied.' I answered that there might be room for difference of opinion about that; and then, after another kind word or two, being warned by the turnkey, I bade him farewell, and retreated to my own den. Poor Walsh! He has a family of young children; he seems broken in health and spirits. Ruin has been on his traces for years, and, I think, has him in the wind at last. There are more contented galley slaves moiling at Spike Island than the schoolmaster. Perhaps this man really does envy me; and, most assuredly, I do not envy him.[79]

A recent biography of Edward Walsh states that this illicit meeting with Mitchel cost Walsh his job, that he was dismissed from the convict service soon after it occurred and spent the rest of the summer of 1848 at home in Kiskeam.[80] However, financial records of the prison show that Walsh was paid up until 22 August 1848, two days before he took up a new post as teacher in the Cork Union Workhouse.[81] The same documents show that Walsh was paid just under £10 per quarter on Spike Island, whereas his Workhouse salary

---

79 Mitchel, p.30.
80 Ó Ríordáin, p.84.
81 PRO, AO19/44/14.

is reported to have been £50 per annum.[82] Whatever prompted his departure from the prison, Mitchel's assessment proved correct and Walsh did not get to enjoy his improved salary for long as he died in 1850 (Fig. 12.5).

Figure 12.5 Plaque commemorating Edward Walsh at the house where he died on Princes Street, Cork. (Image © courtesy of Department of Archaeology, UCC)

By the time of Walsh's departure from his post in August 1848, Thomas Fitzpatrick had replaced the former turnkey, John Hickey, as the assistant schoolteacher.[83] Fitzpatrick was promoted to head school-master and remained in the post for a little over a year before being replaced in turn by Richard Allen in April 1850.[84] Fitzpatrick's and Allen's respective annual reports make it clear that juvenile prisoners attended school every day for four hours per day, while adult convicts were schooled for two hours per week.[85] The curriculum consisted of reading, writing, arithmetic and religious instruction. The latter would

---

82 Ó Ríordáin, p.84; though on salary see: O'Mahony, C. 2005. *Cork's Poor Law Palace: Workhouse life 1838-1890.* Cork: Rosmathún Press, pp.101–3.
83 PRO, AO19/44/14.
84 HMSO, *Prisons of Ireland Report 1850.*
85 HMSO, *Prisons of Ireland Report 1849*; HMSO, *Prisons of Ireland Report 1850.*

have been delivered by the prison chaplains, while the governor reported in 1850 that the transfer of the entire island to the government meant that gardening classes could now be held outside the fort for the boys.[86] In school, the juvenile prisoners were divided into four classes in accordance with the National School system, which also provided their books and other learning materials. In his February 1851 account, Allen provided some measure of his juvenile and adult students' progress but also identified factors that he felt constrained their learning: an inability to understand English; old age; imperfect sight; social class; and the fact that many had never before attended school.[87]

After Allen's report in 1851, schoolmasters' reports were not published again until early in 1856, when the peak of morbidity and mortality had passed as a result of Crofton's reforms and the reduction in the number of convicts on the island. By then a new head schoolmaster had been appointed, Michael Harold, who was to hold the post until 1864. Harold had two assistant teachers in 1856 and one of these, Thaddeus Ryan, was to remain in his post at least until 1877.[88] In his first annual report, submitted in January 1856, Harold noted that literacy was higher among younger convicts while the older men, particularly from the west and south of the country, were more likely to be illiterate. Harold echoed Allen's comments from five years earlier in attributing the educational deficiencies among the convicts to their social class and to their physical condition. In particular, he noted that many of the convicts had problems with their vision and he argued that this was exacerbated by the whitewashed walls of the school. Harold's background was clearly in the workhouses as he mentioned

---

86 HMSO, *Prisons of Ireland Report 1850*.
87 Ibid.
88 HMSO, *Directors' Reports, 1856, 1864, 1877*.

having encountered inmates with this condition in that context, where the whitewashed walls resulted in what he referred to as an individual being 'moonblind' or 'snowblind'.[89] Harold was correct in his diagnosis: the Medical Superintendents reported high levels of ophthalmia among the convicts, particularly in the 1850s. Much of this was likely due to malnutrition and specifically to a deficiency of Vitamin A, one of the early symptoms of which is night blindness. People who are Vitamin A deficient develop an inability to produce tears, which leads to conjunctivitis and painful corneal ulceration that can ultimately lead to permanent blindness. Harold also reported that the worst class of prisoners were despondent to a level that he considered unhealthy. He concluded that the despondency was related to the fact that many of the convicts were addicted to tobacco, an item that was not available in the prison. He reported that this resulted in addicted prisoners being constantly agitated, 'yearning after this pest of social happiness'.[90]

From 1854 onwards, Crofton's new system of convict classification provided for the awarding of marks to convicts based on their progress at school. This must have had the effect of disadvantaging the older men, who were more frequently illiterate than their younger colleagues. It's also hard to imagine the adult convicts making much progress at school, especially when they attended lessons for just three hours per week in 1855. In that year, 200 were writing on slates while 400 were writing on paper; the latter group presumably being the more advanced of the two. The relative value placed on education seems to have diminished over the 36 years of the prison's operation. Classes were moved from daytime to the evenings in the 1850s, in order to free up prisoners for work. This continued in the 1860s when, in July 1866, the day school was abandoned completely so the public

---

89 HMSO, *Directors' Report 1855.*
90 Ibid.

could get the full benefit of convict labour in the construction of the Haulbowline dockyard.[91] Night classes were held in the dormitories, a situation that the teachers did not find satisfactory.[92] By the time of the establishment of the General Prisons Board in 1879, reports on educational matters were omitted from the annual reports.

As previously noted, the original schoolroom doubled as the Catholic chapel and was located between Blocks A and B in the wooden hut that Fr Lyons had found so unsuitable. By the late 1850s, both church and school had moved to the Timber Prison, while the Iron Prison was also being used as a school by 1858.[93] In 1863, Head Schoolmaster Harold was holding classes in what he referred to as B Prison (originally Block F) while his assistants, Ryan and McCartan, were in the Iron Prison (Block D).[94] The schools were regularly evaluated by Inspectors of National Schools. In 1867, Harold was transferred to Mountjoy and Edward McGauran was moved from the Dublin prison to Spike Island.[95] McGauran was still in place at the time of the establishment of the General Prisons Board in 1879, and in his last published annual report he offered the opinion that 'the remarkably low educational status of the convicts of former years is, gradually ... rising to a higher level', though he tempered this statement by saying that the course of instruction was so humble, there was no need to fear that the education offered to convicts would be equal to that made available to the 'lower orders' on the outside.[96] This last statement assumed that all convicts were of the 'lower orders', but Spike Island

---

91 HMSO, *Directors' Report 1866*.
92 HMSO, *Directors' Report 1865*.
93 HMSO, *Directors' Report 1858*.
94 HMSO, *Directors' Report 1862*.
95 HMSO, *Directors' Report 1867*.
96 HMSO, *Directors' Report 1877*.

also had some inmates who were from more affluent backgrounds, and some of these were detailed in the memoir that may have cost Rev. Charles Bernard Gibson his job.

13. The Killer Gentlemen

Gibson's memoir recounts his dealings with the island's more colour-ful characters. One of those characters was Joseph Dwyer who had been convicted of attempted murder and was known on Spike Island as the 'Grave Digger', a moniker he had earned in a most gruesome manner.

Dwyer was a Roman Catholic and, in contrast with most Spike Island convicts, came from a relatively privileged background. He was well-educated, having been a student at Dublin's All Hallows Seminary until his departure due to ill-health. He then served as a teacher in the Queen of Charity School in the city for some five months. However, Dwyer soon drifted into an irregular lifestyle and began to sustain himself by pawning items of clothing or other articles that he could procure by any means. Those who knew him best later testified that he had always laboured under the strains of mental illness and extreme eccentricity. It was alleged that he was a fantasist and told all manner of tall tales, including: his witnessing of an assassination attempt on Napoleon III in 1858; his ownership of a country house in Wicklow; and his visit to the Pope's palace. His continuous claims that he regularly travelled abroad in the company of various princes and other nobility were dismissed as harmless fabrications by most of those who knew him. Nonetheless the pressures of living up to these fabrications may well have driven Dwyer to attempt murder. Whether he felt the need to have his sartorial style match that of his fantasy self or he simply required more clothing to pawn, Dwyer had devised a most ruthless scheme to obtain gentlemen's apparel.

On 27 December 1860, a 'person in the garb of a gentleman' called to a Dame Street tailor in Dublin. There, he placed orders for a large quantity of ready-made clothing, leaving a deposit of five shillings. The goods were to be delivered by a porter named Mulholland to a local hotel. While on his way to this address, Mulholland was waylaid by Dwyer, who admonished him for being late. Having duly chastised the unfortunate porter, Dwyer informed him that he would take him to the office in order to pay him. Mulholland followed Dwyer some distance to the rear of a row of houses on the opposite side of the river. They entered a stable with a 'To Let' sign on the door. As Dwyer began fumbling in his pocket, Mulholland asked him if he needed a match to light a candle. Dwyer replied in the affirmative. As the porter began looking for same, Dwyer pulled a pistol and discharged it in Mulholland's face. Fortunately for Mulholland, the musket ball passed through his nose and lodged in a nearby wall. A struggle ensued, during which Mulholland bit Dwyer's finger and called out for the police. On hearing the footsteps of a constable who reached the scene very quickly, Dwyer fled with a severely wounded finger. Seconds later the constable entered the stable and, when a candle was lit, made a chilling discovery. Against the wall was a freshly dug grave with a pick-axe, shovel and backfill still lying in close proximity. The flagstones had been lifted in order that they could easily conceal the grave as soon as it was filled. William Mulholland had had a very lucky escape.

Three days later, the police descended on Dwyer in a flat he was sharing with a woman on Church Street. They noted his badly wounded finger and duly arrested him. Dwyer burst into tears before being taken to the police station. Mulholland identified him and Dwyer was charged with attempted murder. It later emerged that Dwyer's father's co-operation had led the police to the suspect.

Dwyer was arraigned on 8 February 1861. He pleaded guilty to the charge of 'shooting with intent to kill'. Before sentencing on the following day, a number of depositions were heard by the court.

Dwyer's brother, an inspector at the school where Dwyer had taught, the mother of one of the children he had taught, and a priest who had known Dwyer in All Hallows, all testified that they considered Dwyer insane. The judge dismissed their testimony. He pointed out the fact that Dwyer's parents hadn't testified on his behalf and that his actions had been quite deliberate and calculated. He sentenced Dwyer to 20 years' penal servitude and reminded him that he had only mitigated the life sentence on account of the prisoner's youth.

Dwyer began that sentence in Mountjoy, where he served nine months in separation. He was transferred to Spike Island in late 1861. The Presbyterian chaplain of Spike Island left the following account of his encounters with Dwyer:

> The first time I saw him was on Spike Island, yoked, with a number of other prisoners to a truck. He knit his eyebrows so wickedly at me that I could not avoid making the remark; "That fellow would have no objection to bury me."
>
> The last time I saw him was in the quarry of Spike Island. I called him. He approached with knitted brows. "What on earth" I said to him ... "could have induced you to attempt to commit so terrible and extraordinary a crime?"
>
> My words and manner had a magical effect on him. They exorcised the devil that was in him. His face lighted up – and it is a fair and handsome face – as he replied, "I really cannot say sir, but I suppose I was not quite in my mind."
>
> He told me something of his family and friends and stated – which was evident from his manner – that he had enjoyed some advantages in education...touching his cap as he retired with a sweet – yes, positively with a sweet smile on his youthful face. This is the Grave Digger.[1]

---

1 Gibson, *Vol. I,* pp.78–82.

The 'Grave Digger' was released from Spike Island on 26 October 1874. Like so many of the island's convicts, he crossed the harbour to Queenstown, where it is thought he boarded an emigrant ship.[2]

Dwyer had arrived on Spike Island just as large-scale explosions were beginning to shape it. As such, he, and anyone located within several miles of the lower harbour, heard one of the larger ones on 17 December 1861. The explosion was announced in the *Southern Reporter* that morning and heralded as an opportunity to see 'what powder can do when scientifically applied'. At 11.45am a flag was hoisted above the island, warning any approaching shipping to keep clear. At 12 noon more than 1,000lbs of gunpowder were detonated, 'shattering the mound while dense clouds of smoke rolled heavily away'.[3] Unfortunately, the spectacular blast caused irreparable damage to the leg of an army corporal when a shard of rock almost severed it from his thigh. The unfortunate man had his leg amputated, but died the following day.[4] Undeterred by the accident, large-scale explosions continued to rock the island during the process of clearing away the last remaining bastion of the old fort, just outside the eastern wall of Fort Westmoreland (Fig. 13.1). Then, on 12 May 1862, a second tragic explosion occurred when a convict ignited a gunpowder charge thought to be defective, while opening a seal above it. The convict, known only by his initials, T.D., and an army sapper were killed, while another sapper and three convicts were badly injured.[5] Dwyer worked in close proximity to these explosions and watched

2 For details on Joseph Dwyer, see: *Tipperary Vindicator and Limerick Reporter*, 1 January 1861; *Northern Whig*, 9, 12 & 13 February 1861. See also: NAI, Richmond Prison General Register Male, 1/13/10 and Mountjoy Prison Convict Classification 1857-1866, 1/11/23.
3 *The Cork Examiner*, 18 December 1861.
4 Ibid. and *The Cork Examiner*, 19 December 1861.
5 *Dublin Evening Mail*, 15 May 1862. See also: HMSO, *Directors' Report, 1862.*

Spike Island take on its distinctive man-made shore to fort incline. He also watched the new tramways and rail trucks that greatly reduced the amount of manpower required to move earth across the island. Outside the fort, the island was now changing rapidly.

Figure 13.1 First edition of the Ordnance Survey. This map was compiled about 1840 and shows the remaining bastion of the first Fort Westmoreland on the east side of the island. In the early 1860s, this bastion was removed in a number of blasting operations in which a number of men were killed. (Image © Ordnance Survey Ireland. All rights reserved. Licence number 2016/06/CCMA/ CorkCountyCouncil)

Visitors in 1861 described how they disembarked at the pier and then walked along a 'handsome gravelled esplanade on which a sentinel is pacing up and down and pass the house and pretty plantations of Captain Chesney, military commandant of the island, and ascend a steep hill up which gangs of well fed, well cared-for looking convicts, escorted by a solitary warder, were drawing cartloads of stones and building materials'. They went on to describe the neatness of the fort's interior and the industry of the convicts who could only occasionally speak in hushed tones, ensuring that 'a solemn stillness reigned around'. The convicts' diet was considered most impressive. The visitors also noticed that a broody and 'care worn' attitude prevailed among the island's warders. These men did their duty around near-silent convicts, pacing 'their lonely and solitary rounds on this stony plateau which, though situated in the midst of a much frequented seaport, yet appears as isolated as if in the middle of the Atlantic'.[6] The Spike Island that Dwyer encountered was significantly changed, and yet remained a lonely place for a man contemplating two decades there, especially as it contained few from his relatively privileged social background. That was about to change, however: Joseph Dwyer would soon be joined by two gentlemen killers.

William Herdman was from a highly respectable background, his family being the owners of a milling company located in the north of Ireland. He himself was considerably less industrious, though. He spent some time in America and wrote for an Armagh newspaper for a period, but he was known to move about between odd-jobs and idleness and to rely on an elderly and allegedly eccentric cousin for charity. This arrangement might have continued indefinitely if Herdman's own eccentricities hadn't begun to embarrass his family.

Herdman was known to wear a false nose while walking along Dublin's Sackville Street (now O'Connell Street), using a broom handle as a cane. He would often stand among friends and bang pots and pans while laughing at the din he created. He had an irrational hatred of dogs barking and cocks crowing and would complain to police if he was wakened from his sleep by either noise. On at least one occasion, Herdman dissolved into uncontrollable laughter when the congregation at a religious service began to sing. But perhaps what his family found most embarrassing was his tendency to drink and then

---

6 *Freeman's Journal*, 2 September 1861.

to violently threaten some of those with whom he came in contact. Herdman was aboard the *City of Philadelphia* steamship when she ran aground off Newfoundland in 1854. All of her passengers survived and were brought ashore on the lifeboats; even their luggage was saved. However, the ship's doctor later remembered how Herdman had threatened him during an altercation that occurred after the passengers had been relocated to a hotel The origins of their dispute are unknown. Some claimed that madness ran in Herdman's family. His mother was most certainly a known eccentric and it was claimed that one of his sisters was also mentally ill.

All of these embarrassments may have proven too much for a family as respectable and well-known in the community as Herdman's. Eventually, his cousin cut off his financial support and informed him (through a solicitor) that it would only be reinstated if he left the country. William Herdman argued in return that his allowance should be greater, but did eventually leave the country for Liverpool, whereupon he received payment of the agreed stipend. Shortly afterwards, though, he returned to Ireland and entered into another argument about his allowance and the conditions attached to it. During the course of that argument he aired his suspicions that another cousin, John Herdman, had been instrumental in having the allowance stopped. He then journeyed to Belfast to confront John Herdman and when the latter refused to speak to him, he shot him dead. This crime was witnessed by a woman who had been walking with John Herdman at the time.

Such a vicious crime committed among the relatively well-to-do of Irish society caused a sensation across the country. The case was quite straightforward. Herdman had shot his cousin dead in front of a witness in broad daylight and several other witnesses had seen him fleeing the scene. He was found guilty of murder on 22 July 1862 and sentenced to death a few days later. However, the jury that found him guilty had recommended that he be treated mercifully. In August, the Lord Lieutenant commuted his death sentence to life imprisonment after a deposition signed by Belfast's most influential citizens appealed on grounds of Herdman's eccentricities.

Herdman's wife and four children were dependent on the charity they received from the citizenry of Belfast and an appeal was launched on their behalf. Meanwhile, Herdman began his sentence in Mountjoy. The term of his stay there was far shorter than it should have been and he spent all three months of it in the prison hospital. This indicates that the prison doctor may have feared that Herdman was not mentally fit for the isolation of cellular discipline and had him transferred into association on Spike Island sooner than was normally the case. Mentally ill prisoners were certainly spared the isolation of Mountjoy's separate system on other occasions.

Herdman arrived on Spike Island in October 1862 and was categorised as a 'dangerous prisoner'. Gibson described the general trepidation in which the notorious Herdman was held:

> He is a tall man, about fifty years of age, with grey hair, and dark vindictive eyes, which he proudly or cunningly averts from the face of an honest man; but you feel at the same time, that he is always watching you. His eyes are set in his head like those of a hare, that can see the pursuers without turning around.
>
> "That man can see me when I'm walking behind him," was the remark of the Governor of Spike Island prison.[7]

---

7 Gibson, *Vol. I*, pp.74–6.

Herdman's time on Spike Island was turbulent. His list of prison offences was so long that a new leaf had to be added to the record book. Among other things, Herdman was punished for loitering, refusing orders, collecting prohibited articles and arguing with those in authority. He received all of the usual punishments, often spending two or three days in the Punishment Block on a bread and water diet. In July 1866, he was put in solitary confinement for 72 hours for disobeying an officer and being found in possession of the torn-out pages of a library book. He attempted suicide while in the cells by 'wilfully opening a vein in his arm ... thereby losing a good deal of blood'. This didn't stop the authorities from sending him to the Punishment Block on several other occasions. Although prisoners were periodically transferred to lunatic asylums, Herdman was never among their number. Having spent more than two decades on Spike Island, he eventually left it in February 1883, just a few months before its closure.[8]

As two of only 23 convicts serving sentences in excess of 15 years in 1862, it is almost certain that Herdman and Dwyer knew each other well. Indeed, similarities in their social backgrounds and education and their likely confinement in the Iron Prison may have meant that they gravitated towards each other.[9] If they did, they were about to be joined by another who shared their privileged background. With the closure of the Bermuda convict station in 1863, William Burke Kirwan was about to return to Spike Island.

Kirwan had enjoyed significant status as a celebrity prisoner

8 For the story of William Herdman, see *Northern Whig*, 25 July 1862. See also: NAI, Dublin Prison Classification General Register 1854-1865, 1/9/65 and Mountjoy Prison Convict Classification 1857-1866, 1/11/23.
9 British Library, Add MS 60844–60848. Crofton states that all of those serving life sentences did so in the Iron Prison. Given the gravity of his offence and the limited number of 'lifers', it is likely that Dwyer joined Herdman (and later Kirwan) in that block.

in Bermuda after his arrival there in 1854. It was said that another serious offender had remarked: 'before you came I held first place in these islands but I concede that honour to *Mr William Burke Kirwan*'.[10] It was probably his period as a medical student and associated anatomical knowledge that first led to his working in the hospital. There he had distinguished himself by giving great service to the medical staff on Bermuda during a yellow fever outbreak in 1856. The chief medical officer, Dr Charles F. Edwards, had recommended that Kirwan's release be fast-tracked as he 'was indefatigable in his exertions night and day in attendance on the sick from the commencement of the epidemic until its disappearance'. Indeed, Edwards was forthcoming in his assessment that Kirwan made himself 'more useful than any other three men' during the outbreak.[11]

Kirwan was far too notorious for the authorities to contemplate his release, however. Although the Directors stated that they would reconsider release for some serving life sentences who had rendered service during the Bermuda epidemic as soon as 10 years of their terms were served, Kirwan's case was different. Responding to a query as to whether his release might be considered, they remarked that 'the Kirwan atrocity and recent occurrence of this crime renders any remark unnecessary'.[12] One convict later claimed that Kirwan was eventually removed from the medical department after he revealed the darker part of his personality and gave 'a prisoner he didn't like some pills that didn't agree with him'.[13] He remained on Bermuda until the convict station closed in March 1863, and he was among the

---

10 Gibson, *Vol. II*, p.46.
11 PRO, CO37/162. See also: Hollis Hallett, p.110.
12 NAI, GPO/LB/5/625.
13 Gibson, *Vol. II*, p.47. If Kirwan did indeed administer harmful pills to another convict, it may be relevant to how Richard Downes Boyer (the man who separated/was separated from his wife and sold his property to Kirwan) met his end in 1841.

last group of prisoners to be sent to Millbank penitentiary in London. Kirwan was finally shipped back to Spike Island on 9 May 1863.[14]

Kirwan's distinguished spell in Bermuda's medical department had led to his enjoying some privileges, including an improved diet and being allowed to paint. Shortly after his return to Spike Island he was removed from the labour gangs and sent to the Catholic chapel where he was to complete several religious icons for Fr Lyons. When this activity was noted by the Directors during a visit to the island, they immediately issued orders to Governor Hay and Fr Lyons to discontinue the work and return Kirwan to ordinary labour. They made it clear that a prisoner guilty of such an 'atrocious murder' was not to be employed at work that was 'likely to be an amusement to him'.[15] Their anger at his being permitted to amuse himself may have been a result of his having written representations to the Directors for another prisoner at about this time. This contained what the Directors deemed 'objectionable matter' and the island's authorities were reminded that such representations by convicts should not be permitted.[16]

While upper-class men like Dwyer, Herdman and Kirwan were incarcerated on Spike Island, they were very much the exception. This is perhaps best illustrated by the available prison registers. Of a sample of 617 men received at the prison between 30 March 1849 and 9 September 1850, for example, 509 were listed as 'labourer' while a further nine were listed as having no profession.[17] This represents over 85% of the total and demonstrates that the poor were far more likely to experience incarceration and the dangers associated with it. On Spike Island, those dangers were ever present.

---

14 *The Cork Examiner*, 11 May 1863.
15 NAI, GPO/LB/20/872 & 874.
16 NAI, GPO/LB/20/Margin of Register.
17 NLI, MS 3016.

14. Haulbowline

On the afternoon of 27 August 1864, the prisoners were returned to their wards early in order to wash, shave and change soiled clothes. This was part of the normal Saturday routine at that time. At approximately 4.40pm, convict Patrick Mahony was handed a razor by Warder Michael Reilly. Given the number of prisoners attending to personal hygiene every Saturday, it was impossible for the warders to shave each man individually and the issuing of razors had become a necessary evil.

Patrick Mahony was not the kind of man to be trusted with a razor. He was serving 15 years' penal servitude for a burglary in Kilkenny, and on his arrival in Mountjoy he had been identified as a former juvenile offender who had gone by the name of John Hogan. Mahony's behaviour in Mountjoy was characterised as 'very bad' and he and Warder Reilly had already clashed on Spike Island. Prior to the August incident, Reilly had reported Mahony for his refusal to work, with the result that he had been sent to solitary on bread and water. Now, as Reilly inspected the soiled linen, Mahony saw his chance and rushed the unsuspecting warder. Using the open razor, he slashed Reilly's face and body. Reilly ran for cover through an adjoining ward, and into a third one. Mahony pursued him all the way, but was tackled in the third ward by two of Reilly's colleagues, who took the razor from him. One of them later testified that Mahony had given up the razor quite easily, declaring that he did not wish to injure any man who had not injured him.[1]

---

1 NAI, CSORP/1865/2151 and Mountjoy Prison Convict Classification 1857-1866, 1/11/23. See also: *The Cork Examiner*, 17 March 1865.

Warder Reilly was removed to the hospital, where the doctor expressed the view that the cut would have killed him if it were just a fraction deeper. His health was seriously compromised, however, and he had not fully recovered almost 12 months later.[2] Mahony was taken to the Punishment Block and placed in chains. There he remained, on a reduced diet, while he awaited his trial. On 16 March 1865, Patrick Mahony was found guilty of maiming, disfiguring, common assault, and causing grievous bodily harm. His term of penal servitude was extended to life and he was returned to Mountjoy.[3] Nobody thought it immediately necessary to ban the use of razors by the convicts. Indeed, their use was considered to enhance security as the popularity of facial hair at that time among civilian men made convicts' closely shaven faces somewhat remarkable. Nonetheless that ban eventually came seven years later after a convict 'mutilated himself in a frightful manner with the razor issued to him'.[4] Perhaps the most curious coincidence about the whole affair was the location in which it occurred. The ward in which Patrick Mahony attacked Warder Reilly was the same one where Edmond Power and Patrick Norris had murdered William Reddy some eight years previously. In the wake of the Reddy murder, all of Block A's wards were subdivided into cells to deter convicts from acting in combination. That subdivision may well have been one of the factors that saved Warder Reilly's life.

No doubt William Burke Kirwan heard the commotion that surrounded the attack on Warder Reilly. The violence of prison life had not changed. Nonetheless, he surely reflected on all that had changed in the decade since his initial departure. By the end of 1861,

---

2 NAI, GPO/LB/7/136.

3 NAI, Mountjoy Prison Convict Classification 1857-1866, 1/11/23. See also: NAI, GPO/LB/6/1099 & 1105, GPO/LB/7/25 & 53.

4 NAI, GPO/LB/9/262.

the closure of Forts Camden and Carlisle, along with the continuing reduction of convict numbers generally, had reduced the prison population on Spike Island to a low of 528 from a high of over 2,300 a decade earlier. It was still the largest convict prison in Ireland, but had now been eclipsed by some of the larger English gaols. A process of further expansion was already underway, however. The closure of the Philipstown depot in March 1862 saw the invalids and elderly returning to Spike. At the end of 1863, Fort Carlisle reprised its role as a halfway house between Spike Island and the intermediate prisons. By the end of 1864, almost 200 convicts were working on extending and modernising the fortifications there.[5]

The Spike Island convict prison had been up and running for nearly two decades. After the complete alteration of the island itself, and continual upgrading of the fortifications at Camden and Carlisle, finding sufficient labour for such a large body of men was becoming an issue.[6] In early 1865, the Directors of Convict Prisons commented that:

> At Spike Island the employment of the convicts has been chiefly in completing the works on which for many years they have been engaged, under the Royal Engineer Department, but which appear to be now drawing near a close, when other employment will have to be found for a large proportion of the convicts. It is expected that this object will be attained in the construction of a Government Dock, proposed to be erected in the neighbourhood of the island. It must be

---

5 HMSO, *Directors' Reports 1861–1864*. It is worth noting that Fort Camden lost its status as an intermediate prison in 1860 and became a feeder prison for the intermediate prison at Lusk, Co. Dublin, until the fort was eventually closed as a prison in June 1861. It was not subsequently reopened as a prison (NAI, GPO/LB/18/1804).
6 NAI, GPO/LB/7/1.

observed that the chief work at Spike Island has become of a very desultory character, less capable even than in previous years of actual measurement.[7]

The solution to the issue of labour came in the form of the nearby island of Haulbowline and the biggest construction project in the history of Cork harbour up to that time. Haulbowline had been chosen in preference to Kinsale for the erection of naval storehouses and an arsenal in 1790, and had served as a small depot for the Royal Navy ever since.[8] Now, some seven decades later, Spike Island's neighbour was about to become the site of an enormous construction project. The next 20 years would see the convicts of Cork harbour double the size of Haulbowline Island and build an extensive and modern naval dockyard on the newly created ground. It was a remarkable feat of engineering and construction, and still stands as a monument to its unfree builders.

In the early part of 1864, parliament appointed a 'Select Committee to inquire into and report upon the Basin and Dock Accommodation of the Royal Dockyards of the United Kingdom, and its sufficiency for the public service, having reference especially to the proposed extension of Her Majesty's Dockyard at Portsmouth'.[9] One of the MPs appointed to this body questioned the necessity of a committee having to issue recommendations on a subject matter for which the Admiralty was much better qualified. He feared that MPs appointed to the Select Committee might be tempted to place the interests of their own area, and their own constituents, above those of the state. He was somewhat justified in his fears as MPs from Ports-

---

7 HMSO, *Directors' Report, 1864.*
8 National Maritime Museum Greenwich, Caird Library (NMMCL), ADM/BP/10.
9 Hansard, *House of Commons Debates, HC Deb 25 February 1864, vol. 173, cc1157–8.*

mouth, Norfolk and from Ireland all sat on the committee. Early on in the process, three further members were added: one of them was the Cork-born MP for King's County (now Offaly), John Pope Hennessy.[10]

Back in Cork, the excitement started to build among the city's most prominent citizens. Cork now had a real chance of securing a very lucrative naval dockyard. On 14 March 1864, the lord mayor of Cork and sitting MP, John Francis Maguire, inserted a notice in *The Cork Examiner*, the newspaper that he had founded in 1841. Maguire urged the government to take stock of the great natural advantages of Cork harbour and furnish it with the naval dockyard that had been periodically promised over several decades. Maguire's notice signalled the beginning of a concerted campaign by prominent citizens of Cork to secure a naval dockyard for the lower harbour.

On 9 May 1864, Maguire was one of a number of prominent Corkonians who gave evidence to the Select Committee in Westminster in favour of the Cork harbour location. The following day, Spike Island's more observant convicts may have noted the presence of little red flags flying on the spit bank running eastward from Haulbowline and north of Spike. The flags were flown by ordnance officials who were taking soundings and borings in order to establish the depth of the mud to the east of Haulbowline.[11] They were the first visible sign that the Select Committee was seriously considering the construction of a naval dockyard in Cork harbour. Maguire was determined to maintain the lobbying pressure on the government, and on 19 May 1864 he presided over a meeting of some of the most prominent citizenry of the city. He was keen to emphasise that Cork sought a naval dockyard not for the good of the citizens of Cork but for the greater

---

10 Ibid.
11 *The Cork Examiner*, 10 May 1864.

good of the Empire. He appealed to the government as follows:

> We do not ask the Government to do anything which they are
> not bound to do, nor do we ask them to do anything which it
> is our duty to do ourselves ... It is our right as well as our duty
> to demand from the Government something like a change in
> their policy towards this country – to demand from them for
> Ireland a fair share of the public expenditure of the empire
> (hear, hear). To that fair share of the public expenditure we
> are justly entitled. We contribute taxes, we contribute men,
> we contribute to the efficiency and strength and power of the
> empire; and yet we do not receive in exchange a fair consid-
> eration of our claims from the Government, as subjects of
> the same Sovereign (hear, hear). There happens to be an en-
> quiry held at the present moment relative to a subject of very
> important character to the interests of the empire at large ...
> The navy of the empire – in fact the navy of every maritime
> kingdom – is in a state of transition – is undergoing a process
> of alteration from timber to iron, and there is consequently,
> at present, a greater necessity for dock accommodation than
> when timber ships were universally used (hear, hear). Com-
> pared with France the dock accommodation of the United
> Kingdom is much less than it ought to be. In fact, England
> has only thirty-five acres of dock or basin accommodation,
> whereas France has one hundred and forty acres of floating
> dock (hear, hear); yet the naval force of France is, at least, one
> third less than that of England, and the colonial possessions
> of France are small in comparison to those of England (hear,
> hear). It is our duty to take advantage of the enquiry now go-
> ing on in Parliament, to make our claims on the Government
> known, to say to the Government that now is the time for
> them to, redeem the promises so frequently made even so far

back as the period of the Union (hear, hear). We have in Cork harbour facilities and advantages for dock accommodation that are not possessed in any other part of the United Kingdom, and our object in calling on the Government to erect naval dockyards here, is not to benefit a locality, not to benefit Queenstown, or the city and county of Cork, but we call on them in the interest and for the services of the empire, to avail of the unrivalled advantages which our harbour presents for the purposes I have stated (hear, hear).[12]

Although altruistic notions of serving the public good were foregrounded by the Cork lobby group, so too were more practical considerations of potential benefit to the local economy. It was pointed out that ships were never paid off in Cork. Were this to be altered, and some crews discharged in Cork, they might inject up to £35,000 into the local economy. Furthermore, Maguire claimed that workers employed in naval dockyards at Plymouth, Woolwich, Sheerness, Devonport, Pembroke, Chatham and Dover drew £900,000 in wages annually. Portsmouth dockyard alone employed 3,000 men, who were paid a combined annual wage of £200,000. In contrast, naval workers employed in Cork, which was then Ireland's only naval station, were paid approximately £900 annually. The meeting argued that such a significant inequality should not be allowed to prevail and that Ireland was entitled to a level of investment comparable to that of England.[13] To some degree, the establishment of a naval dockyard in Cork harbour became a national issue as one Dublin newspaper was quite vociferous in its support of the project.[14] A local committee founded at

12 *The Cork Examiner*, 20 May 1864. See also: Brunicardi, D. 2012. *Haulbowline: the naval base and ships of Cork Harbour*. Dublin: The History Press Ireland.
13 *The Cork Examiner*, 20 May 1864.
14 *Dublin Evening Mail*, 21 May & 28 July 1864.

the 19 May meeting continued to lobby the government on Cork's behalf, even sending a deputation to London in order to maintain the political pressure.[15] The Select Committee reported back to parliament and recommended the establishment of a naval dockyard in Cork. Crucially for Spike Island's convicts, the committee observed:

> Your committee received much evidence as to the capabilities of Haulbowline Island for a dock. It is said that the Spit Bank offers an eligible site, and that the establishment of convicts at the neighbouring Spike Island would facilitate the work.[16]

However, the site to the east of Haulbowline was exposed from a military point of view. Consequently, the Select Committee also reported other potential sites in Cork harbour: at Marina, nearer to Cork city, and at the privately owned docks at Passage West. The committee stopped short of recommending a specific location for the new dockyard. The government was left to consider the question.

On 9 February 1865, in response to a parliamentary question from John Pope Hennessy, the Secretary to the Admiralty revealed that the government intended to proceed with the building of a naval dockyard in Cork.[17] Although the response was vague as to the precise location of the facility, press reports continued to indicate that the Spit Bank east of Haulbowline was the chosen site.[18] This was confirmed on 24 May 1865 when the Royal Engineers' plans, as approved by the Controller of the Navy, were published in *The Cork Examiner*:

---

15 *The Cork Examiner*, 27 May & 8 July 1864.
16 *Dublin Evening Mail*, 21 July 1864.
17 Hansard, *House of Commons Debates, HC Deb 9 February 1865, vol. 177, c116*.
18 *The Cork Examiner*, 8 February & 14 March 1865.

Of the very many good sites for stillwater basins and graving docks in Queenstown and Cork outer harbour, I am of the opinion that the 'Spit Bank,' to the eastward of Haulbowline, in direct communication with the existing naval establishment, offers, on the whole, the site most suitable to meet the probable wants of the Royal navy, and presents, in addition to its proximity to Spike Island, where there is a large amount of prison labour available, certain facilities of construction. Adopting then, this site, I herewith submit a general design for the extension of the existing dockyards at Haulbowline. This design consists of a basin of 62 acres, with 30 feet over the sill at the entrance at high water neaps, with 2,000 feet of wharf accommodation, and with space for two docks leading out of the basin. I propose, however, that the construction of only one of those docks should at present be undertaken. The design includes a small factory. The approximate estimate, on the supposition that the largest proportion of the work is to be executed by convict labour, I have taken at £150,000, and the whole should be completed in six years. If it be decided to execute this work with convict labour, it will not require legislative provision for contracts such as is desirable for Portsmouth and Chatham. Should my Lords approve of this design, I propose to commence the works on the 1st of July, at which time the convicts, I am given to understand, will no longer be required by the War Department, and will, therefore, be at the disposal of the Admiralty.[19]

The Royal Navy was about to offer a huge boon to the local economy. The effects would be felt all around Cork harbour for generations to come and in 1865 it seems that some of the locals grasped the

---

19 *The Cork Examiner*, 24 May 1865.

significance of the event. Under the headline 'ROYAL DOCKYARD, CORK HARBOUR – LOCAL REJOICINGS', Maguire's newspaper announced his, and Cork's, triumph:

> Tar barrels and bonfires flashed last night in every direction despite mist, haze, and rain. Parties paraded the high road between Corbally hills and Annmount, where monster bonfires blazed, carrying tar barrels, and followed by hundreds of country lads and lasses, loudly vociferating as they passed the gates of the different neighbouring gentlemen. Some twenty tar barrels were burned on a prominent bridge, directly over the village of New Glanmire, and commanding a view of Passage, Carrigtowill, Midleton and the Intermediate districts. In consequence of the heavy rain which fell during the evening the several local temperance bands were unable to attend as was contemplated.[20]

By early August 1865, the small party of convicts already journeying daily to work at the existing Haulbowline docks and stores was increased slightly. The additional 39 convicts were engaged in opening a stone quarry on Haulbowline.[21] A month later, the ground was visibly marked with flagstaffs and 500–600 tonnes of timber were in the process of being landed on the island.[22] Towards the tail end of the year, convicts were engaged in depositing the mud lifted from a channel dredged between Haulbowline and Rocky Island.[23]

20 Ibid., 25 May 1865.
21 NAI, CSORP/1865/8637. See also: HMSO, *Directors' Report 1865*.
22 *Dublin Evening Mail*, 1 September 1865.
23 *The Cork Examiner*, 22 December 1865.

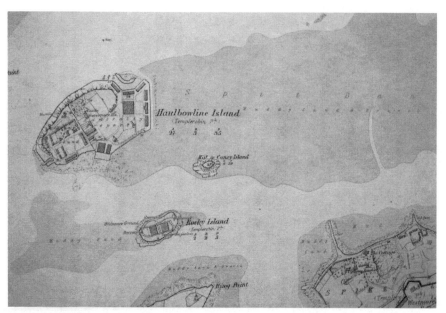

Figure 14.1 Detail of map of Cork harbour showing Haulbowline, Spike, Rocky and Rat islands before the extension of Haulbowline and its incorporation of Rat Island. (Image © PRO: MPH1/188)

Twelve months later, in August 1866, *The Cork Examiner* reported that there was some visible progress in the Haulbowline area. Some of the timber had been used to construct a gantry between Haulbowline and Rat Island, a small islet of a quarter of an acre that was located to the southeast of Haulbowline and was to be absorbed into the enlarged island (Fig. 14.1). It was understood that this gantry would eventually run as far as Spike, forming a land connection with the prison island. Although the newspaper didn't make it clear, the convicts were forming the southern shore of an extended Haulbowline. The new landfill would consume Rat Island, incorporating it into its enlarged neighbour. The newspaper went on to report that the quarry on Haulbowline had already produced one acre of cut stone for the foundations of the extension. Although the same article also complained that the work was not being 'precipitated'. The Directors seemed to echo the concerns of *The Cork Examiner* regarding the lack of progress when they asked Hay for daily reports of the numbers of convicts employed on the dockyards.[24]

There were two reasons why work had not advanced as rapidly as some might have hoped. The first was the dwindling prison population across the entire island of Ireland. In the 12 years since the establishment of the Directors of Convict Prisons in Ireland in 1854, their sweeping reforms had seen the prison population fall by a staggering 52%. Spike Island itself had seen prisoner numbers decrease by precisely the same proportion during the same period.[25] Now, with major construction finally underway at Haulbowline, the Admiralty was finding it difficult to procure the convict labour required. Where it had assumed that 300 convicts could be available from the prison, it had been supplied with only 120 and was informed that, in the short term, the prison authorities couldn't increase that number by more than 80. We have already seen that in July 1866, Spike Island's day school had been discontinued to free its students for labour on Haulbowline, before returning to Spike for night classes. The closure of the day school occurred just weeks before *The Cork Examiner* report referred to above and may have been the primary reason for some visible progress. The authorities also considered replacing the 18 men required to move one of Spike Island's earth-moving hand trucks with horses, thereby freeing more labourers for the naval dockyard.[26] Although this scheme does not appear to have been implemented, Spike Island was able to provide the desired 300 labourers for the dockyards by the end of 1866.[27] The Directors were continually pressured

---

24 Ibid., 7 August 1866. NAI, GPO/LB/21/1207.
25 Prison populations are drawn from the *Directors' Reports* for *1854* and *1865*.
26 NAI, GPO/LB/7/469.
27 HMSO, *Directors' Report 1866*.

to provide labour for the dockyards. They were asked if they could empty Mountjoy, send its convicts southward and make them available for the construction project. The Directors rejected this request on the grounds that the removal of the Mountjoy prisoners prior to the completion of their period of separate confinement would represent 'a grave and dangerous interference with one of the most valuable and important features of the system', although seven tailors and three shoemakers were dispatched to Spike Island due an urgent deficit of same.[28] Finally, in December 1867, the Fort Carlisle prison was closed for the last time and its 200 or so convicts were transferred back to Spike Island and added to the workforce on Haulbowline.[29]

The other key factor slowing progress at Haulbowline was the logistical difficulty in moving such a substantial labour force between the two islands. Relocating large numbers of potentially dangerous men to an unsecure island wasn't an easy process, and it wasn't made any easier by the fact that there had been several recent attempts to escape Spike Island. In January 1863, for example, an unnamed prisoner, possibly Henry Sweers who had been convicted of stealing jewellery, attempted to escape by swimming from the island. He turned around before he reached the mainland and returned to the custody of the prison officers. Two months later, Sweers left a work party on the beach and began swimming towards the mainland. Although the alarm was raised as he entered the water, Sweers brazenly kept swimming. The prison authorities quickly scrambled into boats and pursued the fleeing prisoner. It seems that several boats in the harbour also moved to intercept the swimming convict. He was hauled aboard one of the boats, returned to Spike Island, and ultimately had six months added

28 NAI, GPO/LB/7/524 & 583.
29 HMSO, *Directors' Report 1867*.

to his sentence. The prison authorities sought and received special permission from the government to have Sweers punished by a method outside of the penal code. He was made to wear especially heavy irons, preventing any additional escape attempts and acting as a deterrent for any other prisoner contemplating a similar scheme. Sweers wore the irons for nearly two years before serving out his time and gaining his release in May 1869.[30]

The Sweers case alerted the governor to the possibility of prisoners swimming to freedom and to the difficulty of spotting a man in a vast harbour full of ships. It would be useful if naval or merchant vessels in the harbour might assist in tracking any escapees. To that end, it was agreed that should any prisoner escape the island, a signal flag would be displayed on a pole located on No.1 Bastion. The display of the flag would be accompanied by a canon blast in order that it would receive immediate attention. On days of low visibility, or at night, three cannon blasts would sound from No.1 Bastion.[31] There were no escape attempts in 1864, but 1865 saw yet another convict swimming his way across Cork harbour, having attacked and disabled a warder. The convict was recaptured by one of the several boats launched when the alarm was raised. On his return to the prison, he underwent a practical, but humiliating ritual for many prisoners who were deemed potential escapees. He was stripped naked and placed in a cell. Hidden on his person, the authorities found the cutlass of the warder whom he had viciously assaulted.[32]

---

30 NAI, GPO/LB/6/773, 777, 787, 837 & 1064, GPO/LB/8/247, 249 & 355 and GPO/LB/23/270. Official documents state that the March attempt was the second occasion on which Sweers attempted to escape. As there is no surviving record of any other prisoner having attempted escape at that time, and as both attempts involved swimming to the mainland and occurred within two months of each other, it is considered likely that Sweers was involved on each occasion. It is likely that Sweers served the additional six months in Cork County Gaol as the sentence did not explicitly include penal servitude.
31 NAI, CSORP/1863/8988. See also: *Dublin Evening Mail*, 28 October 1863.
32 HMSO, *Directors' Report 1865*.

It was difficult enough for the prison authorities to detain men on Spike Island. How were they to do it on Haulbowline? As a first step, they sought the assistance of the military on the latter island. Governor Hay wrote to the Under-Secretary in Dublin to request that the military garrison on Haulbowline be kept at a level high enough to ensure that sufficient sentries could be posted around the convicts during work hours, and that other soldiers would be available in the event of 'disorderly conduct'. Hay felt it essential that 70–80 military personnel should be present on Haulbowline at all times, and the administration in Dublin agreed. Indeed within five years, the entire Spike Island security operation was heavily dependent on the presence of military sentries.[33] In this way, the convicts would be heavily guarded by warders and military whilst on Haulbowline, but the problem remained of how they would be guarded during their passage to and from their new workplace.

From 1855, small work parties always rowed to and from Haulbowline. However by 1865, with preliminary works on the dockyard underway, these work parties had already expanded and were expected to grow even further. The boats didn't make the crossing when the weather was bad, or even when it threatened to turn bad. The authorities could not provide secure shelter on Haulbowline nor could they risk convicts being forced to spend a night there. The idea of secure accommodation for convicts on Haulbowline was briefly considered, but in November 1866 it was suggested that sturdier steam-powered boats presented a more cost-effective solution.[34] Governor Hay explained that the use of steamboats would make it more difficult for

---

33 NAI, GPO/LB/8/274.
34 NAI, CSORP/1866/19872.

prisoners to simply row to the mainland, but he added that while convicts were manning boats, further security measures were necessary:

> I would recommend that a Gunboat with some marines on board as a guard be moored near Ring-point with steam always up and in readiness to afford any assistance that might be required ... It must be remembered that 290 convicts, some of them grave offenders will be conveyed in 6 or 7 boats manned and rowed by themselves and they could without much difficulty, unless the guard of marines as above suggested be supplied, reach the mainland in three or four minutes.[35]

The Lord Lieutenant sanctioned the use of steamboats and requested that the Admiralty provide them. Shortly afterwards it was decided that a more effective solution could be provided by a gunboat loaded with Marines towing the convict boats across.[36] By February 1867, convicts were still rowing themselves between Spike Island and Haulbowline. Hay was still concerned that an onboard mutiny could result in an entire boat-load of convicts escaping to the mainland. He now sought sanction to use extreme force if such an attempt was made:

> Sir,
> Now that there are nearly 300 convicts being conveyed daily to and from Haulbowline by means of boats, I have the honour to request instructions as to whether in the event of a boat

---

35 Ibid.
36 NAI, GPO/LB/7/633.

load, or any number of convicts attempting to effect their escape by rowing towards the mainland contrary to orders, the military picket forming the escort would be justified in firing on the convicts with the view of preventing their escape.[37]

The governor had been asked to explain why he had felt the need to order firearms in 1855, and queries regarding the use of firearms in the Irish convict system had been dealt with in 1863. Indeed, in 1865 the authorities had specifically directed Spike Island's warders to register any firearms that they held as personal property.[38] Governor Hay was still unclear in 1866 as to whether he had the authority to fire on escaping individuals, or escaping parties. After several months of correspondence, during which the authorities running the convict prison system in England and Wales were consulted, Hay was finally given very clear authority to fire on escaping convicts. He was told that firearms could be discharged when 'in the judgement of the officer in charge, the escort is in danger of being overpowered, or when weapons of a like kind are used by the assailants'.[39]

No doubt the convicts were informed of the governor's new authority and escape attempts were certainly minimised. Nonetheless there were always those few who still attempted to escape. One of those was 19-year-old Hugh Burns, convicted of theft, who hid himself in a chimney flue at the Haulbowline forge on a May evening in 1867. He intended making his escape after the remainder of the convicts had returned to Spike Island. Unfortunately for Burns, the warders were more vigilant than he had expected. His absence was noted and signals were immediately dispatched to Spike Island. Governor

37 Ibid.
38 NAI, GPO/LB/7/200.
39 NAI, CSORP/1866/19872.

Hay rushed to Haulbowline, bringing every available night-warder with him, and an extensive search began. Marines from two naval vessels in the harbour were also mobilised. Burns was quickly found and returned to prison, where the governor announced his intention to punish him locally rather than resort to the criminal courts.[40]

Figure 14.2   Hand-tinted, late 19th-century lantern slide of Spike and Haulbowline islands and the connecting causeway, completed in 1867. Construction was underway on the coffer dam and landfill on the extension to Haulbowline. (Image © courtesy of Collection of Michael Lenihan)

By the end of 1867, the prospect of a substantial group of prisoners rowing themselves to the mainland was removed when a causeway between the two islands was completed (Fig. 14.2).[41] The cause-

40 NAI, CSORP/1867/8314 and Dublin Bridewell Prison (Richmond) General Register 1864-1883, 1/13/46 and Mountjoy Prison Convict Classification 1864-1875, 1/11/20.
41 HMSO, *Directors' Report 1867*.

way was a substantial project that began in March of that year, with steam engines driving piles into the harbour bed. It was still under construction when inspected by the Lords of the Admiralty in September, and was almost completed by early November.[42] It served as a temporary, watertight boundary on the northern shore of Haulbowline's basin and connected with the northeast corner of Spike Island.[43] Soon the completion of the dockyard became not only a priority for the government but an essential part of Ireland's convict service, providing the principal element of forced labour in the system. The Directors noted that congregating such a large number of men together was actually a useful way to train tradesmen at the hands of other tradesmen, and to avoid any necessity of mixing convict and civilian labour. For that reason they actively opposed requests for convict labour from other arms of government.[44]

For some convicts, though, the daily grind of digging, hoisting, hauling and lifting at the Haulbowline dockyards proved too strenuous. Such men would often find themselves picking oakum or in Dr Jeremiah Kelly's hospital. Unluckily for them, the Medical Officer was about to be engulfed in a storm of controversy. His reputation would be ruined, and his interaction with seriously ill convicts detrimentally affected. Curiously, Kelly's downfall was triggered by his interactions with two of the island's most disorderly inmates.

---

42 *The Cork Examiner*, 6 March & 9 September 1867. See also: NAI, GPO/LB/7/1106.
43 *The Cork Examiner*, 9 August 1867. The remains of the bridge may appear as an embankment in an Admiralty map from 1888 (British Library, Maps SEC.1.(1765)).
44 NAI, GPO/LB/8/72.

15. The Doctor and the Directors

Dr Jeremiah Kelly had replaced Dr Corr as Medical Officer on Spike Island in 1856. From the beginning, he had proved himself an irksome character, prone to clashing with his superiors on a regular basis.[1] The first row erupted soon after his arrival when he had claimed that a technicality in the rules allowed him to come and go from the prison at any hour in order to practice privately on the mainland. Soon after his appointment in 1856, the Directors had expressed the view that a man charged with the care of a prison population that was then still over a thousand convicts, as well as the Island's military personnel, could not absent himself from the prison any time he felt like it and they effectively changed the rules to bar him from carrying on private practice. In 1858, another row erupted when a female servant who resided on the island with Kelly was involved in a quarrel with Chief Warder Cornelius Sporle. The row resulted in Sporle's quarters being searched on the authority of a magistrate's warrant.[2] In 1863, Kelly was involved in an altercation with the Directors regarding the proximity of his quarters to those of lower ranked officers and the slop buckets that they deposited in the corridor.[3] In early 1867, Inspector of Convict Prisons P.J. Murray (who had been appointed in 1863) intervened in another row between Kelly and Sporle's successor, Chief Warder Campbell.[4] All of this may have left a lingering resentment on Kelly's part, and that resentment was about to be exacerbated by the case of Denis Quilty and Bryan Fitzgerald.

---

1 NAI, GPO/LB/5/353 & 610. See also: NAI, GPO/LB/16/1787, GPO/LB/18/885 & 1742 and GPO/LB/22/86.
2 NAI, GPO/LB/17/1048.
3 NAI, GPO/LB/20/135.
4 NAI, GPO/LB/22/86; Murray had previously been Inspector of Reformatory Schools and died in 1872 or early 1873 (HMSO, *Directors' Report 1872*, p.7).

Denis Quilty was convicted of larceny in January 1862. He had a previous conviction for burglary and the authorities were of the opinion that he had 'lived in crime' for the previous five years. He was sentenced to 10 years' penal servitude and found himself on Spike Island by September of that year. His behaviour in Mountjoy had been satisfactory, but it took a turn for the worse when he arrived in Cork harbour. The next five years saw him being reprimanded and punished on multiple occasions for offences such as refusal to work, threatening behaviour and the possession of a knife. He found an ally in Bryan Fitzgerald from Kerry, who landed on Spike Island in 1858. He had been sentenced to 15 years' penal servitude for burglary, having had four previous convictions. He was described as being of 'violent and dangerous temper' and displayed that trait many times while in custody.

In August 1867, Fitzgerald and Quilty were involved in an incident, after which it was deemed prudent to place them in Punishment Block. That form of punishment wasn't suited to the mentality of every convict and it seems that Dr Kelly objected to it in these cases. He had the prisoners removed from the cells to the hospital. He then voiced his concerns in a letter to Governor Hay. Unfortunately, that letter does not survive. It is safe to assume, however, that the doctor had some grounds for objection. It seems that Governor Hay was particularly offended by the tone of Kelly's letter and he promptly forwarded it to the Directors. They replied as follows:

> Herewith I return the file of convict Bryan Fitzgerald, and I have read with astonishment and regret a letter addressed to you and dated the 16th instant, by the medical officer. It appears to me that either through ignorance or petulance that officer forgets your position and duties, and rights, or misun-

derstands his own. You, in separating Fitzgerald and Quilty exercised a wise and sound discretion, and had you permitted them to continue together, I should be compelled to consider you as wanting in judgement and foresight; indeed I am unable to comprehend how anybody acquainted with the character of these convicts could for a moment permit them to be together. There was no question of medical care or treatment involved in the separation of these men, but even if there were, discipline, for which you are responsible, must be observed, and although the keeping of convicts in good health is one of the duties of those entrusted with the management of a convict prison, yet in the case of <u>Refractory</u> convicts, it is not the first and paramount duty.

I deeply deplore the warped state of feeling upon certain matters connected with the discharge of his duty into which the Medical Officer appears gradually to have permitted himself to fall. In place of evincing an anxiety to work in unison with you for the good of the Public Service he appears to have adopted an injudicious and a carping tone, from which nothing but injury to the discipline of your Prison can be expected to arise. I have had to draw his attention on more than one occasion to this very unfortunate state of things, and I trust that I shall not again have to do so; if however, I am thus, through his fault, driven to the consideration of any further unpleasantness (to use a weak term), of this nature, I will, in justice to the Public Service, and to myself, lay the entire matter before the Government for their consideration and directions. This memo is to be read to the Medical Officer by the Inspector.[5]

---

5 NAI, GPO/LB/22/370. See also: NAI, GPO/LB/22/395.

This public chastisement of Kelly seemed to partially contra-
dict orders from 1860 suggesting that the doctor should attend immediately to any convict who became ill while in the Punishment
Block and that any convicts who were on the hospital list could only
be placed in the cells with the doctor's permission.[6] The chastisement
also made it perfectly clear that the maintenance of health was not
'the first and paramount duty' of the governor when dealing with re-
fractory prisoners. Instead, the Directors implied that the governor's
maintenance of discipline should take precedence when dealing with
such men.

The following year, Kelly once again intervened in the case of
Denis Quilty when the convict was being made to wear heavy chains
to prevent him from hurting himself or others. The result was a similar chastisement.[7] By 1870, Fitzgerald had left Spike Island for the
Dundrum mental asylum in Co. Dublin.[8] This is clear evidence that Dr
Kelly's assessment of these men had been correct, that they suffered
from mental illness and one of them was prone to self-harm. However, the doctor had been ordered not to interfere in the disciplining
of convicts, regardless of his opinions as to their state of mind. This
was to have a detrimental effect on the lives of some of Spike Island's
most vulnerable prisoners, one of whom was Michael Terbert.

On 3 July 1863, 19-year-old Michael Terbert, a native of
Killanummery in Co. Leitrim, was convicted of stealing sheep and
he was sent to Sligo Gaol for this offence. Shortly after completing
his sentence, he became a resident in the town's workhouse. On 26
December 1865, Michael Terbert stole eight shillings and a piece
of tobacco from a fellow workhouse inmate. As this was his second

---

6 NAI, GPO/LB/18/1525 and GPO/LB/19/562.
7 NAI, GPO/LB/22/1178.
8 Ibid. See also: NAI, Mountjoy Prison General Register Male 1867-1875, 1/11/5.

serious theft, Terbert was promptly sentenced to seven years' penal servitude. He was removed to Mountjoy on 19 January 1866. Terbert spent the usual six months of cellular confinement in Mountjoy before being sent to Spike Island. It was during those months that Mountjoy's resident doctor, James William Young, noticed that something was amiss with Terbert. The prisoner was certainly treated differently from others whilst in Mountjoy and on his departure from the Dublin prison, Young decided that he should inform his Spike Island colleague of the nature of the prisoner then committed to Kelly's care:

> Some months ago I recommended for removal from this pris-
> on Convict Michael Terbert No. 7,161. The directors did not
> think the grounds of my recommendation sufficient to justify
> them in carrying it out. I do not consider it safe to commit
> this prisoner to confinement in a cell. He has, therefore, been
> kept in hospital over three months. I am still of the opinion,
> as I was before, that although he has had no epileptic seizure
> during all this time, he is not a case for cellular discipline.[9]

Michael Terbert arrived on Spike Island on 9 June 1866. Several of the prison's staff later commented on his weak constitution, hunched back and simple ways. While Dr Kelly was aware of his Mountjoy colleague's assessment of Terbert, he considered that putting the young man to work with other prisoners on Haulbowline was appropriate. However, Terbert soon began to show signs that he was as unfit for hard labour as he had been for cellular discipline. On 19 July 1866, he was punished for his first breach of Spike Island's rules. Between then and the end of 1869, he was punished on 20 occasions for various breaches of discipline. The governor later admitted that

---

9 *The Cork Examiner*, 12 February 1870. See also: NAI, CSORP/1870/2909.

Terbert was among the most troublesome of the island's convicts.[10] His offences were often the result of his failing to live by prison disciplinary codes and his abuse of the staff who tried to impose those codes upon him. On one occasion, when asked to close up in the ranks of a work party, he retorted, 'Why should I close up? Do you want me to stand on the heels of the man before me?'[11] He was also punished for holding a lighted candle in a manner that was considered dangerous. When attempting to assess Terbert's nature, two of his offences stand out. The first was his 'picking up what the officer believed to be tobacco and swallowing it' and the second his 'laughing loudly, talking to himself and taking off and folding his clothes in the ward when forbidden to do so'.[12] These behaviours seem to reveal a man who was certainly recalcitrant, but also perhaps of unsound mind. Terbert's punishment for most of these petty offences involved his being placed in a solitary cell on various reduced diets. This action seemed to negate the whole reason of his removal from Mountjoy. If Terbert was considered 'unfit for cellular discipline', why was he so regularly confined to the Punishment Block?

When Terbert began complaining of pains in his abdomen, his complaints found little sympathy among a prison staff that had identified him as one of their more troublesome charges. Nonetheless, Dr Kelly examined him several times and by 15 January 1869 was concerned enough to exempt Terbert from 'labour on the works' for one month. Three weeks later, on 7 February, Kelly decided that Terbert's condition was indeed serious and that the convict was no longer fit for

---

10 *The Cork Examiner*, 12 February 1870. Hay admitted that there were some 50 prisoners on the island punished 'as often, or nearly so' as Terbert. This placed Terbert among the top 13.5% of the prison's most punished inmates.

11 Ibid.

12 Ibid.

hard labour. He then dispatched the Leitrim man to the oakum room, as was the norm for all infirm patients. It seems that Terbert's physical condition had seen him in the oakum room on several previous occasions and on 20 February 1870 the officer in charge of the infirm class remembered him as follows:

> With reference to Michael Terbert Regt. 12774 I beg respectfully to state for your information that I have had this prisoner in the Oakum room on several occasions during the last three years. Sent there on orders of the Medical Superintendent for periods varying from one day to one month until he was sent in permanently to work there and to be located in my ward (B1 Lower) on the improved invalid diet with white bread on the 7th February 1869. He worked in the oakum room all the time from that date, except that he was sent to the garden at his own solicitations on the 17th June last but he got discontinued there and came back after remaining only two days although he was prevented from being put to any hard work by a note of the Med. Supt. stating that he was only sending him out for the benefit of his health and more for recreation than to do any work.
>
> During the twelve months he was located and working with me he was six times in Hospital sometimes for only one day and at others for longer intervals, he was five times in cells but only three times punished. I never considered him a strong man but I was and still am of the opinion that he put on an appearance of being worse than he really was. I was led to this belief because that if he were permitted to talk and remain idle he would not cease talking at all, but so soon as he would be noticed and checked he would drop his head and in a minute or two afterwards sleep – or rather (as I believe)

pretend to do so. Also on all fine days he got a couple of hours exercise in the open air and then when I would happen to go to the door for any purpose I would observe that he was quite brisk and merry but as soon as he came in he at once let fall his under jaw and assumed the same lethargic appearance. I was also led to the belief that his health was not so bad as he would make appear from observing when changing his clothes on Saturday, that he was quite plump and fat still during this time either from the appearance of his face or his stating that he was unwell I frequently brought him under the notice of the medical officer.

As to his mental health I have never seen any indications of imbecility in his language or acts except as a funniness to do wrong without an adequate motive may always be taken as indicative of weakness of intellect. I considered him however as being of an obstinate and positive disposition that would even suffer a good deal to carry a point, even so small as to the very light work of picking oakum – because it was a forced labour.[13]

So while Terbert was a troublesome and eccentric prisoner, the warder in whose charge he was placed was unable to consider that his peculiarities were caused by anything other than a deliberate desire to misbehave. But the most serious warning of the deterioration of Terbert's mental health came three months after his admission to the oakum room.

---

13 NAI, CSORP/1870/2909.

Figure 15.1 Interior of the Punishment Block with the stairs to a mezzanine landing. There were 18 cells on the two storeys of this main wing and six more in a single-storey corridor at a right-angle to that pictured. The walls would have been whitewashed in the 19th century, but this was removed in the 1980s. (Image © authors)

Figure 15.2 Interior of a cell in the Punishment Block. The slit beneath the window at floor level was for ventilation. The walls would have been whitewashed. (Image © Simon Hill/Scirebroc)

On the night of 19 May 1869, Terbert was again admitted to Spike Island's hospital. He was complaining of pains in his chest and Dr Kelly decided that he should be observed. Kelly went on leave on 21 May and was temporarily (and briefly) replaced by Dr J.P. Doyle. At 2.00 on the morning of 30 May, Warder Patrick Hanlon was patrolling the hospital when he heard Terbert cry out loudly: 'I wish I could put an end to myself.' Shortly thereafter Hanlon entered the ward and found that Terbert had made a noose out of his handkerchief, had tied the noose around his neck and fastened the other end to part of his bed. He was in the process of pulling the handkerchief with all of his might when Hanlon interrupted him. The warder reported that the convict was 'near being choked' when he intervened.[14] Ominously, in the aftermath of the suicide attempt, Governor Hay reported that Terbert 'speaks as if he did not know what he was doing when trying to strangle himself. Says he was in great pain at the time and doesn't care what becomes of him.'[15]

The locum, Dr Doyle, kept Terbert in hospital and continued to treat him for chest pain until 13 June. When he discharged the patient though, he made the following observation:

> Convict Michael Terbert 12774 is discharged from hospital since 7am the usual notification of discharge being sent in, in his case yesterday. I am of the opinion that on account of his having a heart affliction and thereby a tendency to congestion of the lungs and other internal organs he is no subject for any kind of punishment.[16]

---

14 NAI, CSORP/1870/2909.
15 Ibid.
16 Ibid.

Accordingly, Terbert could not be confined to the cells for attempting to hang himself. Instead, Governor Hay merely reduced his classification and returned him to the oakum room. By now the authorities on the island were well aware that several of their staff considered Terbert to be mentally ill. Indeed, Governor Hay himself had referred to the convict as 'more or less weak-minded' in the immediate aftermath of the suicide attempt.[17] They were also aware that the substitute doctor had stated that this mentally challenged convict suffered from physical ailments that made him unfit for punishments. Unfortunately for Terbert, Dr Kelly returned from his period of leave and he disagreed with this assessment.

On 21 July 1869, Terbert was again dispatched to the Punishment Block, this time for idling in the oakum room. When the Resident Apothecary and Surgeon, Mr Maurice O'Connell, visited Terbert in the cells, he immediately expressed the opinion that the convict was 'labouring under heart disease' and consequently unfit for cellular punishment. O'Connell was a former hospital warder who had worked under Kelly in both Philipstown and Spike Island. He had worked his way up to Resident Apothecary having obtained the relevant qualifications. O'Connell reported his opinion to Dr Kelly, who admitted Terbert to the hospital again. Kelly found no evidence of the heart problems alluded to by O'Connell. He did detect some stomach and bowel problems and retained Terbert in hospital for a further three weeks.

Shortly after returning to the prison after this latest stint in hospital, Terbert was sentenced to 48 hours in the Punishment Block on bread and water. This time he was deemed guilty of 'leaving his

---

17 Ibid.

place in the oakum room'.[18] On 27 September, Terbert again fell foul of the prison authorities. This time he was sentenced to seven days in the cells on bread and water for referring to Dr Kelly as 'a bloody butcher'. Curiously, it was Kelly who came to his rescue when he declared Terbert medically unfit to subsist on a bread and water diet, and remitted the sentence after five days.

By 25 October 1869, Terbert was again confined to the prison's hospital. On that date he was reported for 'malingering' and for 'gross insolence to the medical officer Dr Kelly'.[19] It seems that it was during this hospital stay that some kind of physical altercation took place between the doctor and the prisoner. A prison warder later testified that he had heard that Kelly had 'throttled' Terbert after the prisoner 'broke a cup or something'. The doctor claimed that he had merely caught Terbert by the arm after the prisoner deliberately knocked over a tray of medical equipment. Two hospital warders agreed that no throttling had ever taken place.[20] Whatever had happened, the case was referred to Robert Netterville, a visiting inspector. Netterville had the power to hand out punishments in excess of those that the governor could order and he sentenced Terbert to seven days in the cells on bread and water. Two days later, Kelly visited Terbert and ordered that the convict should be returned to a normal diet. However, he did not remit the sentence any further and Terbert served the full seven days in Spike Island's cold and dreary Punishment Block.[21]

Approximately one week after leaving the cells, Terbert was admitted to hospital again. He spent five weeks under treatment, but this time Dr Kelly noted that 'liver disease' had also made an appear-

18 *The Cork Examiner*, 12 February 1870. See also: NAI, CSORP/1870/2909.
19 *The Cork Examiner*, 12 February 1870.
20 Ibid.
21 Ibid.

ance. On 13 December 1869, Terbert was discharged to the convalescent ward but was readmitted to the hospital on 20 December. This time Kelly noted that he was suffering from dropsy.[22] The condition deteriorated and Michael Terbert eventually died on 8 February 1870. A coroner's inquest was convened in Queenstown. The verdict sent shockwaves through the Irish prison system when the jury concluded that:

> We find that Michael Terbert died in hospital at Spike Island Convict Prison on the 8th February 1870, of Dropsey, he was 25 years of age and unmarried. We have also to express in the strongest terms our total disapproval of the frequent punishments he suffered in cells on Bread and Water, for several days in succession during his imprisonment in Spike Island where he had been sent in June 1866, from Mountjoy Prison for the reason that Doctor McDonnell opined that he was unfit for cellular discipline at Mountjoy and we express our condemnation of such treatment.[23]

The verdict provoked a flurry of correspondence to and from the Lord Lieutenant's office. Everybody sought to extricate themselves from any responsibility for Terbert's treatment and death. Kelly sought shelter behind the post-mortem reports of colleagues on Haulbowline and in Queenstown. They concluded that the examination was incomplete but that liver disease, and not heart trouble, appeared to be the cause of death. Governor Hay and Inspector Netterville each pointed out that any punishment they had meted out to Terbert could

---

22 Dropsy was a 19th-century term for swelling of soft tissue due to accumulated fluid, nowadays referred to as oedema.
23 NAI, CSORP/1870/2909.

have been stopped immediately by Dr Kelly. So if Terbert's heart disease was exacerbated by his time in the punishment cells, it was the doctor's fault and not theirs. Nobody was taking responsibility and the civil administration in Dublin Castle wanted greater clarity.

On 26 February 1870, the Chief Secretary ordered an official inquiry into the incident. The results exonerated most of his officials. They found that Terbert was 'stated to have been of a low order of intellect, but neither imbecile nor idiotic'. It was found that the post-mortem had not been able to reach definitive conclusions as to the cause of death. In a seemingly contradictory sentence, the inquiry was nonetheless happy to conclude that the death was caused by liver disease. Perhaps the most interesting aspect of the inquiry was its investigation of McDonnell's certification of Terbert as unfit for cellular confinement. On that subject, they concluded that:

> ... the cause of Terbert's reception into Mountjoy Prison hospital was this; it was Dr McDonnell's invariable practice, when he had a reason to suspect a prisoner of a tendency to fits or insanity, to remove such a prisoner to the hospital for observation, and also for exemption from the cellular discipline of the prison; M Terbert stated he was an epileptic, and his appearance somewhat confirming his statement, he was removed to hospital for observation. His removal to Spike Island was, after a time, recommended by Dr McDonnell, as his case could be closely watched there without detention in hospital, or exemption from employment...[24]

The inquiry reaffirmed that McDonnell had considered Terbert unfit for cellular discipline because of a suspicion that he was

---

24 Ibid.

prone to epileptic fits and needed observation. Yet the inquiry went on to make a rather tenuous distinction between cellular discipline (such as the regime at Mountjoy, characterised as it was by single-cell confinement) and cellular punishment, as was inflicted in the Punishment Block on Spike Island. It seems that the continuous nature of cellular discipline was what McDonnell opposed in Terbert's case. As cellular punishments would normally only endure for periods of a week or less, McDonnell 'did not think he would have objected to Terbert's being punished in a cell if he had misconducted himself while at Mountjoy prison'. It seems contradictory that McDonnell felt that a suspected epileptic should not be confined on his own for long periods but that the same prisoner could spend an entire week alone in a cell. The inquiry did not press the matter.

Dr Kelly was found to be a competent medical practitioner who did not lack in skill. However, his bedside manner was questioned when the inquiry concluded that:

> ... his manner was not so temperate or even with the prisoner as it should have been, but there does not appear to have been such harshness as to justify his removal, a very grave caution as to his conduct in future in this respect and also as to his non interference in discipline matters, would, we believe meet the case; we are influenced in making this suggestion by the fact that many of the Prison Officers spoke of his treatment and rudeness to them in illness; we feel bound also to conclude that Dr Kelly does not appear to have shown that disposition to work harmoniously with the other Superior Prison Officers, which is to be desired from an officer in his position.[25]

25 Ibid.

The Chief Secretary went much further than that. His office wrote to the Directors of Convict Prisons and noted that the doctor's conduct was 'far from satisfactory'. The Chief Secretary continued:

> It is evident that the principal officers of the establishment consider that Dr Kelly's manner towards the prisoners is not what it ought to be, & that many of them have complained, & with apparent reason of his roughness ... Dr Kelly's administration of baths considered to be of a penal character by the prisoners – and also by the Inspector and Governor – for they were ordered to be discontinued upon the officers becoming acquainted with their nature – is an illustration of his feelings towards the prisoners, which is very detrimental to the service and his own position in it. It is scarcely credible how such a state of things could have been continued without the immediate knowledge of the Governor.
>
> It appears that serious charges have been made (although not officially) by the Rev Lyons to the Governor from time to time with regard to Dr Kelly's treatment of prisoners. H.E. considers that any serious statement, involving, as this matter did, the good discipline of the establishment, should not have been received otherwise than officially and that greater watchfulness over Dr Kelly's manner & general demeanour towards the prisoners, on the part of the Inspector & the Governor should have been the immediate result. It appears to have been considered that the medical officer was almost irresponsible for his conduct in the absence of distinct charges; and that gentleman evidently fails to realise that there is superior authority to himself on the island.
>
> ... Persons conversant with prisoners are aware that there are some who will malinger & scheme. An allowance may be made for a Medical Officer's manner in his endeavour to

defeat such attempts; but it is his duty to take care that his desire (or as Dr Kelly terms it, his <u>zeal</u>) to detect impetration does not lead him to a general suspicion of all cases brought before him.

... His Excellency desires that you will point out to the Medical Officer the responsibility of his position and the importance which is attached to an impression on the minds of the prisoners that he is kind and humane towards them and state that the Government will not consider any person qualified for such an appointment whose general practice does not produce that impression.

Mr Hay's statement that his remarks were not well received by Dr Kelly and that he therefore refrained from making them, shows that the latter has mistaken his position & failed to realise the subordination of his authority to that of the Governor of the prison, who also appears to labour under some misconception upon this point. His Excellency desires that you will inform Mr Hay that for the future he is to consider it his duty to notice any point or shortcoming which may be calculated to act detrimentally to the establishment which he governs.[26]

The Chief Secretary was making it perfectly clear that he was deeply dissatisfied with the medical practice, and regulation of same, on Spike Island. He would not tolerate any further abdication of responsibility on the part of the governor and pointedly informed Dr Kelly that if his bedside manner did not improve, he might find himself without a post. The Chief Secretary also agreed with the inquiry report that an external medical examiner should visit Spike Island on a regular basis. It is a noteworthy tacit admission of Spike Island's

26 NAI, CSORP/1870/88841.

difficulty with mentally ill convicts that one of the authors of that report was the Inspector of Lunatic Asylums, Dr George Hatchell.[27] The entire senior staff had now had their cards marked. Unfortunately for them, worse was to follow.

Patrick Lambe arrived on Spike Island on 22 April 1871, some 11 months after the Terbert controversy had subsided. After an initial examination, Dr Kelly certified the 24-year-old prisoner as fit for 'light labour' only. On 11 May, Kelly seemed to think that Lambe's condition was improved enough for him to be recertified as fit for 'ordinary labour'. A few weeks later though, Lambe presented at the hospital again, this time complaining of palpitations. Dr Kelly put him back on light labour for a month and in June, Lambe returned to Haulbowline for quarry labour and excavation of mud. In August he complained of palpitations again and Kelly placed him in the oakum room as a precautionary measure. After a few days, Lambe requested that he be returned to the Haulbowline works, where a larger gratuity could be earned. On 14 October, he again complained of palpitations but was returned to work after examination. When he presented with the same symptoms a week later, he was kept under observation until 1 November. Lambe then returned to ordinary labour, working in the quarry at his own request. In late January 1872, he was returned to the oakum room after once again complaining of palpitations. Finally, on 30 January his condition worsened and he was readmitted to the hospital. He died of complications brought on by typhus fever on 10 February 1872.[28]

The day after Lambe's death, the coroner arrived on the island to carry out an inquest. To his surprise, he found that Lambe

---

27 NAI, GPO/LB/23/907.
28 NAI, CSORP/1872/9182; HMSO, *Directors' Report 1872.*

had already been buried. The prison authorities later claimed that the coroner had stated on the previous day that no inquest would be necessary. If such a statement had been made, the coroner had evidently changed his mind over night; he ordered that the body be exhumed. The inquest was perplexed that a prisoner initially certified as being fit for only light labour could suddenly be returned to ordinary labour three weeks later and issued the following verdict:

> Patrick Lambe died at Spike Island on the 10th February 1872, from suppression of urine consequent on a febrile attack. He was 25 years of age and unmarried.
>
> We are of the opinion that having regard to the original medical certificate that his work should be light, that he was not fit for the heavy work to which he was put subsequently, and his repeated complaints of illness show that the original certificate was correct though changed on the 11th May by Dr Kelly, and in June by Dr Falkner, showing he was fit for ordinary labour.[29]

The verdict was forwarded to the Chief Secretary along with a statement from Captain J. Barlow, by now promoted to Director of Convict Prisons in Ireland, to the effect that 'the responsibility if any, of the deceased being placed at labor, for which his state of health rendered him unfit, rests entirely with the medical officer of the prison, Dr Kelly and his substitute during his absence, Dr Falkner'.[30] Barlow didn't hesitate to blame Kelly, and that lack of restraint might have been motivated by *The Cork Examiner*'s reporting of Kelly's remarks

---

29 Ibid.
30 NAI, GPO/LB/9/283. It is worth noting that questions had previously been asked of Kelly's certification of some convicts as fit for hard labour (NAI, GPO/LB/23/241).

during the inquest. When asked about cellular punishment, the doctor was reported to have said: 'I have nothing to do with punishment, there is quite enough of that without me.' As Director of the convict system, Captain Barlow was certainly annoyed at that remark and made his feelings on the matter known.[31] Based on the inquest's verdict, the Chief Secretary ordered an investigation into the circumstances surrounding the death of Patrick Lambe. Due to what he claimed were pressures of work in an understaffed Convict Department, Director Barlow did not report back until June. When he did so, he made a joint report with Dr George Hatchell, the Inspector of Lunatic Asylums.

Barlow and Hatchell exonerated Spike Island's medical staff. Their conclusion came as a result of evidence that hadn't been produced at the inquest. They explained that Lambe's initial certification for 'light labour' was as a result of his having a whitlow on his hand when he first arrived on Spike.[32] Thus, when Kelly later certified that the prisoner was fit for ordinary labour, he was not contradicting an earlier diagnosis but rather acting as a result of Lambe's whitlow being healed. Hatchell and Barlow concluded:

> Having made careful inquiry into his treatment medical and otherwise whilst at Spike Island Prison we feel bound to report that there does not appear to us to be any ground for the supposition that his treatment with respect to his labour or otherwise in any way affected or accelerated his death.[33]

On this occasion, Dr Kelly was found to have done no wrong

---

31 NAI, GPO/LB/24/581.
32 A whitlow is an inflammation of the deeper tissues of a finger or toe, especially around the nail, usually producing suppuration.
33 NAI, CSORP/1872/7989.

and, in the wake of the Terbert affair, he may have breathed a deep sigh of relief. Nevertheless his name had now been connected with medical negligence on two occasions in the space of as many years. The sudden appearance of evidence regarding a whitlow on Lambe's hand, some four months after the inquest, is certainly suspicious. It is possible that it was also regarded as suspicious in 1872. But during those four months of delay, Kelly had been at the centre of yet another controversy. That began less than a month after Lambe had died, with the death of another convict, Patrick Mahony.

Mahony was reported to be a habitual thief who was serving a seven-year sentence for larceny (and should not be confused with the convict of the same name who had attacked Warder Michael Reilly with a razor in 1864). Although his previous behaviour in prison had been good, the medical authorities on Spike Island developed an opinion that he was 'malingering'. Although he also received frequent treatments in the hospital, Mahony was accused of malingering and placed in the Punishment Block on several occasions. The result of his regular confinement was the further deterioration of his health. However, neither Dr Kelly nor the Resident Apothecary, Maurice O'Connell, seem to have noted this and on several occasions when Mahony presented himself as ill, he was not even treated. The convict eventually lost all faith that those who were supposed to attend to his illness could do anything other than accuse him of malingering. As a result, he appears to have come to welcome confinement in the Punishment Block. On one occasion, when unable to work, he expressed the wish that the warders should take him directly to the cells and not bother calling the doctor. Some two weeks before his death, he presented himself at the hospital. Instead of retaining him there, as was normal in cases of serious illness, the doctor insisted that he return to his ward every night for the first eight days of his treatment. Unlike the prisoners' wards, the hospital was heated by a fire all day long. Mahony complained of having to leave its warmth and head out into a cold February evening, and then trying to sleep in an unheated ward. His complaints were ignored until eventually, on 24 February 1872, Mahony was admitted to hospital on a full-time basis. By 2 March, it was obvious that he was dying when the authorities allowed the convict's mother to visit him in the last hours of his life.[34] He died on 5 March and the cause was listed as heart disease.[35]

This time the coroner adjourned the inquest from Spike Island to Queenstown in order to obtain the opinions of medical men unconnected with the convict establishment. Having obtained such opinion, he wrote:

> I have no doubt upon my mind but that the Medical gentlemen at Spike Island are influenced, to a considerable extent, by the necessity that exists, of maintaining discipline, and of exercising very great caution, in order to prevent convicts from evading labour, by pretending they are ill when they are not so in reality, but as this feeling may be carried too far, as I believe it was in this instance, those placed over the Doctors may order them to be less rigorous, and more slow in pronouncing a man free from disease, because its symptoms are not apparent.[36]

A few days later, Dr Kelly was hit by another crisis when convict James Connell died. When the severity of Connell's punishments was raised by the coroner, Dr Kelly stated that he didn't have the pow-

34 NAI, GPO/LB/24/605 & 606.
35 HMSO, *Directors' Report 1872.*
36 NAI, CSORP/1872/4127.

er to reprieve a convict from punishment. He pointed out that only the governor had the power to do so. In stating this publicly, he again aggravated the Director of Convict Prisons, Captain Barlow. The Director pointed out that Kelly was dealing in technicalities and that any recommendation of his would have been implemented. He went further in opining that the medical officer's publicly implying that the prison authorities were disposed to treating convicts harshly, regardless of their medical condition, went 'far to prove his unfitness for the very important situation held by him'.[37] Kelly was on borrowed time.

For the fourth time in two years, medical negligence was alleged to have occurred on Spike Island. In truth, the doctors were hampered by their profession's rudimentary understanding of some common ailments and by their constant attendance on a specific category of prisoner. That category was generally referred to as 'weak minded' and it consisted of prisoners with various forms of mental illnesses and handicaps. This category of prisoner had been removed from Spike Island along with most of the invalid class in 1855, but the closure of Philipstown in 1862 saw their return to the harbour prison.[38] In anticipation of the arrival of mentally ill prisoners, Spike Island had prepared by fitting up a special padded cell in the Punishment Block, but otherwise little was done to meet the special needs of these men.[39] Terbert's death had highlighted the need for a greater understanding of, and an environment more suited to, these prisoners. However, as Terbert was never officially considered 'weak minded', despite manifesting several characteristics that should have qualified him for that category, the problem was allowed to fester.

---

37 NAI, GPO/LB/9/320. See also: GPO/LB/24/694.
38 NAI, GPO/LB/9/260.
39 NAI, GPO/LB/19/966. The padded cell was located in number one cell in the Punishment Block.

Yet Terbert's death did seem to spur some action on this issue. In July 1871, a full return containing names, crimes, sentences and remarks on each of Spike Island's 47 weak-minded convicts was forwarded to the Chief Secretary's office.[40] By October it was clear that Governor Hay wasn't entirely convinced of his medical officer's judgement regarding this class. Knowing that two of the 47, John Doyle and Francis Donnelly, were due for release that month, the governor approached Dr Kelly to ascertain whether or not the men were 'capable of finding their way to their destinations when released or whether warders should be sent in charge of them'. Kelly assured the governor that the men 'were fit to take charge of themselves'.[41] However, Hay remained unconvinced and brought the matter to the attention of Director Barlow. Having observed the men and made further inquiries, Barlow decided to call in an expert in such cases, Dr W. Townshend, the visiting physician in Cork's Lunatic Asylum. Townshend certified that the men were indeed unfit for release. He declared Doyle to be a person 'of weak intellect and quite unfit to be set at large as he is incapable and unfit to take care of himself'. Donnelly was 'a lunatic of the idiotic class and incapable'.[42] Donnelly returned to his Belfast home accompanied by a warder, while Doyle was accompanied to Enniscorthy.[43]

Having seen Townshend effectively overrule Spike Island's medical officer, Director Barlow wrote to the Chief Secretary requesting that an outside medical officer with expertise in mental health be allowed to examine all of Spike Island's weak-minded convicts. The Chief Secretary agreed and Dr George Hatchell was again dispatched

---

40 NAI, CSORP/1874/4814.
41 NAI, CSORP/1871/19144.
42 Ibid.
43 NAI, Mountjoy Prison Convict Classification 1857-1866, 1/11/24 & 1/11/23.

to report on the situation on the island. Hatchell performed his inspection in December, when he found that two of the convicts then held among the weak-minded class were not fit for prison discipline and should be dispatched to the asylum for the criminally insane in Dundrum, Co. Dublin. He also found three convicts whom he considered were not weak-minded and should be returned to the general population. Of the remaining mentally ill prisoners, Hatchell reported:

> I consider the remaining twenty six to be unfit for treatment in a prison so constituted as Spike Island. Some of those are of a violent and uncontrollable temper, and have been so frequently punished, that prolonged punishment could not be carried out consistently with safety to their health. Also several of these are, and have been for a considerable time unfit for punishment from heart and other diseases, whilst of the rest, although not fit objects for the central asylum, they are to a great extent irresponsible.
>
> The convicts of the last two classes are well aware that owing to frequent exemption from punishment they can annoy their fellow prisoners, idle at the works, and set discipline at defiance.
>
> The twenty six convicts as alone mentioned should in my opinion be removed to a prison where they could be kept apart from their fellow prisoners, and where at no time could their bad conduct interfere with or influence the well conducted convicts.[44]

In the wake of Hatchell's report, the Chief Secretary immediately sought new accommodation for Spike Island's mentally chal-

---

44 NAI, CSORP/1871/484.

lenged prisoners. Mountjoy was considered as an option, as was the intermediate prison at Lusk. It was also proposed that separate, purpose-built accommodation be erected on Spike Island, outside of Fort Westmoreland. However, officials from all these locations had very strong opinions about where weak-minded convicts should not be held. The debate seemed to grind to a halt in February 1872. Then, on 14 May 1872, the Chief Secretary requested that Director Barlow and Director Murray examine the feasibility of reopening the old Smithfield depot in Dublin for the detention of weak-minded convicts. The Chief Secretary's motivation seems obvious. He wrote his request the day after convict John Mahony killed his fellow inmate, Patrick O'Neill.[45]

John Mahony had been detained on Spike Island since 1868. He had been removed from Mountjoy on medical grounds before he had completed the cellular component of his sentence. Although this was his first time on the island, Mahony was no stranger to prisons. He had 21 previous convictions and had been sentenced to 15 years' transportation for larceny in 1855. He had served some of that sentence in Philipstown, but his Convict Classification record clearly noted that he was removed from that prison and placed in the asylum at Dundrum, Co. Dublin, on 24 June 1862. Having been released from the asylum, Mahony did not evade the criminal justice system for very long as he was convicted of receiving stolen goods in July 1868. By July 1871, Mahony had been officially placed among the 'weak-minded' class on Spike Island.[46]

Although Spike Island's officials were aware of Mahony's past mental health problems, his behaviour while on the island was

45 NAI, CSORP/1872/7188.
46 NAI, Dublin Bridewell Prison (Richmond) General Register 1864-1883, 1/13/46; NAI, CSORP/1874/4814.

exemplary and he was soon part of the A class. As such, he laboured with all of the other convicts at Haulbowline, now under the steward-ship of a warder foreman specially transferred from Chatham Royal Dockyards, downriver from London.[47] On 13 May 1872, Mahony was employed in a quarry on Haulbowline. There were five other prison-ers in the gang in which he worked. At about 5.20pm the prisoners were involved in attaching a sling to a stone in the quarry. One of them, Patrick O'Neill, had lain on his side to see to the fastenings. Suddenly, without any warning, Mahony struck O'Neill a vicious blow over the head with a hammer. A second blow was struck be-fore the warders and some of the other prisoners were able to restrain Mahony. O'Neill was taken to the hospital where he lingered for a little more than a week before dying there on 21 May 1872. Mahony was immediately placed in the Punishment Block and subsequently charged with murder. He made no comment upon hearing the charge, stating that he 'had plenty to say, but would not say it now'.[48] On 23 July, Mahony was tried at the Cork Assizes. The verdict recorded was 'Not Guilty on the grounds of insanity'. He was returned to the Cork County Gaol, from where he was subsequently dispatched back to the Dundrum asylum.[49]

While O'Neill lay dying in Spike Island's hospital, he shared that space with Michael Hayes from Co. Mayo, who had been con-victed of theft. Hayes died just as it became apparent that O'Neill would not recover. More controversy followed when the coroner ruled that Hayes's death was caused by 'disease of the heart accel-erated by harsh treatment'.[50] This was the fifth accusation of medical

47 NAI, GPO/LB/24/299.
48 NAI, CSORP/1872/11113.
49 NAI, Cork County Gaol General Register 1870-1876, 1/8/50.
50 NAI, CSORP/1872/7711.

negligence in two-and-a-half years. Dr Kelly drove the final nail into the coffin of his own career when he accused convict witness John Gildea of 'rascality' when Gildea's testimony at the inquest wasn't to his liking. The convict denied the accusation. Resident Apothecary O'Connell reported that he had heard Dr Kelly's remark, but that the convict was not intended to hear it. Unfortunately for Kelly, the convict did hear it and seemed to imply that he feared repercussions when he asked the coroner to protect him from Kelly. A week later, Director Barlow effectively ended Dr Kelly's career when he wrote to Dublin Castle:

> The conduct of Dr Kelly in speaking of a convict when under examination was most improper, the evidence of the convicts examined appears to me to show a harsh and irritating manner on the part of Dr Kelly to the convict Hayes and taking into consideration former cases in which Dr Kelly has been concerned, I feel bound to recommend very strongly that he be removed from the service. The prisoners have no confidence in Dr Kelly's treatment and I should add here that this feeling on the part of the convicts is not the general disposition shown by them to a medical man, on the contrary in three different instances when, in Dr Kelly's absence medical gentlemen acted for him, whilst there were far fewer exemptions from labour or punishments on medical grounds, the convicts were satisfied and the working and discipline of the prison much improved.
>
> Until Dr Kelly is removed, I cannot hope that things will be as they should be in Spike Island prison: perhaps as Dr Kelly has good service, he might be permitted to retire.[51]

---

51 NAI, GPO/LB/9/374.

Barlow had already taken offence when he interpreted Kelly's remarks at James Connell's inquest as implying unnecessary cruelty on the part of the prison regime. Barlow accepted that Kelly's comparatively recent lapses in judgement might have been explained by his ill health. Having explained that the doctor may never have fully recovered from an illness which lasted several months during 1860, the Director suggested that 'failing health may have been the cause of the unsatisfactory manner in which several convicts appear to have been treated by him'.[52] Dr Kelly was quietly retired from the convict service in August 1872.[53] Although Apothecary O'Connell applied for the post of Medical Officer, he did not get it. Indeed, the apothecary post was abolished and a new man took up residence as both apothecary and doctor. Spike Island's controversial medical department was entirely cleansed.[54]

There is sufficient evidence to suggest that Kelly was an arrogant and argumentative man who hadn't endeared himself to Spike Island's management while also managing to isolate himself from its warders.[55] But it is also clear that he had been expected to do a job that was almost impossible. He was under constant pressure to root out 'malingerers' while caring for potentially violent and mentally unstable men whose conditions were not fully understood. Five years before he was retired, he had been severely chastised for interfering with the governor's disciplinary procedures. Yet, after the deaths of several convicts, Director Barlow and Governor Hay had pointed out that Dr Kelly could overrule them on convict discipline, if he felt that convicts' punishments were detrimental to their health. Indeed,

---

52 NAI, GPO/LB/9/413. See also: NAI, GPO/LB/18/952 & 1955.
53 NAI, GPO/LB/9/438. See also: HMSO, *Directors' Report 1872*.
54 NAI, GPO/LB/9/520.
55 NAI, GPO/LB/23/668 & 674.

Barlow, just a few months before the doctor was retired, was still complaining of Kelly's tendency to exempt convicts from labour on medical grounds.[56] In reality, Dr Kelly had been at war with Spike Island's management for several years, and like Deputy Governor George Downes and Rev. Charles Bernard Gibson before him, it was a war he ultimately lost and paid for with his career.

The doctor's daily routine was fraught with difficulty. There were prisoners who were most certainly, and often dangerously, physically or mentally ill. Yet there were also prisoners who feigned such illnesses, which placed a huge burden on Dr Kelly to distinguish between the two and make the right decisions in highly pressured circumstances. Those who feigned illness often had very good reason to do so. An example of one such character is provided by the peculiar case of convict John Cuddy.

---

56 NAI, GPO/LB/9/374.

16. Ribbonmen and Whiteboys

John Cuddy arrived on Spike Island in November 1870. He was approximately 36 years old and had worked as a farm labourer near his birthplace: Derrymore, near Kinnegad in Co. Westmeath. Like most of the labouring class, Cuddy was a Roman Catholic, and also like many of his class by the 1870s, he was fully literate. At 5ft 6½in. (1.7m), he was neither small nor tall. His teeth were described as 'uneven' and the fact that he was missing two fingers from his right hand was also recorded (Fig. 16.1). Other than those slight physical peculiarities, there didn't seem to be anything different about John Cuddy. And yet, nearly a century-and-a-half later, we now know that he might have been hiding his involvement in an infamous crime.

Figure 16.1 Convict John Cuddy, in civilian attire. (Image © courtesy of National Archives of Ireland)

On 1 March 1870, Cuddy was convicted of stealing a gun from a private dwelling. His crime was a manifestation of growing tensions between landlords and their tenants in counties Meath and Westmeath. Tenants were arming themselves and several murders and attempted murders had occurred. The authorities were well aware that Cuddy's offence was connected to this violence, as they had clearly declared his crime a 'Whiteboy Offence' and sentenced him to five years' penal servitude.[1]

---

1 NAI, Mountjoy Prison General Register Male 1867-1875, 1/11/5 and Dublin Bridewell Prison (Richmond) General Register 1864-1883, 1/13/46.

The agrarian agitators of counties Meath and Westmeath tended to refer to themselves as 'Ribbonmen' rather than the older term 'Whiteboys', which was still preferred by the authorities.

Cuddy's first year on Spike Island was uneventful. He laboured on Haulbowline, as all of the able-bodied convicts did at that time. After 12 months of this routine, something began to change. Cuddy lost his appetite and consequently began to lose condition. On 10 November 1871, Cuddy was admitted to the prison hospital. Five days later, Dr Kelly wrote:

> Convict John Cuddy was admitted to hospital on the 10th instant suffering from total loss of appetite and loss of flesh; he is in a very nervous state, and there is decided evidence of mental disturbance. He is quite unfit for removal from hospital and I consider it necessary to have additional medical aid in his case, viz Dr Townshend Cork.[2]

In the aftermath of the Terbert affair, Dr Kelly was clearly unable or unwilling to act alone in the cases of intellectually impaired convicts. Cuddy would remain in the 'weak-minded' class while the medical officers examined his case. During this time it is likely that he became well-acquainted with Patrick Mahony, the convict who was accused of malingering and whose death in 1872 was to contribute to the downfall of Dr Kelly. Mahony visited the hospital on numerous occasions in 1870 and had one four-day stay there during Cuddy's convalescence.[3] However, Cuddy may well have had more on his mind than making friends. Unlike the sickly Mahony, Cuddy's illness seemed to come at a very opportune time for the convict.

2 NAI, CSORP/1872/948.
3 NAI, CSORP/1872/4127.

Almost two years before John Cuddy was first arrested, a shocking murder had occurred on 15 April 1868 near the Co. Westmeath village of Killucan. On that evening, a local landlord and Deputy Lieutenant of the county, Mr Howard Fetherstonhaugh (b.1819), was making his way from Mullingar railway station to his home at Bracklyn House (Fig. 16.2). During the journey, Mr Fetherstonhaugh and his coachman were ambushed at a location known locally as Knocksbaden Hill and the landlord was shot dead. Newspapers all over the country later reported the crime and speculated on the motive for the killing. Almost a week later, one of them left the following account:

> It is now a well ascertained fact that the deceased gentleman had for some time before he was murdered rendered himself obnoxious to a certain section of his tenantry, because, it is stated, he had raised their rents. A number of them belonging to a particular townland presented themselves at Bracklyn House on the preceding Monday for the purpose of discharging their liabilities, but Mr Fetherson-H declined to receive less rent than that which he had on a former occasion intimated to them they should pay. A few of them consented to undertake the increased responsibility imposed upon them, while the majority refused. It is generally believed that the murder was perpetrated, not by a stranger, but by some person or persons well acquainted with the fact that Mr Fetherson was expected to return home that night from Dublin, in addition to being aware that the horse was a very restive animal, and that the coachman would walk him up the hill at a slow pace. The assassin lay down in some brushwood that grew on the side of the hill, and

awaited the arrival of his unsuspecting victim. When the car reached the highest point at this part of the road, the murderer, who is supposed to have previously divested himself of his shoes, emerged from his place of concealment unobserved, and, stealing round by the back of the vehicle, discharged the weapon he carried with fatal effect. After receiving the contents of the blunderbuss, the deceased articulated merely a single observation, and died instantaneously, falling over heavily on his servant, who sat beside him. Fulham, the coachman who had been twenty two years in his master's employment, proceeded to the house of a man who lived within a few yards of where the occurrence took place, and requested his son to give some assistance in conveying Mr. Fetherston to his residence, but this was bluntly denied him. A like result followed in giving a similar appeal to one of the deceased's tenants ...

Although the actual perpetrator of this crime has not yet been detected, the inquiries which have been officially made leave little doubt that it is the result of a local Ribbon organisation, and that the murderer was the emissary of others who employed him to commit the crime. There is no doubt that Mr Fetherston - Haugh, who acted as his own agent, had some difference with some of his tenants, and to this may probably be attributed his murder. A report that more than one man had taken part in the outrage is incorrect.[4]

The prime suspect was a man called Thomas Coughlan, who had fled to America not long after the event. A few years later, a lo-

---

4 *The Belfast News-Letter*, 21 April 1868. Text was reportedly taken from *The Irish Times*.

cal man called Luke Peppard, whose family were heavily involved in agrarian violence, informed a policeman that Coughlan was the murderer.[5] Peppard had met the policeman while they were both resident in Mullingar Lunatic Asylum. The County Inspector went to interview Peppard in the asylum and, having ascertained from the doctor that the inmate knew wrong from right and was 'perfectly clear in memory and understanding', he took the following statement:

> In 1868 I lived with my father Christopher Peppard who has two acres of land at Croboy, County Meath. I joined the Ribbon Society through fear like many others. William Dixon (Blacksmith) of Croboy was a leader. A cousin of mine Laurence Peppard was more implicated in the society of these boys than I was, and could give more information than I can. The intention to murder Mr Fetherston was talked of for nearly twelve months before it took place. After it occurred I heard from several persons (my cousin and Dixon amongst them) that Mr Fetherson was shot by Thomas Coughlin of Anniscannan, and that John Cuddy of Derrymore was present – assisting him. About three weeks after the murder there was a collection among the Ribbonmen generally to send Coughlin to America. I gave William Dixon a shilling towards the fund. Coughlan went to America shortly after, and was, I heard, living in New York. He was not a tenant of Mr Fetherston's but was married to a girl named Corcoran – whose family were tenants of his ... I have nothing but hearsay as to Mr Fetherston's murder, but it was well known the two men I have named did the act.[6]

---

5 NAI, CSORP/1871/19748.
6 NAI, CSORP/1871/17942.

John Cuddy was now implicated in one of the most serious agrarian crimes that had occurred in many a year. On the receipt of Peppard's information, a detective was immediately dispatched to Spike Island to take a statement from Cuddy, but the latter refused to make any comment.[7]

Figure 16.2 Bracklyn House, Delvin, Co. Westmeath, home of Howard Fetherstonhaugh, who was murdered in 1868. (Photograph by Shannon Images © National Inventory of Architectural Heritage and courtesy of the Murphy family)

On 9 November 1871, the magistrate for Co. Meath wrote to the Under-Secretary requesting that Cuddy be 'brought to Dublin and confronted with' Luke Peppard. By a remarkable coincidence, or perhaps the intervention of a sympathetic and loose-lipped prison warder, Cuddy presented himself in Spike Island's hospital on the very next day. He could not be moved to Dublin. Peppard had to be returned to his home in Westmeath, where he claimed that his life was endangered by his family's suspicions regarding his trips to Dublin.

---

7 NAI, CSORP/1871/18599.

On correspondence related to Cuddy's illness an unidentified official wrote: 'It may be that Cuddy's illness is brought on by apprehension that he will be prosecuted for the murder.'[8]

Cuddy's illness might indeed have been a result of his uneasiness about a forthcoming prosecution. Its timing might also have been very convenient. But even if there was initially just the pretence of being unwell, a serious illness appears to have developed. By early December 1871, Director Barlow was able to inform the Under-Secretary that Cuddy 'had been very seriously ill of fever', but that he was now 'recovering, and will be convalescent in about a fortnight probably'. By this time, it seems that the prison authorities had disregarded Dr Kelly's earlier 'evidence of mental disturbance' and concluded that 'he has not been insane, nor has he shown symptoms of insanity, at any time'.[9] The net seemed to be closing around John Cuddy and the confrontation with his accuser was no longer avoidable. However, Cuddy was a more robust character than his accusers might have imagined and was not about to be intimidated.

Cuddy was transferred back to Mountjoy on 15 January 1872.[10] A few days later, the resident magistrate for Westmeath, accompanied by the inspector and sub-inspector of police as well as by Luke Peppard, went to confront Cuddy. If they had hoped for a confession or to turn Cuddy into one of their informants, they were to be disappointed. The magistrate later reported:

> I have to report that accompanied by Inspector Kirwan and Sub Inspector Harvey, I had an interview with convict "John

---

8 NAI, CSORP/1871/20079.
9 NAI, CSORP/1871/21142.
10 NAI, Mountjoy Prison General Register Male 1867-1875, 1/13/46. See also: NAI, GPO/LB/9/257.

Cuddy" at Mountjoy Prison on yesterday. Altho' I had him paraded with other prisoners (about his own height) he was at once identified by "Luke Peppard." Mr Harvey having subsequently informed him (most judiciously) that only information of a reliable character which he might give would in all probability benefit him. I questioned him in reference to the several statements made by "Luke Peppard" ... all of which he seemed perfectly oblivious.

As I could not obtain any information from him, I closed the enquiry, explaining to him, that he could communicate with the Governor should he wish to make any statement.[11]

John Cuddy was not the kind of man that would make any statement. Unlike Luke Peppard, he seemed to consider loyalty to his co-conspirators of utmost importance. Peppard returned to his home and to his hostile and suspicious family in Croboy, Co. Meath, while John Cuddy returned to Spike Island. By now he was plotting further mischief but while he did so, the island found itself at the centre of yet another controversy.

On 22 March 1872, *The Cork Examiner* accused the prison's administration of assisting in the operation of a ferryboat monopoly to and from Spike Island:

Spike Island has been frequently brought under the notice of the public lately in connection with matters of a very serious kind. An affair of apparently a very trivial nature has been brought under our attention. There is a Ferry Boat plying between Spike Island and Queenstown which is the monopoly of one or two officials of the prison. The garrison has set up

---

11 NAI, CSORP/1872/1100.

a Ferry Boat also. Now it appears that if the wife or son of a prison warder happens to travel by the garrison boat he will be fined, and the consequence is that the people have often to wait for hours together.

Now is not this funny? And yet the thing is sanctioned by the Director of Convict Prisons in Ireland! Straws show how the wind blows and very trifling indications will often point to the existence of grave faults in the principles of a system.[12]

The Chief Secretary immediately ordered an explanation from his subordinates in the prison service. Governor Hay and Director Barlow explained that many of the prison warders' wives and families now lived on the island and needed to commute to Queenstown on a regular basis. Those warders with wives and families on the mainland also had great need for a regular service to take them to and from their homes. With these needs in mind, the warders had been given permission to establish a regular ferry service in 1860. They purchased a boat and operated it themselves for a period, but soon found it more convenient to have a contractor in Queenstown own and operate the boat on the understanding that its hours of operation would be dictated by the prison authorities.[13] Soon the ferry was transporting all of the island's residents, as well as those who had business there, to and from the mainland. In 1865, the authorities expressed concern at this practice and stated that 'the ferry boat was first started for the use of the officers and their families ... and ought not to be used as a ferry boat for the general public'.[14] The Directors later rescinded this concern and by 1872 members of the public with business on the island

12 *The Cork Examiner*, 22 March 1872 in NAI, CSORP/1872/4694.
13 NAI, GPO/LB/9/324.
14 NAI, GPO/LB/21/88.

were regularly using the boat.[15] The ferry was contracted for regular hours of arrival and departure and a warder was placed on the pier in order to supervise its comings and goings and to ensure that no unauthorised person entered, or exited, the island prison.

Shortly before *The Cork Examiner* ran its piece, the military contracted a second ferry for their purposes. Governor Hay found this action objectionable. The military's ferry was entirely under their control and as a result, it could arrive at the pier at any time, day or night. On some occasions, it had landed passengers after the pier warder had retired, thereby compromising the prison's security. Governor Hay made it clear that the military ferry took 'all comers notwithstanding orders', thereby removing any monopoly enjoyed by the boat contracted by the warders. He also stated that the 'prison officials can one and all avail of any island or Queenstown boat without ... hindrance. So that in no sense is the ferry boat a monopoly.' He neglected to mention that Barlow had ordered that all warders persisting in using the military boat should be removed from their accommodations on the island.[16]

While the ferry had been operated by a number of providers since its inception, the governor had to concede that it was then operated by 'a young man resident in Queenstown and the son of a Prison Warder'. The Chief Secretary seemed satisfied with this explanation. He did remark, however, that officers should be encouraged to be mindful of security concerns and to reward all of the staff who were equally mindful, by giving them higher preference when awarding cottages on the island. The warder's son was therefore to be allowed to continue his operation of the ferry without any investigation as to

---

15 NAI, CSORP/1872/5248 and GPO/LB/21/162.
16 NAI, GPO/LB/24/370.

how he obtained the contract.[17] In reality, the operation of the warders' ferry had been an irritant to the watermen at Queenstown since
1865 and this newspaper article was likely to have been their latest
attempt to gain control of the island's lucrative ferry business.[18]

As an imprisoned convict, it is unlikely that John Cuddy would
have been aware of the ferryboat controversy in 1872. It wasn't the
only thing of which he was unaware. Unbeknownst to Cuddy, he was
being watched very closely by one of his acquaintances, a man called
John Brady from Kells in Co. Meath.

On 23 April 1870, a particularly daring crime had sent shockwaves through Co. Meath and in the days that followed it made head-
lines across the country. The crime was an audacious attempt on the
life of a local magistrate. As far away as Cork, a local newspaper
reported as follows:

> A correspondent writing from Kells, on Saturday, says:- At
> two o'clock p.m. on this evening, as John Radcliffe Esq., J.P.,
> was riding from this town to his residence at Willmount, a
> man met him about half a mile from Kells, and caught his
> horse by the bridle. Presently another man rushed out of a
> laneway and fired at Mr. Radcliffe, but fired too high, so
> that the contents of the pistol lodged in the top of Mr. Rad-
> cliffe's beaver hat. Immediately on being fired at, Mr. Rad-
> cliffe turned upon his assassins, one of whom he recognised
> as Edward Gearty, a carrion butcher of this town. Both im-
> mediately fled and Mr. Radcliffe rode to the constabulary
> station, where he reported the occurrence. The constabu-
> lary, under the command of John H. O' Farrell Esq., turned

17 Ibid.
18 NAI, GPO/LB/7/19.

out and, after a lengthened search arrested Gearty and a man named Brady, both of whom Mr. Radcliffe identified – Gearty as the man who fired and Brady as the man who stopped the horse ... The cause to which this attack has been attributed is that some time ago a man named James Gearty, a friend of the prisoner Edward Gearty, was committed to gaol for three months, by Mr. Radcliffe, for having in his possession a sheepskin for which he could not account.[19]

On 9 June 1870, 39-year-old Edward Gearty and 20-year-old John Brady were each convicted of attempted murder. Gearty was sentenced to penal servitude for life, while Brady's sentence was limited to 10 years on account of his comparative youth. It also seems that while in prison, he had offered some information regarding local outrages. Both of the convicts arrived on Spike Island in mid-March 1871.[20] This was just four months after John Cuddy had reached the island. As agrarian/political activists living in close proximity to each other, it is quite likely that the men already knew one another. But if John Cuddy thought that John Brady was a friend and ally, he was mistaken. Unbeknownst to those around him, John Brady was beginning to distance himself from his turbulent past.

Prior to his arrival on Spike Island, Brady had already written to the John O'Farrell who was mentioned in *The Cork Examiner* report, offering him further information regarding the plot on Radcliffe's life. After his arrival on the island, Brady renewed his correspondence with the County Meath constabulary. This time, he suggested that he could offer further information on five specific outrages committed

19 *The Cork Examiner*, 26 April 1870.
20 NAI, Mountjoy Prison General Register Male 1867-1875, 1/11/15. See also: NAI, CSORP/1872/8943.

in counties Meath and Westmeath, though it is unclear what benefit he sought in exchange for this information. On the recommendation of the constabulary, a detective was ordered to review Brady's correspondence and report as to whether he should be removed from Spike Island in order to secure further information from him. Having reviewed the papers, the detective reported:

> I have carefully read this file. As it may not be deemed prudent to remove the convict – John Brady – from Spike Island convict prison – his removal might give rise to suspicion on the part of the convicts from whom he expects to receive information regarding the murder of Mr Fetherstonhaugh. I beg to suggest that I may have a personal interview with him at Spike Island.[21]

With Brady now circulating among the prisoners at Spike Island seeking out further information, a detective was dispatched to interview him. The authorities had to establish whether the convict's information was reliable and from where it had been gathered. The result of the interview was an assertion by the detective that while the information provided by Brady would be of little use in any court case, it could provide the basis for further investigation. One avenue the authorities sought to pursue was placing an undercover detective in Kells railway station. This detective was to befriend a local called Nicholas Mullen, whom Brady had claimed was central to much of the agrarian violence in the area. Brady had also intimated that Mullen was likely to become 'soft in the mouth' if he were to be plied with alcohol. In the end, this plan came unstuck when the railway

---

21 NAI CSORP/1872/11696.

bosses objected to participation in a scheme that might ultimately endanger their passengers. The Ribbonmen around Kells had a record of violence and would have to be investigated with caution. Brady was asked to continue his infiltration of his fellow prisoners in order to gather further information.

It appears that Brady did as he was asked and that one of those with whom he associated was Michael McCormack from Kilnahinch, near Moate in Co. Westmeath. McCormack was serving five years' penal servitude for writing threatening letters to a local landlord, but he also claimed to know quite a bit about local Ribbonmen's operations.[22] Unfortunately for his former associates, it seems that he shared his knowledge with Brady. The latter was still keen to be of service to the local magistrates and on 17 August 1873 he wrote the following, poorly penned letter:

> Mr. Mcarty I am sendenngin, you word with regard to the Murder of Misses Trellyy. I have been talking to Michel Mc-Cormick with regard to the Murder of Misses Trellyy he told me that he was at a metting at terls Pass that is a metting held on the bad land lords and tenants of Westmeath. he told me that the Murder of Mises Tlelly was introduced among them by a boy of the name of Sheridan and he said that the best place to murder her would be on the tulamoar road leding from her house or inside her own gate to fier on her and shote her on the avenew or a place a way from the gate so the man that would go to do it would have the Choice of shoting her Either at home aboute her own place or in a house in Dublin that she was in the habiot of stoppining in he also told me

---

22 NAI, Mountjoy Prison General Register Male 1867-1875, 1/11/15 and Dublin Bridewell Prison (Richmond) General Register 1864-1883, 1/13/46.

that he was at several metting on all the harm she don on the people about her McCormick was another of the boys that attended the party society he knows more than Cudy Knows with Regard to the depredations that hapend in the County. I am going to say a few words regarding Cudy's Intentions when he leaves this he intends to hold Communications with the Party men of Kells and about it and to be and friten Mester the Ballif by getin tretten letters sent to him thinking that Mester Ballif get him out by fritnen him he says that he has only six mons to go in Spick Iland that he will twerl the blak thorn on some of the big fellows heds yet I will give tree chers for the Irish republic yet in west Meath when no tyrants dar ...[23]

Brady's letter is nothing if not confusing. He was clearly only partially literate and portions of the letter seem contradictory. The murder to which he referred was almost certainly the murder of Mrs Harriet Neill in Rathgar, Dublin, on 27 May 1872.[24] Mrs Neill owned property in counties Offaly and Westmeath and had been in a dispute with some of her tenants near Edenderry. Hers was the only prominent murder of a woman at around the time that Brady wrote. It is also worth noting that her dispute with her tenants occurred within 18 miles of Tyrrellspass and that somebody had called to her Dublin home to warn her that she was in as much danger in Rathgar as she was in Westmeath. Why, then, did Brady's illegible scrawl seem to indicate that her name was Trellyy? It could be that he intended to write Neilly, a name which some older records use interchangeably with Neill and O'Neill. It might also be that he was referring to her by her maiden name, Tyrell. Equally, it may be that he had misheard

---

23 NAI, CSORP/1873/12747.
24 *The Belfast News-Letter*, 28 May 1872 and *Freeman's Journal*, 28 May 1872.

a name with which he was unfamiliar. It was curious, though, that he implicated somebody called Sheridan in the crime. The authorities were convinced that the perpetrators were a local family known as Walsh.[25] It is perhaps because of this belief that they did not act on the information regarding the murder. They hadn't forgotten about John Cuddy though and now Brady had reminded them that a very serious agrarian offender, whom it seemed had strong republican sympathies, still waited on Spike Island. While Cuddy did so, he plotted revenge.

John Cuddy was telling Brady one story, but he was telling his gaolers something entirely different. He had informed them that upon his release he intended going home and, after a short period, leaving the country.[26] Thanks to Brady's information, the authorities were not inclined to believe him. As a result, when Cuddy finally left Spike Island on 17 February 1874, he was specifically forbidden from entering counties Meath or Westmeath for the duration of his licence. Police in those counties were furnished with a photograph (perhaps that in Fig. 16.1) and all other relevant particulars of the convict, so they could ensure that he complied with the terms of his release.[27] Records do not allow us to say with any degree of accuracy whether or not Cuddy returned to his home-place after his licence had expired. Neither can we say whether or not he was really guilty of one of the area's most infamous murders. We can merely say that he was, for a time, a chief suspect.

John Brady left Spike Island in February 1876. His licence was revoked when he was convicted of assault and imprisoned in Lifford, Co. Donegal, a year later. A man of the same birth year and name

---

25 *The Belfast News-Letter*, 28 and 30 May 1872 for explanation of the circumstances surrounding Mrs Neill's death.
26 NAI, CSORP/1874/742.
27 NAI, CSORP/1874/2612 and NAI Mountjoy Prison Convict Classification 1870-1880, 1/11/25.

(albeit a relatively common one) died in Kells in 1925.[28] If it was the same John Brady, he returned to his home town and lived to see the birth of an independent Irish state. By then, Whiteboys, Ribbonmen and Spike Island were just a distant memory from a turbulent past. Indeed, by the time Brady left Ireland's most infamous island, it had but six years of its convict operation remaining.

---

28 NAI, Mountjoy Prison Convict Classification 1870-1880, 1/11/25. General Registers Office (GRO), Irish Deaths 1864–1958 (Kells, April–June 1925). This was the only John Brady of similar age to the convict John Brady whose death was registered in the convict's home town.

17. Fenians

The serious information that Cuddy had imparted to Brady indicates that the men were likely to be friends rather than mere acquaintances. Given that Cuddy was never aware of Brady's role as an informer, it is likely that their friendship continued. If that were the case, the two men probably discussed the great crisis that struck Spike Island during Cuddy's final summer in Cork harbour. That emergency was an outbreak, in 1873, of what was described at the time as choleraic diarrhoea.

This illness is now called 'summer diarrhoea' and is the result of an acute gastroenteritis, usually due to the presence of *Salmonella* or *Shigella* bacteria. It is more common in hot weather and is associated with poor hygiene as it is usually the result of bacterial contamination of food or the water supply. The condition made its appearance on the island on 14 August 1873, when 14 prisoners presented with symptoms. Within days, a further 66 patients were isolated as possible cases of cholera. Each prisoner was issued with new clothing, wide-scale disinfection was commenced and the diet was changed. White bread was substituted for brown and the use of oatmeal and vegetables temporarily discontinued. By 27 August, the spread of the disease was contained, although by then the outbreak had already taken the life of one 30-year-old prisoner who was reported to be of a weak constitution before he contracted the disease.[1]

On investigation, the source of the outbreak was found to be Spike Island's water supply. Much of the convicts' drinking water was obtained from the large tanks that had been excavated in the centre

---

1 NAI, OPW/1233/78 (1874/11065). The dead convict is known only by his initials, P.N. (HMSO, *Directors' Report 1873*, p.26).

of the Parade Ground. The pipes that channelled rain-water from the roofs of the prison buildings were reasonably new, having been replaced after an earlier contamination with sewage in 1871.[2] At times of high rainfall, the subterranean tanks were prone to overflowing and to combat this had been fitted with an overflow pipe that discharged into a nearby sewer via a ventilation shaft from the latter. This shaft had filled with foul water and, on inspection, was found to come within 1in. (2.5cm) of the overflow pipe emerging from the drinking-water tanks. The inspecting doctor from the local government board was therefore able to report that he had 'no doubt sewage passed into the tank through this pipe'.[3] It turned out that this wasn't the only problem. When samples of water were taken from the wells, they also tested positive for contamination by sewage. It was obvious that the island's sewers were leaking. The result was the commencement of another great engineering project and the associated withdrawal of some convict labour from Haulbowline.

The prison's sewers were relaid with glazed earthenware pipes. Much of the foul earth surrounding the tanks was removed. In addition, a new pump was fitted to the well located in No.3 Bastion in order to draw water up to the tanks located on the ramparts. Fitting these pumps involved emptying the wells (one of which contained 85ft (26m) of water) with buckets. Considerable civilian labour was also used in the sewer project.[4] By the beginning of 1874, Spike Island had an upgraded sewerage system and an improved supply of clean drinking water. The prison's difficulties with the water supply did not end there, however, as although surrounded by saltwater, Spike Island had never enjoyed access to an abundant supply of fresh water.

2 NAI, OPW/13471/1871.
3 NAI, OPW/1233/78 (22041/1873).
4 NAI, OPW/1233/78 (11065/1874).

In the first half of 1876, rainfall in Cork harbour was considerably lower than usual and as a result its most infamous island was teetering on the edge of disaster. For a few short weeks, it seemed quite possible that the 680 prisoners on Spike Island might run out of drinking water. The matter was first reported to the executive in Dublin by Governor Hay on 17 June, when he wrote as follows:

> I have the honor to report that the supply of water in the prison has run very low and I fear that with continued dry weather, the wells may not give a sufficient supply. Under ordinary circumstances the depth of water in the wells varys from 30 to 50 feet, but at present there is only from 3 to 6 feet of water in three of those from which the supply for cooking and drinking purposes is obtained, and one becomes exhausted daily. In former years the main tank which would contain about 328,000 gallons, was always full, or nearly so, after the winter rains, but after the rains of last winter there was only about 4ft 6 inches of water in the deepest chamber, and 1ft 6 inches in the second chamber, leaving the other three chambers entirely empty, the chambers vary in depth from 14 to 8 feet.
>
> On the 2nd March last I wrote to the Royal Engineer Officer in command here, pointing out the difficulties that would be caused by want of water, requesting that the necessary steps may be taken for making the tank a sound receptacle for water...
>
> The wells and tank, have not been, for many years, so low as at present ...'[5]

---

5 NAI, OPW/1233/78 (1876/10552).

It was the governor's opinion that the prison had only a week's worth of water remaining, and he added that the water stored for fire-fighting was depleted and would not be adequate should that threat become reality. By late July 1876, the purchase of water and the use of marine soap for saltwater washing were being considered.[6] Nobody outside of the prison system could have known how close the Spike Island convict depot had come to disaster. In the end, it appears that the rainfall increased and the crisis was averted.[7] Correspondence regarding the impending drought on Spike Island seemed to end in an unresolved debate about securing funds for the upgrade of the tanks.[8] That debate was part of a growing tension between the military and the prison service on the island. Each had to co-exist with the other, but that co-existence was not always harmonious. Yet, on some matters, co-operation was vital and one of those issues was the security of the island's Fenian prisoners.

The British authorities applied the umbrella term 'Fenian' to republican activists who were members of the Irish Republican Brotherhood (IRB) or their allied North American group, the Fenian Brotherhood. Both organisations had been founded in 1858. The Fenian Brotherhood staged a number of raids attacking Crown forces in Canada between 1866 and 1870. In 1865, the authorities discovered plans for a Fenian uprising in Ireland and in 1866 they suspended the writ of *habeas corpus*, effectively allowing them to intern suspected Fenians without trial. These untried Fenians were imprisoned in various county and city gaols, but were ultimately collected in Mountjoy and released by the end of 1868.

---

6 NAI, GPO/LB/23/953.

7 *Freeman's Journal*, 23 August 1876. An article in this edition referred to the improvement of the crops due to increased rainfall in the previous week. See also: NAI, GPO/LB/30/92. This document refers to an order for waterproof clothing for Spike Island's warders being made prior to 19 August.

8 NAI, OPW/1233/78 (11313/76).

The IRB staged a number of small, uncoordinated revolts throughout 1867. Indeed, in March of that year, works on the Haulbowline dockyards were temporarily suspended when it was 'considered advisable not to send the convicts from Spike Island to Haulbowline for the present owing to the disturbed State of the country'.[9] Just before the convict labour was withdrawn, warders John and Thomas O'Neill had absented themselves from duty. Rumours alleged that they had defected to the Fenians and planned to use sympathetic convicts in order to seize the arsenal on Haulbowline. They were dismissed from service and prohibited from landing on Spike Island.[10]

Most of the IRB members directly involved in the revolts of 1867 were convicted of treason felony, while any Fenians who had been members of the British armed forces were court-martialled for military offences. These men all ended up in various English prisons or were transported to Western Australia. Fenians convicted of less overtly political offences went through the Irish penal system and, like most other convicts, eventually made their way to Spike Island. The Fenian organisation was broken by an extensive network of Crown informers within the ranks of the Brotherhood. As their conspiracy unravelled, the most committed Fenians were appalled at the extent to which they had been infiltrated. Their revenge was swift and brutal, and one of the first to feel it was John Warner.

Warner was a former sergeant in the North Cork Militia who rose to the rank of captain within the IRB. In 1866, Warner testified to the Royal Commission in Cork regarding key members of the IRB and their activities. His testimony resulted in numerous convictions and this notorious informer was relocated to Dublin. Nonetheless he

---

9 NAI, GPO/LB/7/763.
10 *Dublin Evening Post*, 13 March 1867. See also: NAI, GPO/LB/22/115.

was not as cautious as he should have been and just a few months later he was attacked and badly beaten in a public house in Clontarf. That may well have led to the IRB tracking him down to his Howth residence, right next-door to the police station. On the evening of 21 May 1866, while out walking in the town, Warner encountered a man who identified himself as Edward O'Connor. Warner's new acquaintance spoke with an American accent and claimed that he was formerly a soldier in the Confederate army. As a veteran of the Crimean war, Warner was interested in the many stories that O'Connor could spin and invited the latter back to his home for tea. This proved a near-fatal mistake. O'Connor's real name was Patrick Tierney. He had been a soldier in the Royal Irish Fusiliers but was now a committed member of the IRB. When Warner made the mistake of turning his back on his guest while showing him something in the garden, Tierney proved just how committed he was. He took a dagger from his pocket and plunged it into Warner's neck. A struggle ensued and somehow Warner, with the aid of his wife, managed to hold Tierney. The would-be assassin eventually wriggled free, leaving his coat and waistcoat in his victim's hands. A revolver was found in the pocket of his coat. The police were immediately alerted to these happenings and officers were dispatched in all directions to find Warner's coatless attacker. They caught up with Tierney near Sutton and he was taken into custody. Fearing that his real identity might expose other Fenians in the ranks of the Irish Fusiliers, Patrick Tierney still insisted that he was Edward O'Connor, an ex captain of the Confederate army.[11]

Tierney pleaded guilty to attempted murder and was sentenced to a lifetime of penal servitude on 14 June 1866. He served

---

11 See Connecticut Irish American Historical Society. 2013. 'New Haven Monument Honors Forgotten Hero', in *The Shanachai*, Vol. XXV, No. 4, pp.3–5. See also: *The Waterford Mail*, 23 May 1866.

eight months' cellular discipline in Mountjoy before being transferred to Spike Island in February 1867. He later claimed that he was singled out for special attention by a warder as soon as he set foot on the pier. He alleged that he was frequently brutalised and that Governor Hay was supportive of his warders' efforts to make life difficult for the Fenian. This might have been what led to his escape attempt on 18 May 1867, just a few months after his arrival. On that evening, having returned from Haulbowline, Tierney and 50 other convicts were being marched back to their cells when convict John Duffy seized a cutlass from one of the warders. He immediately ran for the boats on the beach, shouting for Tierney to follow him. Duffy was a badly behaved convict with a long criminal record. Some of his offences appeared to be of a political nature and this may have been his motivation for wanting to help Tierney regain his freedom. Warders intervened and a scuffle ensued, but Tierney broke away and got as far as a boat that was occupied by the nine-year-old son of one of the island's gunners. Tierney showed the boy little mercy, hitting him over the head with an oar and dumping him into the water. Tierney then pushed off and managed to move the boat some yards into the harbour before a warder made it down to the shore of the island. With his revolver drawn, the warder ordered Tierney back to shore and the Fenian decided to obey. Corporal punishment was unusual at this time but because they had used violence during their escape attempt, Tierney and Duffy were both flogged and placed in the Punishment Block. Thereafter, like other escapees, they wore heavy chains.[12] While Tierney remained a prisoner on Spike Island, the Fenian conspiracy continued to unravel.

---

12 NAI, GPO/LB/7/886 and Mountjoy Prison Convict Classification 1866-1868, 1/11/24. See also: *The Shanachai*. 2013. Vol. XXV, No. 4, pp.3–5; HMSO, *Directors' Report 1867*.

The British administration had placed three key informers at very senior levels of the IRB. They were later identified as J.J. Corridan, Pierce Nagle and Constable Thomas Talbot. Assuming the identity of a water bailiff called John Kelly, Talbot became the leader of an IRB circle in the vicinity of Clonmel and Carrick-on-Suir, Co. Tipperary, and attended IRB meetings in several counties. His information was key in alerting the authorities to the rising planned for March 1865 and his testimony assisted in the conviction of numerous Fenians (many of them British Army personnel) during the years that followed. Talbot had been baptised into the Church of Ireland, but during the course of his undercover work he had attended Roman Catholic services and partaken in the communion of that Church. This deception was particularly abhorrent to many Irish Catholics, as was his testimony against young men who he had sworn, and perhaps inveigled, into the IRB.[13] Unlike other key Fenian informants, Constable Talbot chose to remain in Ireland and retired on a pension of £80 per annum.[14] His decision was to prove fatal, as on 11 July 1871, the Fenians got their revenge:

> A most determined and murderous assault was perpetrated
> on Monday night, about twelve o' clock, on Head Constable
> Talbot, who, it will be remembered, occupied a prominent
> position in the last Fenian trials. About the hour we have
> mentioned, Talbot was proceeding along Hardwicke Street,
> Dublin, in the direction of George's Place, when he was con-
> fronted by a man, who, without delay, levelled a revolver at
> him, lodging the contents in the side of Talbot's head, and

13 Ó Concubhair, P. 2011. *The Fenians were Dreadful Men: The 1867 Rising.* Cork: Mercier Press, pp.83–4. See also: Ó Broin, L. 1971. *Fenian Fever: An Anglo-American Dilemma.* London: Chatto & Windus Ltd, pp.12, 137, 140, 146 and 222.
14 *The Cork Examiner*, 4 January 1869.

inflicting a wound from which recovery is impossible. Immediately on the discharge of the shot Constable Mullen, 146 D, and Grimes, 50 D, who were on duty in Eccles Street, made to the spot, and came at once on the offender. He was challenged, we believe by the constables, but his only reply was to again level the revolver and fire on the constables. The shot, we are sorry to say, took effect; and inflicted a fresh wound on one of the legs of Mullen. By this time Constables Connor, 141 C, and Walsh, 129 C, came up from Dorset Street, and, after a chase and a struggle, the three constables succeeded in securing the perpetrator of this audacious and daring outrage. Seeing that Talbot was most seriously injured the constables had him at once taken to Richmond Hospital, where he received prompt attention, but the medical men in attendance we understand, entertain no hope, and probably ere this paragraph is published Talbot will have ceased to exist. The prisoner, who is a low-set, closely shaved man, who refuses to give his name or any particulars, was at once taken to Sackville Lane station, and will be brought up at the Head Office. The Chief Magistrate Mr O'Donnell, accompanied by his clerk, attended at Richmond late on Tuesday night, to receive the depositions of Talbot who was sinking fast. The wound inflicted on Constable Mullen is not of a serious nature; but Constable Grimes had a narrow escape, as the ball which lodged in Mullen's leg closely grazed the breast of Grimes. The outrage was of the most determined, deliberate, and daring nature.[15]

Talbot died in hospital a few days later. The nameless assassin was identified as Robert Kelly (Fig. 17.1) and he was charged with

---

15 *The Belfast News-Letter*, 13 July 1871.

murder. What followed was one of the most remarkable court cases of the 19th century.

Figure 17.1 Robert Kelly, in later life. (Image © courtesy of National Archives of Ireland)

Kelly's trial began on 30 October 1871. His audacious crime made him as notorious as the infamous spy he had killed and it is clear from contemporary accounts that members of the general public wanted to see Ireland's most famous assassin. The *Freeman's Journal* described the prelude to one of the most eagerly anticipated trials that Ireland had seen in some time:

The trial of Kelly, alias Pemberton, for the alleged murder of T. Talbot, a detective, was commenced yesterday in the Courthouse Green Street. The opening of the proceedings was, it is needless to say, awaited with intense public anticipation and interest, as well from the character of the charge as from the nature of the defence which it was rumoured would be made. Extraordinary precautions were taken by the authorities to ensure the safe transit of the prisoner, who was escorted from Kilmainham Jail by three full troops of cavalry and a large body of mounted constables. Indeed the appearance of the cavalcade would lead one to suppose the passage of some historic captive whose treason had shaken the pillars of the

State. The line of route was thronged by crowds of people who gazed curiously on the cortege as it went by with the black van in its midst. There was not an utterance of any kind by the people, nor any demonstration whatever. The Courthouse and its precincts were held by a numerous posse of the Metropolitan Police, who were distributed in parties at the corners of the streets opening on the building, upwards of forty or fifty of them also being distributed among the audience. The utmost rigour was exercised in the matter of admission, no person being allowed to pass the gateway unless they had a ticket.[16]

Indeed, it seems that crowds had been gathering outside the courthouse for several days beforehand, hoping that Kelly would appear.[17] The rumoured defence that the newspaper referred to was one of the most inventive in legal history and was deployed on Kelly's behalf by Isaac Butt, William Burke Kirwan's former defender and by now a leader of the Home Rule movement (see Fig. 7.3). Butt conceded that Kelly had shot Talbot, but argued that the gunshot did not kill the constable. Indeed, according to Butt, Talbot's condition only became fatal when doctors attempted to remove the bullet from his body, therefore Kelly was not responsible for Talbot's death and not guilty of murder.

At the time, Butt's defence was seen as being almost as brazen as Kelly's crime. How could somebody who admitted firing a shot at another person who subsequently died not be guilty of murder? Yet, on 10 November 1877, the jury seemed to agree with Butt's defence when Kelly was sensationally found 'not guilty' of murder. Republi-

---

16 *Freeman's Journal*, 31 October 1871.
17 Ibid., 26 October 1871.

cans as far away as Cork marched through the streets in celebration of an incredible verdict. Their celebrations may have been tempered somewhat by the fact that Kelly was not a free man. He was remanded in Kilmainham while the Crown considered its next move. The famous assassin of a notorious spy could not be allowed to go unpunished.

Robert Kelly was tried for the second time on 9 February 1872. This time, his case didn't attract nearly as much public interest as he was arraigned on the lesser charge of 'shooting at Constable James Mullen with intent to murder'. The verdict was guilty. Kelly was promptly sentenced to 15 years' penal servitude. He began that sentence in Mountjoy and it was later reported that his wife and child clung to him while he was escorted from the courthouse after the trial. Eight months later he was dispatched to join Tierney on Spike Island.[18]

A few days after Kelly began his labours in Cork harbour, the Fenians struck again. This time their target was a Dublin-based journalist called Daniel Murphy, who had also been involved in the IRB and was suspected of passing information to the government. On 10 October 1872, he was gunned down on a Dublin street. Murphy survived the shooting and went on to identify the gunman as Edward O'Kelly. After two mistrials, O'Kelly was finally convicted of attempted murder on 23 June 1873 and he was sentenced to penal servitude for life. O'Kelly was moved to Spike Island in September of that year, having spent a little under four months in Mountjoy. The reason for his early departure from the Dublin prison was a concern regarding the state of his health after he began complaining of dizzy spells.[19] On Spike Island, he renewed his acquaintance with Robert

---

18 Ibid., 5 August 1878. See also: NAI, GPO/LB/24/899.
19 NAI, Mountjoy Prison Convict Classification 1870-1880, 1/11/25.

Kelly, as it was later thought that the two men were already known to each other having been engaged in the same conspiracy.[20] He also renewed his acquaintance with John O'Farrell, who was a witness for the prosecution during O'Kelly's trial but was himself already convicted of burglary.[21]

Figure 17.2 The Fenian Edward O'Kelly. (Image © courtesy of National Archives of Ireland)

Kelly and O'Kelly served the next four years on Spike Island among the general prison population and both became friends with Patrick Tierney. They were there during the choleraic diarrhoea outbreak in 1873 and Edward O'Kelly was hospitalised during that period.[22] It is almost certain that the Fenian prisoners worked on Haulbowline like the overwhelming majority of convicts at that time. While they did so, they, along with several other detained Fenians, were the subject of petitions presented to Queen Victoria after mass meetings of London's Irish community in Hyde Park on St Patrick's Day in 1873, and again in 1875. The petitions were redirected to the Secretary of State, where they ultimately fell on deaf ears. Kelly, Tierney and O'Kelly remained on Spike Island.[23]

---

20 NAI, CSORP/1876/13298.
21 Hansard, *House of Commons Debates, HC Deb 29 January 1878, vol. 237, cc618–19.*
22 *Freeman's Journal*, 20 February 1878.
23 PRO, HO 45/9331/19461D.

In April 1876, the authorities received alarming information from one of their many Fenian informants and immediately wrote to Director Barlow, informing him that a potential embarrassment was threatened:

> Private information has reached the Government which leads to the conclusion that it will be prudent to see that all reasonable precautions are taken for the safe custody of the convicts Robert Kelly and Edward O'Kelly who are in Spike Island. Will you please to give directions accordingly.[24]

Barlow did as he was asked; the threat of two Fenians breaking out of Spike Island prison with assistance from outside was taken very seriously. Although the authorities were not then aware of it, the above communication was penned as a breakout from a convict prison in Western Australia was in the final stages of preparation. That occurred some two weeks later when a ship called *Catalpa*, which had been procured by the Fenians, dropped anchor off the coast of Rockingham, near Fremantle Prison. Six Fenians who had been in work gangs outside the prison boarded the ship and sailed to freedom. On Spike Island, Governor Hay immediately enhanced his security.

By day, Kelly and O'Kelly were put to work in a trade shop within the walls of Fort Westmoreland. They toiled under the charge of special warders transferred from Lusk and assigned exclusively to these two Fenians. At night they now slept in the Punishment Block. The fact that this building was the only purpose-built prison block of single cells on the island made it far more secure than the alternatives. The solid walls of the Punishment Block, its purposely secured

---

24 NAI, CSORP/1876/5116.

windows and separately constructed cells, ensured that any escapee would have to open three separate locks just to get out of the building. One warder patrolled the corridors through the night, while another slept in special quarters. On the detection of the plot to free Kelly and O'Kelly, Governor Hay placed an additional warder on patrol in the Punishment Block.[25] It was known that one of O'Kelly's children was living with a known Fenian in Queenstown and Kelly's wife was a regular prison visitor.[26] These visits were closely monitored and specifically remarked upon in the convict classification book.[27]

Meanwhile, Director Barlow identified two other prisoners then on Spike Island whom he considered potential flight risks. The first of these was Patrick Tierney, whom Barlow still referred to as Edward O'Connor. The second was a former soldier in the British army named James Dillon, who had shot at Royal Irish Constabulary (RIC) personnel when they raided a house where Fenians were meeting in Co. Tipperary. Dillon had been sentenced to 20 years' penal servitude in 1866. Barlow now recommended that all four of these Fenian convicts be transferred to an English prison. He also recommended that William Jeffreys Mulcahy and Robert O'Sullivan, alleged Fenians then located in Mountjoy and due to be transferred to Spike Island, be sent to an English prison instead. An alleged plot to rescue these latter two men while in transit to Spike Island had been uncovered. The discovery of that plot had uncovered the initial information regarding the potential escape of Kelly and O'Kelly from Spike Island. It was considered that a sympathetic Irish population made the likelihood of Fenian escapes from Irish prisons far greater than was the case in

---

25 NAI, CSORP/1876/7185 and GPO/LB/29/673.
26 NAI, CSORP/1876/7111.
27 NAI, Mountjoy Prison Convict Classification, 1870-1880, 1/11/25.

England. Indeed, a key part of the escape plan appeared to involve bribing prison warders on Spike Island.[28]

In the end, the Chief Secretary ordered that Kelly, O'Kelly and the two Mountjoy prisoners be transferred to Millbank Prison in London. That plan seems to have fallen apart after Barlow asked whether Kelly and O'Kelly could be placed directly aboard the civilian steamer that plied from Cork to Bristol. There is no recorded reply to his question and both men remained on Spike Island.[29] Due to the presence of its military garrison, the security of Spike Island was considered superior to that of Mountjoy and this is probably the reason why it was decided not to remove its Fenian convicts to English gaols.[30]

Security concerns continued to exercise the minds of the island's authorities and the military orders issued in connection with protecting the convict prison in 1875 were reviewed in 1877. The military patrolled the outer perimeter of the fort, with sentries placed on the ramparts and in the moat. Two additional soldiers were posted on the landing pier, with orders to challenge any boat that approached the island. Soldiers were to challenge all who approached to provide a password, known as a parole, and after designated hours an altered password, known as a countersign. All of these military sentries were ordered to call out their post number along with the phrase 'All's well' every fifteen minutes after the evening tattoo. In addition, the sentries were authorised to do all in their power to prevent the escape of a prisoner, short of taking that prisoner's life. Nonetheless, should any prisoner threaten a soldier's life while that soldier sought to

---

28 NAI, CSORP/1876/14437.
29 Ibid.
30 Ibid.

prevent an escape, the soldier was ordered to discharge his firearm in self-defence.[31]

Throughout the 1870s, the treatment of Irish political prisoners was continually raised in parliament and periodically reported on by the newspapers. By January 1878, a series of amnesties ensured that only eight of the Fenian political prisoners remained in prison. Four of those were detained in English convict prisons, with the remaining four – Dillon, Tierney, Kelly and O'Kelly – on Spike Island.[32] Releases of political prisoners from English prisons in late 1877 and early 1878 provoked huge celebrations in Ireland. There was an outpouring of grief when one of them, Charles McCarthy, died soon after his release.[33] In parliament, John O'Connor Power, himself a former Fenian and now an MP, raised issues regarding the treatment of O'Kelly and Tierney on Spike Island. This was part of an ongoing campaign directed by O'Connor Power and greatly assisted by O'Kelly's and Tierney's sisters. The latter each visited their brothers on the island in 1878 and reported alleged mistreatment of political prisoners to the newspapers.[34]

On 28 April 1878, James Dillon was transferred to Mountjoy. He was released from there just a few days later.[35] A few days after that, on 10 May 1878, Robert Kelly was also transferred to Mountjoy. By that time, he had spent two years in the confines of the Punishment Block. By the time of his transfer to Mountjoy, it was clear that the atypical security restrictions had taken their toll on his health. As he

---

31 NAI, CSORP/1878/1937.
32 *The Belfast News-Letter*, 4 January 1878 and *Freeman's Journal*, 16 January 1878.
33 McConville, S. 2003. *Theatres of War - Irish Political Prisoners 1848-1922*. London and New York: Routledge, p.310.
34 *Freeman's Journal*, 6 February 1878, 12 March 1878 and 20 April 1878.
35 NAI, Mountjoy Prison Convict Classification, 1/11/24. See also: *Freeman's Journal*, 4 May 1878.

was one of Ireland's most famous prisoners, it wasn't long before the press had heard of his plight:

> Information from a reliable quarter has reached us that Robert Kelly, convicted of having fired at with intent to kill the policemen who pursued him on the night when Talbot, the informer, was wounded, has been removed from Spike Island and transferred to the hideous economy of Mountjoy. Kelly is in bad health and when seen with the two warders who had charge of his safe transport showed unmistakable signs of breakdown. Another prisoner, Edward O'Kelly, now in Spike Island, is, according to the statement of a contemporary last week, in a miserable state. He is allowed but half an hour for recreation and exercise in the day. He is lodged in close proximity to a hapless wretch, half of whose face has been devoured by cancer. Will it be believed that Kelly, seeing this poor creatures condition, is forced to use the same drinking vessel and endure the constant pain which such a sight must produce? Prison regulations are rigid, and discipline is the basis of government; but we do think the higher authorities might abate the miseries which are not included in the horrid code of penal servitude. Governors and warders must need do their duty, and mayhap the system may induce a tendency to overdo it. We cannot believe however, that the sort of hideous, disgusting persecution we have indicated should find place in any institution...It is a positive scandal to humanity and a downright disgrace to England that prisoners should be treated in such a manner.[36]

While the newspaper reflected a contemporary tendency to

---

36 *Freeman's Journal*, 14 May 1878.

define many unknown medical conditions as 'cancer' and then potentially misrepresent the nature of their contagion, it also demonstrated the knowledge that Kelly and O'Kelly had been the recipients of exceptional treatment whilst on Spike Island. On 3 August 1878, Robert Kelly was finally released (Fig. 17.3). A journalist from the *Freeman's Journal* conducted an interview with him and what he reported must have made uncomfortable reading for the authorities. Kelly claimed that during his time on Spike Island he had experienced little other than cruelty. The island prison had broken the spirit and the body of Ireland's most famous assassin:

Kelly passed eight months in Mountjoy in what is known as the "probation class" during which interval ... he was obliged to work extremely hard in his close cell, and was allowed but very little exercise. Still when the dreaded order came for the convict's removal to Spike Island he was sound in mind and body. Indeed his health, considering all he has passed through, was wonderfully robust, but he abhorred the notion of detention in a prison which has forever been known amongst the convict class as a "hell upon earth." To Spike Island then Kelly was removed ... But the stories he had heard of the prison in the harbour of Cork fairly terrified him, and it was with awful forebodings and a sick and sorry heart that he stepped on Haulbowline's rocky shore to commence penal life.

IN SPIKE ISLAND

It was here Kelly's life and health were broken down, and it was his treatment in this fearful living hell that today has made him, in his 42nd year, a worn, shattered, emaciated, enfeebled old man, looking fully three score of years. When he went to Spike Island he was, as we have said, a stalwart,

314

hale and hearty prisoner; but when in March last, he crept, or crawled – for Kelly now crawls rather than walks – out of Spike Island, he was a dying half dead man. The tale he tells of his life in Spike makes the listener shudder, and ask, "Is Spike Island in a Christian land?" and "Were its officials made by the same God who created its miserable captives?"... The locale was altogether too harsh for the prisoner, and he suffered intensely from the strong biting winds that swept across the place from the Atlantic. As many as fifteen and twenty convicts often constitute a gang in charge of one warder but Robert Kelly and Edward O'Kelly – another political prisoner at Spike – were regarded as such desperate men that the Governor (Mr Hey [sic]) deemed it advisable to place a special warder over each of them. These special warders haunted the men like their very shadows. When O'Kelly worked with his last and awl his special warder was at his back and Kelly never drove a nail or sawed a piece of wood but his special warder was at his elbow. The functions of these warders did not end with the setting of the sun, for they watched the wretched prisoners go to sleep, and they watched them wake again. Never out of the right hand of each of these worthies was a heavily lead laden baton, nineteen inches long and weighing over 11lb, a most deadly weapon grasped in the strong sinewey hand of a stout well fed warder, to chastise, if deemed necessary, these half starved, wholly broken down, men. Once at Spike, for a period of four days, Kelly was confined in a filthy foul smelling cell, without chair or table, his only seat being on a low foot stool or boss. His food was served to him on the floor, and he adds, "when I could I eat it like a beast off the ground." The food was so bad at Spike that he ate it with great difficulty, and then the work was downright killing, the prisoner being frequently obliged to stand out in heavy rain until his clothes became soaked through. The tender care with which the official watched both of the political prisoners, was ten-fold increased when the telegraph wires told the news of the Fenian's escape from the penal prison in Australia. No trouble was too great to keep both of the men under half a dozen eyes night, noon, and morning, and guard was mounted at the bedposts of these poor fellows as though they had secreted on their person a powder magazine and an army's firearms. Kelly's quarters very recently – and O'Kelly is still confined there – were in the worst part of the prison, wherein all the "degraded" convicts are locked up. Kelly shuddered on Saturday afternoon last when he described this place to a representative of the *Freeman's Journal.* He said; "Most of the men here are chained, and many of them suffer from terrible diseases, such as scrofula, ulcers, and skin affections. We were obliged to drink out of the vessels used by these men; this was most revolting." The political prisoners had been for a long time confined in what were known as the penal cells, and it was on the 4th of March last that Kelly and O'Kelly were removed to the section of the prison for "degraded" prisoners, the cause of the change being for what reason they could not say. Speaking of the severity of some of the prison's regulations, Kelly remarked, "I knew one poor fellow from Ship Street Dublin, named Brannigan, to be handcuffed with his hands behind his back for eight months. I once heard him pray aloud to the jailers to take off the manacles, if even for a few moments. That night I saw him kicking in his cells and he died. A Coroner's jury said that the death was natural." ... Another instance of the severe discipline adopted towards the political prisoners is to be found in the fact that a warder named Coogan, who was found speaking to Kelly otherwise than in strict duty, was

suspended for a month and fined £5, whilst a Dublin prisoner, who only inquired after Kelly's health, was sent to the
punishment cells for three days. In the second week in March
last, Kelly's health at length gave way...His ailments were
not two, but many, and he suffered terribly from the kidneys
and liver. His strength had now waned down to nothing, and
his teeth were lose and rotten, his tongue was always dry,
dirty and furred and; yet no drink could moisten it; and his
eyesight became impaired. This was Kelly's condition at the
conclusion of his Spike Island experience. Soon after his ad-
mittance to hospital he prayed permission for a visit from
Edward O'Kelly and he thus speaks of the meeting:- "O'Kelly came to see me in the hospital and the poor fellow looks
completely broken down. He complained of not being able to
eat and seems in a wretched state."[37]

Kelly's interview seemed to expose a darker side of Spike
Island. It suggested that the Fenian prisoners suffered systematic
abuse that wasn't inflicted on many of the ordinary prisoners. While
any Fenians remained in prison, they represented a stick with which
Irish MPs and newspapers could beat the British administration in
Ireland. This sustained pressure led to the establishment of a Royal
Commission to enquire into the operation of Irish convict prisons and
the treatment of political prisoners. The commissioners visited Spike
Island on 18 September 1878 and interviewed the last of the Fenian
prisoners, O'Kelly and Tierney.[38]

The final two Fenians held in English prisons were released
in November.[39] Tierney was released on 4 December 1878. He later

---

37 Ibid., 5 August 1878.
38 *Freeman's Journal*, 20 September 1878.
39 *The Irish Times*, 15 November 1878; *Freeman's Journal*, 15 November 1878.

claimed that his release had been shrouded in secrecy and that he was taken by special boat from the island to a steamship that conveyed him directly to New York. His immediate emigration was a condition of his release. Before he left the prison, he requested that he be permitted a final farewell to the island's last Fenian, Edward O'Kelly. The two men shook hands and Tierney left Spike Island and Ireland.[40]

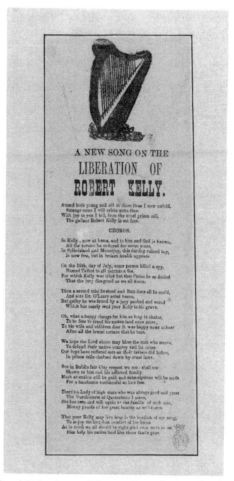

Figure 17.3 Ballad published to celebrate the release of Robert Kelly. (Image © courtesy of National Library of Scotland)

40 *The Shanachai*, 2013. Vol. XXV, No. 4, pp. 3–5. See also: NAI, Mountjoy Prison Convict Classification, 1/11/24.

O'Kelly didn't have to wait too long for his own release. A little more than two months later, on 14 February 1879, the last of the Fenian political prisoners departed from Spike Island's pier.[41] In his mid-thirties by the time of his release, O'Kelly also emigrated. The *Freeman's Journal* claimed that he 'was placed' aboard the ship, implying that his decision wasn't entirely voluntary.[42] No doubt O'Kelly watched Spike Island from the decks of the *Marathon* steamship before she set out from Cork harbour. It was from that ship that he sent his final farewell to his mother with the following telegram:

> Free: Sailing in the Marathon. Hearty thanks to all kind Friends. Loving remembrances to sisters and yourself.[43]

On his arrival in New York, O'Kelly was soon reunited with Tierney. It was reported that while O'Kelly was being welcomed by Irish-American friends and supporters, he heard somebody call out, 'Where is 13938?' On hearing his old prison number, O'Kelly asked that its user might identify himself. It was then that Tierney stepped

---

41 NAI, Mountjoy Prison Convict Classification 1870-1880, 1/11/25. Kelly was certainly the last prisoner on behalf of whom the Fenians campaigned and frequently referred to as a 'political prisoner'. However, there were other convicts who had probably been engaged in 'fundraising' for the Fenian organisation. As their crimes involved robbery, they were not considered 'political prisoners'. Two of those men (William Jeffreys Mulcahy and Robert O'Sullivan) served out their sentences in Dublin prisons.
42 It is worth noting that Britain had no legal right to effectively transport two of her prisoners to the USA. Indeed, in 1873, enquiries by the American ambassador as to whether Irish convicts were released on condition of their emigration to America were met with outright denial by prison authorities (NAI, GPO/LB/623). However, O'Kelly and Tierney claimed that they were released on condition of their emigrating. Official records do not refer to their emigration being a condition of their release, but do state that they emigrated. It is likely that the men (as stated by Tierney) agreed to emigrate before they were released. Thus, it was their 'choice' to emigrate and the authorities did not choose their destination, but they did put them on ships to the destination of their 'choice'.
43 *Freeman's Journal*, 15 February 1879.

forward and the two old friends greeted each other.[44]

Like Robert Kelly before him, O'Kelly gave a damning interview, this time to a reporter with the *Irish World* newspaper. The *Freeman's Journal* claimed it was they who had sent the *Irish World*'s employee and then reprinted the interview with O'Kelly. In it he stated:

> Upon my arrival in Spike Island I was immediately put in the punishment cell. Here I had to sleep and take meals but was allowed to work during the day time. I was put at the most disgusting kind of work – cleaning closets sunk several feet into the rock, down which I was compelled to go. A severe illness ensued. I was put into the hospital from which I was removed to my cold cell while still very sick; was again sent back to hospital, where I was kept altogether nine days, and again ordered to work. During that time I was given three and a half pounds of bread – nothing else. The doctor ordered me to the oakum house, which is especially set apart for invalids, and in which the restrictions are unbearable. I was given two days exercise which consisted of sitting on the steps of the oakum house in frosty weather. I was attached to a working party that was sometimes sent outside of the prison, but on such occasions I was detached. For over two years a warder was kept over me, although at work. There was no one in the prison treated like me except the other Fenian prisoners. My health was completely broken down when released from the punishment cell ... I was finally put to shoe-making, and, instead of being kept in the same place as the others engaged in similar work, I was put into the carpenters shop and made

---

44 *The Shanachai*. 2013. Vol. XXV, No. 4, pp. 3–5. It is worth noting that 13938 was indeed O'Kelly's prison number. This lends considerable credibility to the report.

to undergo what might be termed a process of slow congela-
tion.[45]

After a prolonged illness, which the *Freeman's Journal* didn't
hesitate to blame on his confinement on Spike Island, Edward O'Kelly died in New York five months after his release. One of the darkest
chapters in the island's history was concluded. Indeed, Spike Island's
infamous convict prison was about to meet its own end.

---

45 Ibid., 24 March 1879.

18. The End of the Convict Era

The Kelly affair had seen the military and the prison authorities working together to enhance the island's security. That co-operation couldn't mask the reality that the competing interests of the military and the prison service often clashed, rendering the administration of both the fort and the prison inefficient and ineffective. Former Director Walter Crofton (1815–1897) later revealed that the War Department had sought the dismantling of the convict depot in the 1860s, but the Haulbowline works and associated requirement for convict labour had saved the prison.[1] Now the building of the dockyard on Haulbowline necessitated an upgrade of the seaward defences on Spike Island.

By 1877, the military were spending significant money upgrading Fort Westmoreland and were not about to allow the needs of the prison to interfere with their plans. Prior to an overhaul of defences on the southern side of the fort, prison authorities were informed of the military's plans to draft in civilian labour. In addition, it was proposed to create a temporary entrance and a bridge across the moat on that seaward side of the fort. Given the threat of Fenian escape still prevailing at that time, the prison authorities could not allow these plans to proceed. Accordingly, Director of Convict Prisons Barlow wrote to the Under-Secretary and outlined his concerns for the prison's security. He proposed that the necessary labour be found by transferring convict labour from Haulbowline back to Spike Island. The Under-Secretary agreed and by March 1877, Spike Island's convict labour force had left Haulbowline in order to complete the defence works on their own island.[2]

---

1 British Library, Add MS 60844–60848.
2 NAI, CSORP/1877/3812.

By September of that year, the military were frustrating the prison establishment again. This time, Governor Hay made a rather simple request when he wrote the following to the Chief Secretary:

> I have the honor to report that the Royal Artillery propose firing the 25 pound guns mounted on the ramparts, 3 rounds of shot from each as soon as the range seawards can be got clear of ships and I am apprehensive that the concussion from such large guns may do damage to some of the prison buildings and also break a great deal of glass in the windows. It has been suggested to remove the sashes but it would be quite impossible to do so, and owing to the construction of the windows generally, the iron bars will admit of only a small opening of a few inches in each window.[3]

Director Barlow forwarded the governor's communication to the Chief Secretary with the recommendation that the proposed test firing be deferred until the following summer. He was certain that the chapel, then under construction, would be completed by the summer and also argued that any repairs to buildings could be more efficiently conducted at that time.[4] It was clear, however, that the defence of Cork harbour was considered of greater priority than the maintenance of Spike Island's convict prison. Having sought the advice of the military, the Chief Secretary was simply told that while they had considered Hay's concerns, they still felt that the firing of the guns should go ahead as scheduled. They also promised to take every care in trying to avoid damaging the prison buildings. The Chief Secretary had no power to interfere with the running of the War Office, and the protests

---

3 NAI, CSORP/1877/14955.
4 Ibid.

of Barlow and Hay were dismissed. It was but one of the incidents that contributed to a growing tension between the competing interests on Spike Island.

On 18 January 1879, William Burke Kirwan finally left Spike Island as a free man. He had spent 27 years in captivity, some 17 of those on Spike Island. Two years after he had been stopped painting religious imagery in the chapel in 1863, he had had a parole application rejected.[5] Then, in 1867, he had been allowed to return to his work in the chapel, this time touching up a painting for the altar.[6] On his release, the prison records say that he 'went to Queenstown'.[7] By now, the man convicted of the notorious murder on Ireland's Eye was 63 years old. At the time of his departure from prison, he was described as 'an aged and very respectable looking gentleman, white haired, bent, and feeble, and with nothing in his aspect or manner to suggest that he was guilty of the awful tragedy on Ireland's Eye'.[8] Nonetheless, his love for one of the women with whom he had lived seems to have been every bit as intense as it was at the time of his conviction. Having departed Queenstown, it is thought that William Burke Kirwan lived out his days with his former mistress, Teresa Kenny, and their family, all of whom had departed Ireland for America shortly after her failure to claim his property in 1853. Unsubstantiated rumours also circulated that Kirwan revisited the scene of his brutal crime. A source dating from before 1900 claimed that 'years rolled on and one day an old man hired a boat to Ireland's Eye and spent some hours testing how far the human voice was capable of making itself heard at

---

5 NAI, GPO/LB/7/585.
6 NAI, GPO/LB/22/219.
7 NAI, Mountjoy Prison Convict Classification, 1/11/23.
8 *Freeman's Journal*, 3 February 1879.

the mainland'.[9] Whether or not Kirwan ever returned to Ireland's Eye must remain the subject of speculation.

Kirwan had first seen the Spike Island convict prison at the height of its overcrowded wretchedness, just six years after its conversion to a convict depot. Now he departed a much smaller prison that was gradually drifting towards its closure. In his report for 1877, Director Barlow disparaged Spike Island as a poorly constructed prison where the maintenance of discipline and security was an unnecessarily expensive process.[10] Later that year, as the governance of the convict prisons passed from the Directors of Convict Prisons to a newly constituted body called the General Prisons Board (GBP), the Secretary to the Treasury asked the new Board to be mindful of the desirability of returning Spike Island to the exclusive use of the military.[11] The final nail in the coffin of the Victorian prison at Spike Island came when a Royal Commission on Penal Servitude, reporting in 1879, recommended a raft of changes to the entire system. Its concerns about Spike Island were specific and damning:

> The management of the prisons for males and females at Mountjoy calls for little remark. The condition of both prisons appears to us generally satisfactory, and to reflect credit on the Irish prison administration. We regret that we cannot say the same of the prison at Spike Island, which was originally an old barrack. The very defective construction of the prison itself, and especially of the sleeping cells, renders it impossible to enforce proper discipline, whilst the constant opportunities of seeing the outside world afforded to the pris-

9 Fitzpatrick, W.J. 1900. *History of the Dublin Catholic Cemeteries.* Dublin: The Offices, 4 Rutland Square, p.62. See also: *Derry Journal*, 24 September 1928.
10 HMSO, *Directors' Report 1877*.
11 PRO, Treasury (T) 1/12695. See also: NAI, GPB/LB/108/751.

oners both when at work and in going to and returning from Haulbowline greatly impair the severity of the punishment. Indeed Captain Barlow goes so far as to say that "penal servitude as at Spike Island has very little terror to criminals." The intermixtures also of the convicts on the works with free labourers and with soldiers on the ramparts, though limited as much as possible, is most objectionable; and generally the system appears to be more lax than in the English convict prisons. Sir Walter Crofton informed us that it was contemplated before he left Ireland that the convicts should be removed from Spike Island. He strongly condemns the establishment as "unfitted for every branch of prison treatment," and is anxious it should be abolished and broken up altogether without delay. No doubt some of the objections to it might be obviated by the construction of a new prison upon approved principles; but it appears from Sir Walter Crofton's evidence that the War Office has been constantly writing to request that the prison should be given up and the convicts taken away. Unless, therefore, the objections of the War Office are removed, the only alternative is to transfer the establishment to some other more suitable place, and we strongly recommend that no time be lost in taking steps for this purpose.[12]

Spike Island's days as a convict prison were numbered. It was still the largest single prison in Ireland and its closure needed to be managed appropriately. The prison population would have to be distributed among other gaols and that would take time. The dispersal of Spike Island's convicts and their labour was the subject of substantial administrative debate.

---

12 Hathi Trust Digital Library, *Royal Commission on the Penal Servitude Acts Report, 1879*, p.lxii.

The first attempt to begin removing convicts from the island came when appropriate labour was identified at prisons in Cork city and Maryborough (now Portlaoise). By the end of 1879, 69 convicts had been removed from the Spike Island establishment in order to assist in prison repairs at those locations. Spike Island's prison population had by then been reduced to 514 convicts. Deciding on where the remainder of the labour force should be located was complicated by the convicts' lack of skill. While over three decades they had transformed Cork harbour, most of the convict work consisted of digging, moving earth, blasting and chipping rock, as well as cutting and lifting stone. The number of convicts who had the skills to become involved in the repair and construction of buildings had been comparatively small. Indeed, the Royal Commission's report made it clear that external free labour had supplemented the island's skills deficit quite frequently. So while the practical transfer of skilled labour to Cork and Maryborough continued into 1880, a more fanciful scheme involving the construction of a new convict prison in Galway began to gain traction. The idea of providing convict labour for works at Galway harbour had been considered at intervals over the previous two decades, but it was only in Spike Island's twilight years that such consideration became serious.[13] The proposed Galway prison would accommodate some 500 prisoners and they would be employed in constructing breakwaters in Galway harbour. This scheme had many opponents, one of whom was Barlow. In his opinion the transfer of Irish convicts to English convict prisons would be far more cost-effective.[14] While the debate about how to close it continued, Spike Island entered its final years as a convict prison.

---

13 NAI, GPB/MB/1/28 March 1878.
14 PRO T 1/15663 & T 1/12695.

Sporadic violence still haunted the prison. In 1879, there were nine separate cases of attacks on prison warders. Three of those cases involved three to five convicts combining to attack an officer. Barlow remarked:

> The difficulties of maintaining discipline ... have always been considerable owing to almost unrestrained communications of the convicts necessitated by the temporary nature of the cells erected in buildings originally intended for military barracks; for years the class of convicts has been becoming worse, more inclined to violence and less reclaimable ... Whilst the conduct and industry of many of the convicts have been good, there has been, during the last few years, an increasing tendency to acts of violence, and to combination to cause disturbance on the works. In some cases the offenders were prosecuted, and in others corporal punishment was inflicted. As I have stated in previous reports, I do not consider any marked improvement in discipline can be expected until the convicts are located in a properly constructed prison.[15]

The critique of Spike Island as a convict prison was now becoming unanimous and continuous. Even Fr Lyons, in his third decade as Roman Catholic chaplain on the island, was publicly critical of the prison's lack of separate cells.[16] In the first three years of the 1880s, there were just a few minor assaults on prison officers. As Spike Island entered its final year as a convict prison, the most serious disturbances of its history were about to seal its fate.

In 1879, the Irish National Land League was founded and

15 HMSO, *GPB Report, 1879.*
16 HMSO, *GPB Report, 1881-82.*

tenant farmers began a campaign of civil disobedience in order to secure ownership of the land that they rented. Their primary weapons were withholding rents and boycotting landlords who sought to enforce the collection of rents, as well as boycotting tenants who undermined the campaign. Although the Land League did not condone violence, the older Whiteboy/Ribbonmen tradition was still alive and well, and much of this agrarian agitation resulted in violence. The British reaction was the passage of new legislation in 1881, known as the Coercion Act. This effectively empowered agents of the Crown to intern land agitators without trial. Spike Island never received any such prisoners, but it did receive many of those who had been convicted of agrarian offences in connection with the Land League. These men considered themselves political activists and it appears that they resented being forced to associate with what they regarded as 'common criminals'.

By 1883, almost all of Spike Island's convicts had returned to labour at the dockyard on Haulbowline. On 27 January that year, a fight broke out between two prisoners working on the docks. The fight was later claimed to be the result of tensions between agrarian offenders and those with a more ordinary criminal background.[17] As soon as the warders sought to intervene, they were set upon and Warder Tynan, against whom some of the convicts bore ill-will, received the brunt of their attack. The deputy governor called on the assistance of the police and military guard. The presence of these groups only served to escalate the violence and soon almost all of the convicts were fighting amongst themselves and with those seeking to regain authority over them. It was later reported that 'several warders

---

17 Hansard, *House of Commons Debates, HC Deb 10 March 1883, Vol. 277, cc3–125 (CS Parnell)*.

were knocked down and kicked when on the ground, stones were thrown, batons and cutlasses taken from the warders, the warders were assaulted with batons, stones and shovels, and many were cut and bled profusely'.[18] The only convicts who didn't join in the fracas were the convict tradesmen, who were not among the unskilled labour gangs. The *Freeman's Journal* reported as follows:

> The yelling of the convicts apprised the others that something exciting was going on, and a general riot took place among the several gangs, the warders each being badly treated. Constable Thompson and seven policemen, armed with loaded guns and bayonets fixed turned out, clubbed the convicts with the butts of their guns and rescued the warders, several of whom were badly cut and bruised, while Constable Thompson got a bad wound on the right side of the head from a blow of a shovel, for which he is at present treated in the naval hospital, Haulbowline. Sailors from the guardship and the Revenge were at once brought to Haulbowline under arms, and about 100 marines were also called out, but they did not interfere. The determination of the police and the advice they tendered to the convicts succeeded in restoring order. The row lasted about an hour and a half. When order was restored the convicts returned to the prison on Spike Island, and on the journey, which is about a mile in length, they indulged in defiant yells and singing. They were guarded into prison by the marines.[19]

With what might have been the rebellious songs of the agrarian class ringing out towards the hills of Queenstown, Spike Island's

---

18 NAI, GPB/MB/2/26 February 1883.
19 *Freeman's Journal*, 29 January 1883.

problems were plain for all to hear. The agrarian offenders did not see themselves as criminals. They were part of an organised political campaign, and while much of what they did was probably motivated by the prospect of improving their individual circumstances, they also campaigned on behalf of all Irish tenant farmers. As such, they quite probably resented being placed among thieves and other so-called common criminals. On Spike Island, where the separation of prisoners was impossible, that resentment had turned to anger and as they lay in their makeshift cells on the night of 27 January 1883, their anger hadn't abated.

On 31 January, while having their midday meal in Haulbowline's Tank House, the prisoners decided *en masse* that the milk presented to them was not fit for human consumption. They refused to drink it and demanded a change in the prison diet. 'They threw milk and tins about, upset the tables and were so disorderly that they had to be removed to Spike Island prison.'[20] The authorities later expressed their annoyance that the campaign was organised by a few ringleaders on the verge of release. These men were removed from association and six of them were corporally punished. In mid-February, 40 insubordinate prisoners were removed from Spike Island and placed in segregation in Cork City Gaol. A further 20 were returned to Mountjoy a few days later.[21]

In the days that followed, Director Barlow issued a report into the disturbances and claimed that he had 'never before experienced such bad and mutinous conduct, and owing to the construction of the prison, the Governor was comparatively powerless. In a properly constructed prison matters would have been far more easily dealt with,

---

20 NAI, GPB/MB/2/26 February 1883.
21 NAI, GPB/LB/112/319, 324, 338 & 339.

but under the circumstances very strong measure became necessary.'[22] The insubordination on the island, as well as the public reporting of it, had placed further pressure on a prison that should have already been closed.

In December 1882, another Royal Commission had been appointed to inquire into the condition of Irish prisons. One of the matters with which it was specifically tasked was to establish the extent of progress in relation to the recommendations of the previous commission's report in 1879. The 1882 Royal Commission might have been satisfied to simply report upon a previous report, issue similar recommendations and then watch a further four years go by while the various arms of government argued about how they should implement those recommendations. Given the course of events, however, the disturbances on Spike Island pushed the commissioners to act. On 15 February 1883, a little more than two weeks after the riot on Haulbowline, the Royal Commission issued an interim report. It spelled the end for Ireland's most infamous prison:

> Having regard to the Report bearing date 14th July 1879 ... and also to subsequent reports made by the General Prisons Board of Ireland, Your Commissioners have carefully examined both Mr Bourke the Chairman, and also Captain Barlow, a member of the Irish Prison's Board upon the subject.
>
> Your Commissioners have been convinced of the urgent necessity for action being at once taken in this matter; and we may refer to the open mutiny which has twice recently taken place as confirming this view.
>
> Without therefore waiting for any final decision of Your Majesty's Government as to the best means of perma-

---

22 NAI, GPB/MB/2/26 February 1883.

nently employing the Irish convicts in reconstructing prisons, reclaiming waste land, or carrying out harbour works, Your Commissioners would earnestly press the urgent necessity for removing without further delay all the prisoners from Spike Island, and closing the prison within three months of this date, or earlier if possible.[23]

The commissioners also noted that if all other Irish prisons were combined, there was considerable vacant space that might be used to accommodate Spike Island's convicts, although it stopped short of making any specific recommendations on prisoner redistribution. On 3 March, the Chief Secretary endorsed the commission's report and 'informed the Prison's Board that he should insist on Spike Island being closed as a Convict Depot three months hence and earlier if possible'.[24] During parliamentary questions on 12 March 1883, Sir Richard Cross asked the Under-Secretary, George Trevelyan, when the prison would finally be closed. Trevelyan assured him that the government was doing everything in its power to arrange for the transfer of Spike Island's convicts. He also assured his questioner that the deadline set by the Royal Commission and endorsed by the Chief Secretary would be met.[25]

The Spike Island convict prison had initially been established as a temporary solution to overcrowding in the Irish prison system. Now, under significant political pressure, the General Prisons Board proposed another temporary solution. It moved all of the female prisoners out of Mountjoy's female wing and into a designated convict

---

23 HMSO, *Preliminary Report of the Royal Commission Appointed to Inquire into the Administration, Discipline, and Condition of Prisons in Ireland 1883.*
24 PRO, T1/15418.
25 Hansard, *House of Commons Debates, HC Deb 12 March 1883, Vol. 277, c190.*

wing of the female prison at Grangegorman Lane. This created enough space for most of Spike Island's convicts. Its remaining able-bodied men formed working parties that were dispatched to local prisons in Cork, Galway and Tralee, while the men in the invalid class were sent to Maryborough. At the time, it was understood that a purpose-built convict prison was a necessity and should be built in the near future.[26] However, the plans for such a prison in Galway fell through and there was no official replacement for the Spike Island convict prison.

Finally, almost two months later than the deadline set by the Royal Commission, the last of Spike Island's convicts left Cork harbour on Friday, 13 July 1883. While the first convicts had arrived in the harbour by ship 36 years previously, the last cohort of prisoners made their departure by the railway that had since been completed.[27] Governor Hay, having spent 28 years as Spike Island's most successful and reforming governor, also departed the island. He took up a position as the governor of Mountjoy Gaol. Deputy Governor Murphy and Medical Officer Dr O'Keefe also took up positions in the Dublin prison.[28] Some of the warders were happy to retire on superannuation. All of them were informed 'that should they desire re-employment the board will consider their applications with a view to re-appointing them to the local or convict service if found suitable'.[29]

After 36 years as Ireland's most dreaded prison, Spike Island reverted to military use. On inspecting the old prison blocks, engineers noted that substantial expense would be incurred in returning them to military use. New flooring joists were required and the glass in the windows had to be broken when removing the heavy iron bars.

26 HMSO, *GPB Report, 1882-83*.
27 NAI, GPB/LB/112/645, 654 & 772.
28 NAI, GPB/LB/112/895.
29 NAI, GPB/MB/2/ 7 & 16 May 1883.

The timber structures that had once served as workshops and a chapel were to be broken up and used as firewood, along with the remaining stockades. Although a police guard was posted, the cottages of some of the former prison staff dotted along the island's shore had fallen victim to vandalism. The military had wanted the island back since they were forced to temporarily turn it over to the prison service more than three decades previously. Now that they had it, they complained bitterly of its condition and sought payment from the General Prisons Board for returning it to military use.[30] Just over a century later, in 1985, the military of an independent Irish State was once again ordered to turn Spike Island's fort over to the civilian prison service. But that is another story.

Figure 18.1 Aerial view of Fort Mitchel, Spike Island, taken before the renovations carried out in 2016. (Image © courtesy of National Monuments Service)

---

30 NAI, CSORP/1883/13472 and GPB/LB/112/534.

Figure 18.2 General view of Spike Island from the south with Cobh (formerly Cove and Queenstown) in the background. (Image © courtesy of National Monuments Service)

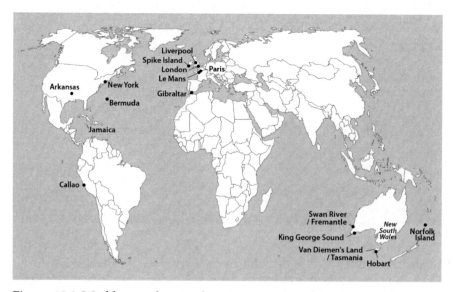

Figure 18.3 World map showing locations mentioned in the text. (Image © courtesy of Department of Archaeology, UCC)

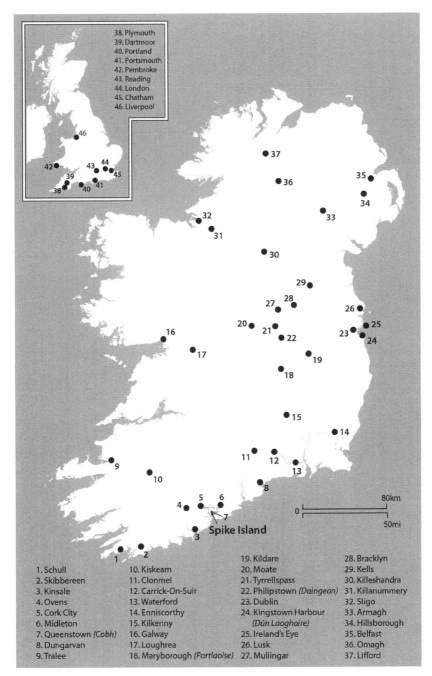

Figure 18.4 Map of Ireland and Britain showing locations mentioned in the text. (Image © courtesy of Department of Archaeology, UCC)

Index

Governors
    Grace, Richard   46, 62, 125, 141
    Hay, Peter   141, 204
    Hogreve, Francis   140
    Stewart, William   126, 139, 190

H

hammocks   30, 43
Harness, Capt. H.D.   110
Hatchell, Dr George, Inspector of Lunatic Asylums   266, 268, 272
Haulbowline   vii, 30, 50, 91, 148-149, 190, 217, 230, 233-234,
        236-242, 244-248, 253, 261, 266, 275, 280, 297, 300,
        302, 308, 314, 322, 326, 329-332
Hennessy, John Pope   234, 237
Hillsborough, Co. Down   82
Hitchins, Henry   86, 193
Hobart   35, 89, 207, 339, 344-345
Hodder, Colonel   58
Hoddersfield   58
Hoffman's anodyne   196
Home Office   xii, 26, 203
Home Rule Movement   306
homosexual activity   198
Hope, Colonel   12
hospital   51-53, 61, 76-78, 88, 91-92, 101-103, 116-117,
        127, 129, 148-149, 171, 189, 191-192, 207, 226, 228, 231,
        248, 250, 252-253, 255, 258-262, 266, 269-270, 275, 280,
        284, 304, 317, 320, 330
Hospital for the Insane, Hobart   207
Hospital Sergeant   192
Howth, Co. Dublin   94-96, 98, 104, 301
hulks   9-10, 90, 109, 205, 208
Humphreys, Matthew   65

I

Intermediate Prisons   xi, 38, 118, 201-202
invalid class   271, 334
Ireland's Eye   94, 96-98, 104-105, 324-325
Irish Board of Ordnance   12
Irish College, Paris   186, 189, 199
Irish Republican Brotherhood (IRB)   299
Irish World   320